Philosophy of mind

Fundamentals of Philosophy
Series editor: John Shand

This series presents an up-to-date set of engrossing, accurate, and lively introductions to all the core areas of philosophy. Each volume is written by an enthusiastic and knowledgeable teacher of the area in question. Care has been taken to produce works that while evenhanded are not simply bland expositions, standing rather as original pieces of philosophy in their own right. The reader should not only be well informed by the series, but also experience the intellectual excitement of being engaged in philosophical debate itself. The volumes serve as an essential basis for the undergraduate courses to which they relate, as well as being accessible and absorbing for the general reader. Together they comprise an indispensable library of living philosophy.

Published:
Piers Benn
Ethics

Alexander Bird
Philosophy of Science

Colin Lyas
Aesthetics

Alexander Miller
Philosophy of Language

Stephen Burwood, Paul Gilbert, Kathleen Lennon
Philosophy of Mind

Forthcoming:
Richard Francks
Modern Philosophy

Dudley Knowles
Political Philosophy

Philosophy of mind

**Stephen Burwood, Paul Gilbert
and Kathleen Lennon**

University of Hull

Published in the UK in 1998 by UCL Press

UCL Press Limited
Taylor & Francis Group
1 Gunpowder Square
London EC4A 3DE

The name of University College London (UCL) is a registered
trade mark used by UCL Press with the consent of the owner.

ISBNs: 1-85728-590-5 HB
       1-85728-591-3 PB

British Cataloguing-in-Publication Data
A catalogue record for this book is available
from the British Library.

Cover printed by Flexiprint, Lancing, West Sussex
Printed and bound in Great Britain by
T.J. International, Padstow.

Contents

Acknowledgements

The authors would first like to thank each other: writing a book with two other people may sound like a fractious enterprise; in fact, it has been an intellectually rewarding experience. We would then like to express our gratitude to a number of colleagues and friends who have either read or heard earlier versions of much of this material and were always ready with stimulating and pertinent comments. In this respect, we must give special thanks to our research students and those on the MA Philosophy of Mind course at Hull (past and present), as many of the arguments contained herein started life in seminars as responses to, or developments of, questions, objections, insights and positions which were theirs. We also have, of course, a singular indebtedness to our series editor, John Shand, not simply for his useful comments on early drafts, but also for his patience, encouragement and support throughout the writing process. Last, but by no means least, we wish to thank Chris Coulson and Lisa Carter who, despite having produced the typescript and bibliography while running two university departments, never failed to keep a sense of humour.

P. H. G., K. L. & S. A. B.
Hull, May 1998

Chapter 1

The Cartesian legacy

The dominant paradigm

Modern philosophy of mind begins with Descartes. This is not to say that this field of philosophy was born into a vacuum in the middle of the seventeenth century: one could begin an historical survey of its central concerns by reviewing positions before Descartes. One could begin profitably, for example, by examining the arguments of Plato, Aristotle, Aquinas, or any number of the other great thinkers of the past. What one could not do, however, is to begin such a survey by looking at historical positions that come *after* Descartes. Why is this? We can begin to understand why this is so when we realize that modern philosophy of mind is almost exclusively concerned with the mind/body problem; how meaning, rationality and conscious experience is related to, or arises from, a material world which, in itself, is devoid of such characteristics. In its present form this is a problem we owe almost entirely to Descartes and his contemporaries. Thus, the straightforward answer is that the Cartesian turn in philosophy sets up this problem and then proceeds to give us both a classic statement of the issues involved and a particular position which philosophers have continued to argue for and against.

Nevertheless, this straightforward answer will not do, at least not by itself, as it presents only a part of the complete picture. As every first-year undergraduate knows, Descartes himself provides us with one of the main solutions to the problem; a form of psycho-physical dualism in which body and mind are considered to be distinct substances able to causally interact. This position has come to be known as Cartesian dualism. However, one is able to read Descartes' work in such a way that he is much less of a pure Cartesian in this respect than those who came after him. Very few philosophers now argue for and against the philosophical position Descartes himself may have actually held. The second reason why the straightforward answer is inadequate is that the Cartesian dualism we are familiar with, whether or not it can be directly or solely attributed to Descartes himself, is simply not a going concern in modern philosophy of mind. Despite the evident popularity of psycho-physical dualism as a theory of mind among the general public, and despite the fact that it still occasionally receives spirited professional defences from practising philosophers (sometimes very eminent philosophers), the simple fact is that most professionals working in the philosophy of mind do not see any form of psycho-physical dualism as a viable option, let alone a form anything like that to which Descartes may have been committed. The complete answer is rather more recondite. Descartes' singular contribution does not consist simply in providing us with a new puzzle and providing a possible solution to it; rather it consists in the way he has shaped our understanding of both body and mind. One of the curious things about the current scene in the philosophy of mind is that, even where it is rejected, habits of thought associated with Cartesian psycho-physical dualism continue to play a defining role in theory formulation.

Presently the dominant paradigm in the philosophy of mind sees its task as articulating a conception of the mental consistent with the investigation of the mental by natural science. From the point of view of philosophers working within this paradigm, philosophy of mind is something like what the philosopher of science Thomas Kuhn constrasted with mature science; different schools of thought vie with one another and there is constant disagreement over fundamentals.[1] Consequently they often see themselves as doing what might be called "pre-science": the clearing of the conceptual ground in preparation for the problem being tackled, and ultimately solved, through empirical investigation and the application of specialized scientific knowledge and methods. Where there is a large degree of agreement among such philosophers it concerns the method for this ground clearing: the preferred method is reductionist. In general terms, reductionism claims that, given two fields of discourse, there is an equivalence of either meaning or reference between the statements of the two fields so that anything explicable in terms of one field is explicable in terms of the other. In practice one of the fields of discourse is normally privileged over the other and is seen as being more basic as a means of explanation: so, for example, heat is reducible to kinetic properties. With respect to the specific case of the mind and body, the claim has been that anything explicable in terms of mental entities, attributes, or descriptions is explicable in terms of physical entities, attributes, or descriptions. Given that the physical is invariably privileged, this has meant that reductionists have argued, classically, that we can reduce mental states or their descriptions to physical states or their descriptions or, more recently, that we can reduce the intentional idiom of the mental to a non-intentional functionalist idiom.

This paradigm is therefore one which is assuredly materialist, and often stridently physicalist but, in any case, unquestionably monist. It is also a paradigm which is often characterized by what some would see as scientism. What we mean by the dominant paradigm being monist and materialist is that, in contradistinction to Cartesian dualism, it is committed to the view that the world consists of only one type of thing, material things. It is physicalist in the sense that the nature of the material is articulated in terms of physical science and scientistic in that it privileges this mode of articulation to the exclusion of all others.[2] In all these respects, but especially in its rejection of immaterial substance and its explanation of mind entirely in physical terms, the dominant paradigm stands in *prima facie* opposition to Cartesian conceptions of mind and its relation to the physical world. Sure enough, its constituent theories are often presented as an advance on the obfuscations of dualism and their proponents are extremely vocal in their denunciations of Descartes. Nevertheless, those very same theories often continue to work within a framework of Cartesian categories and assumptions. This will be an important theme running through the course of this book so that, while we avoid giving a detailed critique of dualist positions, we need to be clear what we have inherited from the Cartesian turn in philosophy.

Cartesian dualism

In a sense, Descartes himself was also doing pre-science, though to a different end. Descartes' overall project into which his philosophy of mind fits was to provide the foundations of a universal science based on reason. His philosophy of mind was motivated partly by a concern to respect the distinctive place of the mental within a metaphysical framework encompassing this new science. The establishment of this science required him to initiate a radical break with a largely Aristotelian past and to construct a new starting point in philosophy by laying bare a self-evident truth which would form the axiom of an epistemological enterprise. Although his project was to establish an objective conception of reality, Descartes' method was famously first-personal, so that by the systematic application of doubt he believed he could discover the axiom in the surety of his own existence. This surety was encapsulated in the famous phrase *cogito ergo sum* – "I am thinking, therefore I exist."[3] Whatever else I might doubt I cannot doubt this, that I exist, for the very act of doubting presupposes someone who is doubting. Thus the *cogito*, his intuitively apprehended existence of self, became the foundation for his epistemic edifice, the security of which was further guaranteed by being cemented together by the assurance of God's existence and beneficence. But the self this process revealed was, for Descartes, notoriously not an embodied or social self such as we might uncritically take ourselves to be, but rather a self shorn of all corporeal characteristics and recognizably human attributes and relations.

Descartes' new science thus elevated epistemology above all else, with all the philosophical, as well as political, ramifications this entailed.[4] In terms of our specific interests, his epistemological project quickly turned into a metaphysical treatise which succeeded in changing our understanding of both ourselves and the world around us. Cartesian dualism, as traditionally understood, therefore stands upon two interrelated epistemic and metaphysical doctrines:

(a) *The primacy of the mental* (the epistemic doctrine): we can only be epistemically secure about our own minds and not about the physical world in general and our bodies or, indeed, the minds of others: it is our own mind which is best known and which really counts.

(b) *The autonomy of the mental* (the metaphysical doctrine): there is no dependency between the mental and the physical: bodies can exist independently of minds and, perhaps more importantly given (a), minds can exist independently of bodies. The relationship between the two is external and contingent.

Presenting things in this crude way has the benefit of exposing an extremely important feature of dualistic thinking: it does not consist simply in the positing of a dichotomy between the mental and the physical, but involves notions of exclusion, autonomy and privilege. It is fashionable nowadays to list a set of dichotomies that are seen as being central to the history of Western thought; self/other, subject/object, universal/particular, mind/body, private/public, male/female, master/slave, reason/emotion, culture/nature, and so on – the list is almost endless. It also sometimes seems that the mere mention of a presupposed binary opposition is enough to condemn a theory as being dualistic; but an opposition between two terms does not, by itself, constitute dualism. What is noticeable about the role the above dichotomies have played in our thought is that they have been seen as exclusionary (that things are one or the other but not both), autonomous (each exists separably without the implication of the opposed term), and that the first term in each case is in some sense privileged (that it is of primary importance and something to which the second term plays a secondary and oppositional role). What is crucial here is not the simple positing of dichotomy or difference but the way this is construed in terms of an agonistic or combatitive opposition between the concepts comprising the binary opposition.

If a theory can be explicated in terms of such an agonistic opposition then it can be properly construed as dualistic; and Cartesian dualism is clearly dualistic in this sense. For example, a troubling feature of Cartesian dualism is the way it presents phenomena as being either exclusively mental or exclusively physical so that all human attributes can be divided up exhaustively into two distinct categories. Thus, when referring to a phenomenon such as, say, pain, either we are speaking about something objectifiable and quantifiable such as muscle spasms and nerve impulses, or we are speaking about something entirely non-corporeal and subjective such as how the pain is perceived from the perspective of the person in pain. As we shall see in the next section, not even Descartes himself was entirely convinced of this, as there are clearly phenomena that cannot be dealt with so expeditiously. Nonetheless, it follows directly from the way he defined the mental and the physical in opposition to each other: the first consisting in non-extended thought and the latter solely in extension. This was not an incidental feature of his philosophy but central to his new science, which was premised upon a withdrawal from the perspective of the individual in understanding the material world. The world was not to be understood from the point of view of someone engaged with it, either in perception or action, but simply in terms of its abstracted geometrical properties. Thus, in the *Principles of philosophy*, Descartes argues that "The nature of matter, or body considered in general, consists not in its being something which is hard or heavy or coloured, or which affects the senses in any way, but simply in its being something which is extended in length, breadth, and depth."[5]

Similarly, in order to understand the mind, one should again abstract from engagement with the physical. On the Cartesian model, mind is seen not only as something entirely distinct but also as something essentially independent and autonomous of the body and its physical environment. An important lesson learnt from the exercise of systematic doubt in the *Meditations* is that the mind could be as it is regardless of the nature of the world external to it, or even if such a world did not exist. In order to understand the nature and contents of the mind we do not need to pay heed to the nature or contents of this world. Thus the mind of an individual (any individual), on this view, is something "disengaged"; both from embodied relations to physical things in its environment and from cultural or social relations to others and shared projects with them. As we shall see, this rather solipsistic picture (from the Latin *solus* and *ipse* meaning "I alone"), although now divorced from a project of epistemic foundationalism such as Descartes', continues to inform our understanding of the mind. To gain some purchase on why this should be the case we must examine the flip-side of this model of mind. What is sometimes called the Cartesian hyper-separation of mind and body not only changed our conception of mind but also our conception of body and the physical world.

The secret life of the body

It might seem rather perverse this early in a book on the philosophy of mind to start speaking about the body, but it is impossible to understand the impasse which is the mind/body problem without reflecting upon both sides of that divide. We philosophers are often forgetful of the double-edged nature of our Cartesian legacy and how our presently held conception of mind was forged in the same crucible as our presently held conception of body, including the human body. After all, Descartes was not only the father of modern philosophy, as he is often called, but also one of the architects of modern science. During the Renaissance and the Baroque periods people were beginning to investigate the world in new ways and this required them to formulate new ways of modelling its workings and their relations to it. Part of this conceptual shift was a remodelling of the human body with the invention of new discourses by which it could be described and understood. What was true of "body considered in general" was equally true of individual human bodies. A second curious feature about modern philosophy of mind is that, while it is, as we have said, almost exclusively concerned with the mind/body problem, research in the field pays little or no attention to the question of the body. Research within the field is focused almost exclusively on the nature of mind and attempts to provide adequate accounts of this – as if questions concerning the mind/body problem could be satisfactorily addressed without some reference to the conception of the body such questions presuppose. The problem, it seems, lies all on one side. Consequently the body has become the forgotten and invisible term in the debate.

It is tempting to think that the reason for the body's invisibility is that, as we have said, the body in the mind/body dichotomy has played a secondary and oppositional role to the mind. This is too simple. In fact, nowadays the opposite is nearer the truth for, in many ways, modern physicalism reverses the traditional privileging of the mental over the physical. Thus many philosophers confidently believe in the explanatory adequacy of the sciences, especially the physical sciences, as presently conceived. The problem is that the nature of the physical goes unchallenged, so that the invisibility of the body in our thinking is the invisibility of the normal. This is not to say that physicalism does not operate with a theory of the body, but that this theory is tacitly understood: it is simply unquestioned and viewed as being relatively unproblematic. As a result, many philosophers, at least those in the Anglo-American analytic tradition (and most philosophy of mind is firmly embedded within this tradition), write as if it is obvious what the human body is, even if we continue to be puzzled by the nature of mind. Three hundred or so years after the Cartesian-Galilean revolution which gave birth to modern science, we might now feel that we have a firmer grip on what a physical body is than on what the mind is; but what if this body is a human body? What sort of body is this? Consider what Keith Campbell says (in what has become a standard introductory text in the philosophy of mind):

> Provided you know who *you* are, it is easy to say what your body is: it is what the undertakers bury when they bury you. It is your head, trunk, and limbs. It is the collection of cells consisting of your skin and all the cells inside it. It is the assemblage of flesh, bones, and organs which the anatomist anatomizes. It is the mass of matter whose weight is your weight.[6]

In contrast, one supposes, even if we know who we are, it is not so easy to say what our minds are. Perhaps this is true; but is it so clear that the picture Campbell presents of the body is simply what our bodies are? Are our bodies no more than an assemblage of flesh, bones and organs? Are our bodies (as he seems to suggest) no more than animated corpses? Campbell slides seemlessly from the innocent recognition of the body as a materiality to a reductive understanding of the body as something which is merely an object and the sum of its anatomical parts (where the relationship between the parts is to be understood *simply* in causal-mechanical terms).[7] But this body, in many ways, is something we have inherited from Cartesianism. The habits of thought that inform Cartesian dualism have left us not only with a picture of the mind as an absolute interiority independent of its physical environment, but also a picture of the human body as an absolute exteriority divested of meaning. Given that this exclusionary dichotomy still informs our conceptualizations, that there continues to be an explanatory gap between the mental and the physical should really be of no surprise. The French phenomenologist Merleau-Ponty puts it this way: "How significance and intentionality could come to dwell in molecular edifices or masses of cells is a thing that can never be made comprehensible, and here Cartesianism is right."[8] But if Cartesianism is right in this we should not be surprised, for it was the Cartesian turn in philosophy which was largely responsible for us having this exclusionary dichotomy. Because both dualism and modern physicalism share these habits of thought, what they also assume in common is a conception of the physical devoid of meaning, and thus a conception of the human body concomitant with this broader conception of the physical. The conception of the body as a "mass of matter" or that which the "anatomist anatomizes" is simply the only conception of the body presently on offer.

Because of the cultural dominance of this conception, a peculiarity of our Cartesian inheritance is that it is assumed to be simply commonsense to regard things so. Yet things were certainly not so clear cut for Descartes and his contemporaries and Descartes himself would probably not be completely content with such a view. Although he argued passionately, if not entirely successfully, that body and mind are distinct substances, the essence of one being extension and the other thought, Descartes recognized that there was something unique about human beings, that they are a subtle unity of the two and not merely an accidental union. The experience of our everyday lives teaches us that human beings are a compound of these two substances. This was most clearly seen, he thought, when experiencing sensations such as hunger or pain and was the point of the famous "pilot·in a ship" example in the *Sixth meditation*. Cartesian dualism tempts us into thinking of the mind as a sort of humunculus, a little man imprisoned within the body. Descartes vigorously tries to resist this picture and argues that I, my mind, am not simply housed as a foreign element in my body but is intimately connected with it. When my body is damaged I am not simply aware of the fact intellectually, I *feel* the pain. His problem was in combining this insight with what he saw as the conclusions reached by reasoned argument, that mind and body were nevertheless distinct substances, and the view of the human body his dualism presupposed, as something completely external to the mind. This tension is never completely resolved by Descartes and had important consequences for the way he understood body and mind.

Descartes' philosophy of mind was of a piece with the new science he was attempting to establish, in which the physical world should be understood in terms of a large mechanism and causal relations within it as a function of material objects' extension – as the push of one thing on another. As human and animal bodies are material objects, they too could be understood mechanistically. Descartes' philosophy thus dispenses with Aristotelian notions such as a "vegetative" or "sensitive soul", or a "principle of movement", as a *causa vitae* and he occasionally indicates that such bodies could be thought of in terms analogous to watches or other automata; that is, machines that are able to move themselves by the mere arrangement of their internal organs, as watches move themselves simply by the arrangement of their counter-weights and wheels.[9] Nevertheless, there remained certain anomalies.

As we have seen, Descartes recognized the difficulty this model has in accommodating sensations and the same is true for sense perception and, he thought, imagination. All three appear, on examination, to be "hybrid" phenomena that are not graspable in terms of the either/or dichotomy of the mental or the bodily. Consequently, he also sometimes seems to think of human and animal bodies as "sentient machines", as such phenomena can only be understood in the context of a body.[10] Sensation and imagination were thought by Descartes to be faculties *of the mind* which were, nevertheless, not exclusively mental but something that could only be understood in the context of both mental and physical categories. This seems to suggest that, with respect to these phenomena, the exclusive nature of the dichotomy between mind and body is compromised, at least to some degree: that the body is not simply a machine external to the mind and the mind itself is not a completely autonomous entity. Indeed, he occasionally goes so far as to say that these attributes "cannot belong to the mind simply in virtue of it being a thinking thing; instead they can belong to it only in virtue of its being joined to something other than itself . . . namely what we call the human body".[11]

However, the rhetorical power of the clockwork metaphor of the body has been difficult for subsequent philosophers to resist and Descartes himself never quite succeeds in freeing himself from it (it is simply too central to his general metaphysical theory). One could say that Descartes was the victim of his own rhetorical eloquence. In order to accommodate the foregoing anomalous phenomena in a way consistent with the mechanical understanding of the body required by his dualism, he makes a startling move that has a resonance in the philosophy of mind down to the present day. Using modern idiom we may put it like this: only when construed "broadly" do these phenomena need to be understood in the context of the body; but then they can be reduced to and explained in terms of the mechanical functions of the body. On the other hand, when construed "narrowly" they are simply modes of thought which can be perfectly grasped from the perspective of the thinker, without explanatory recourse to the body or the physical world. If we put ourselves in the position of Descartes' doubter, we can be sure that we *seem* to see a light, hear a sound, or feel warm, for example, even if we cannot be sure the source of the light, sound, or heat actually exists. As he says in the *Meditations*, the fact that I seem to see, hear, or feel warm, in this narrow sense, cannot be unreal for "what is called 'having a sensory perception' is strictly just this, and in this restricted sense of the term it is simply thinking".[12] In other words, the autonomy of the mind is reinstated since sensation, sense perception and imagination are, strictly speaking, modes of thought and thought is the essence of the mind alone and not of the body or the mind/body union.

Two important assumptions underlie this move and result in two important and interrelated consequences. The assumptions are that disparate phenomena can be brought together under the auspices of the mental and that the mark of these being mental states, that is – according to Descartes – thoughts, is that they are conscious states. As he says, "I use this term [thought] to include everything that is within us in such a way that we are immediately aware of it. Thus all the operations of the will, the intellect, the imagination and the senses are thoughts."[13] The two consequences are that the body can continue to be understood simply as a causal, mechanical system, external to the mind proper, which itself is understood as something essentially private and "inner". The dominant paradigm in modern philosophy of mind rejects the gloss Cartesian dualism puts on this in terms of the opposition between two types of substance; but what it continues to take on board is a conception of the body as something explicable simply in terms of medico-physical sciences and, in varying degrees, the notion of the mind as a self-contained inner realm.

The Cartesian theatre

What has emerged from the foregoing discussion of Descartes is how he thought that what really counts is how things seem from the perspective of the person who has mental states: from their particular subjective point of view. He therefore emphasizes an extremely important characteristic of the mental – its subjectivity. Any complete philosophy of mind must be able to say something about this. However, in doing so he left us with a particular model of the mind which is not very appealing. What Descartes assumes is that the content of a person's mental states could be what they are irrespective of how the world is: the world may be radically different from how she believes it to be and, indeed, may not even exist.[14] In other words, even though her intentional states fail to refer to, or her phenomenal states do not have, the physical cause she supposes, or no physical cause at all, they nevertheless have the content they do simply because they seem that way to her. This is the model of the mind as the Cartesian theatre, something like a self-contained black box in which thoughts, feelings, and so on successively strut and fret their hour upon the stage in splendid isolation of states of affairs external to it. It is a view which has given rise to the peculiar philosophical vocabulary of the "inner" and "outer": a private world of subjective conscious experience and a shared public world of objective facts. This model of the mind raises important epistemological and ontological questions: questions concerning self-knowledge and knowledge of the world and others on the one hand, and on the other hand questions concerning what it is for something to be a mental state. We shall look briefly at each of these in turn.

As we have seen, Descartes' philosophy of mind was based initially upon a distinction he drew between our knowledge of the world in general – that is the physical world of matter, including knowledge of our own physical attributes, as well as the minds of others – and our knowledge of our own minds. For Descartes, and many philosophers who came after him, our knowledge of the "outer", the shared public world, is essentially indirect and lacks immediacy because it relies on the causal interaction of our bodily sense organs with the objects constituting that world, that is inanimate objects such as tables and chairs as well as the animated bodies of other sentient creatures. Furthermore, each of us can only know the mind of another indirectly, by observation of their behaviour. On the other hand, as mental states are conscious states, our knowledge of our own "inner" worlds, our subjective conscious states, is both direct and immediate. In fact, Descartes defines thought – in his broad understanding of that term – as any mental state of which we are immediately aware. Because of this, each of us is thought to be authoritative about our own mental states in a way we cannot be about the minds of other people, states of affairs in the world external to our minds, or in a way others cannot be about our mental states. From each of our subjective points of view, therefore, our own minds are transparent to themselves whereas the material world and the minds of others remain opaque to us. One can see from this that this view of the mind is of a piece with the sceptical doubts with which the

Cartesian project began. Viewing the mind as an "inner" realm of which our knowledge is privileged naturally leads to a radical scepticism concerning an "outer" realm of material objects and other human beings. Even if the existence of a material "outer" world is accepted, this epistemic asymmetry may still encourage a scepticism concerning either the *nature* of minds other than our own (that is, are the beliefs, experiences, and so on of others congruent with mine?), or the *existence* of other minds (that is, does anyone else have any beliefs, experiences, and so on at all?).

The doubt expressed in the first way is familiar enough, for there are times when we are not sure what another person is thinking or feeling; but the philosophical difficulty associated with the Cartesian model goes beyond these everyday concerns and asks if you can ever be sure what it is like to be someone else, or if she experiences things as you do?[15] For example, there is no way of telling, from her behaviour or what she says, that the colour sensation she experiences when she sees a red tomato is congruent with the colour sensation you experience when you see a red tomato – she may, for all you know, experience what you both call green. However, the problem may be even more radical than this. You see your neighbour speaking and behaving as you do; but does this constitute evidence for a mind at work at all? The lights are on, but is anyone at home? For all you know she and everyone else may all be cleverly constructed automatons or perhaps even zombies. This may seem a bizarre, possibly even insane, speculation; yet it follows directly from the model of mind and body Descartes bequeathed to us. On this model, we absolutely cannot ever know directly what someone is thinking or feeling for her mind is shut away, hidden from view, and all we have access to is her body described simply in terms of a physical, mechanical system.[16]

The idea of the mind as a self-contained theatre also raises, as we have said, questions concerning the nature of mental states and not simply our knowledge of them in ourselves or others. As far as Cartesian dualism is concerned, the mind is self-contained because it is an immaterial substance and thus a mental state – for Descartes a thought – is essentially a modification of this immaterial substance. No philosopher nowadays believes this. However, even if Cartesian immaterialism is rejected as a way of picturing the mind as self-contained, this latter idea continues to influence the way philosophers understand the nature of the mind. If the idea of the mind as a Cartesian theatre assumes that our mental states have the content they do irrespective of how the world is, then it assumes that these states are "narrow" as opposed to "broad" in terms of what determines their content. This is a question about what sort of facts are constitutive of, say, a belief. Are they facts only about you – for Descartes facts about how things seem to you – or do they include other sorts of facts as well, facts about things external to the mind's black box?

Nowadays the view that mental states are narrow is often termed individualism or internalism; its opposite is externalism. We have to be careful here because, for the present-day internalist, the relevant facts about you may also include facts about the internal states of your body such as states of the central nervous system. As far as they are concerned, the boundary between the "inner" and the "outer" lies at the surface of someone's skin, or somewhere within its surface – for example at the boundary of the brain. Thus, for these philosophers, certain physiological facts may be constitutive of what a mental state is; indeed, for some these may be the only relevant facts. For Descartes this was not, nor could it be, the case, for he could not assume his body or brain existed. All he could assume was what was available to consciousness. The distinction between broad and narrow content is important, for some philosophers have suggested that, even if there is some content which is broad, it is only narrow content which is important to psychology and that psychological explanation should therefore focus on this narrow content. In this respect, at least, there is some agreement between modern internalists and Descartes, even if they reject his immaterialism.

The domain of reason

Descartes thought that two principles governed bodily movement; the first is simply a causal-mechanical principle by which the motion of a body can be explained without reference to the mind, and the second is the will, which he calls a faculty of the rational soul. According to Descartes, many forms of bodily movement could be explained mechanistically without invoking conscious states. In this respect he is often thinking of the automatic functioning of the body's internal organs; but he also makes it clear that this category includes what he calls "waking actions" such as walking, which can occur without our conscious attention, as well as reflex actions such as sticking out one's hand in order to protect oneself in a fall.[17] Indeed, he thought that all animal behaviour was just of this sort and that it was because we often confused the two principles that we mistakenly attributed souls to animals.[18] Whatever the merits or otherwise of this particular argument, when it comes to explaining a large amount of human behaviour Descartes believed that we require the attribution of thought. Sticking out one's hand to protect oneself is a spontaneous and natural thing to do, but sticking it out to grasp a cup is an entirely different thing.

The distinction here is the familiar (though by no means straightforward or clear-cut) one between a bodily movement and an action. Descartes seems to have thought that the distinction lay in the fact that actions have their origin in a certain mentalistic event, an act of will, which then triggers the required physiological changes in the body, and that they are a type of "doing" of which the "doer" has some form of conscious awareness. While each of these criteria might be thought to be sufficient in themselves, it is arguable whether either are, either singularly or in combination, actually necessary. Nonetheless, what he also wished to emphasize was that human beings are *agents* so that, while many of our bodily movements can be characterized in purely causal-mechanical terms, there are many others which are also susceptible to another economy of explanations. As rational, purposive creatures with goals of our own, we are not, he argued, merely machines performing set tasks. Human reason is, Descartes thought, a "universal instrument" which allows us to respond to different circumstances in different ways: "hence it is for all practical purposes impossible for a machine to . . . act in all the contingencies of life in the way in which our reason makes us act".[19] This other mode of explanation is, as a consequence, quite different from the causal-mechanical one. Causal explanations are nomological (from the Greek *nomos* meaning "law") and descriptive, whereas this other mode of explanation, in referring to reasons, is normative and evaluative.[20] Reasons act as norms which guide rather than govern our behaviour (causes compel, reasons do not) and, because of this, what reason-giving explanations explain may be seen as justified or unjustified, appropriate or inappropriate – concepts quite out of place in causal explanations.

What Descartes recognized was that human behaviour enters into the domain of reason. Thus, an agent has a reason for believing α or doing β if this belief or action is justified or appropriate, and what makes it justified or appropriate is, in part, her other psychological states. What this shows is that there is a network of rationalizing links which holds, on the one hand, between the state which constitutes the *explanans* (that fact which does the explaining) in this mode of explanation and, on the other, between this state and the *explanandum* (that fact which is explained). Indeed, one may go so far as to say that part of what makes these states what they are, and what individuates the acts they explain, is that they are positioned within this network of relations.

The causal relevance of the mind

One last feature of Descartes' thinking is important in its influence on the modern scene, his belief in the causal relevance of the mind. Despite the fact that he regarded the mind as something autonomous and distinct from the body and the material world, he also recognized that, in practice, the mind was able to causally engage with the world and was able to do this, he thought, through its mysterious union with the body. This was such a clear lesson of experience, he argued, that it was not to be gainsaid.[21] The causal engagement of mind and body runs in two directions: the mind affects the body and the body affects the mind. As we saw in the last section, Descartes thought that two principles governed bodily movement, one of which was the will. From childhood, he argues, experience teaches us that bodily movements often occur in obedience to the will. An example of this would be having the intention to kick a ball, which results in the forward movement of a leg and foot in the direction of the ball. Conversely, to use one of Descartes own examples, when a sword strikes our body and cuts it, a sensation of pain is produced in us by the physiological changes which occur in the body. Both examples involve a causal relation obtaining between the mind and the body. The problem for Descartes was in providing an account of *how* mind and body interact in this way. His difficulty had two interconnected sources: first, the autonomous and exclusionary nature of the mind/body dichotomy his dualism maintains, in which they are posited as logically distinct substances, and secondly, his general understanding of causation in terms of the push of one thing on another. Even if such an explanation of causation works in the case of causal relations between extended, material things, he recognized that it obviously cannot work if the relation is supposed to be between an extended, material thing (the body) and an unextended, immaterial thing (the mind).

Descartes does attempt an account, but it is less than convincing. The reason for this is that he tends to wrap up what is essentially a philosophical difficulty in the cloak of seventeenth-century physiological sophistication. Despite his own insistence that the soul (mind) is really joined to the whole body, he proceeds by nominating the *conarion* or pineal gland – a small gland in the centre of the brain – as the principal seat of the soul: that is, the place in the body where the soul "exercises its functions more particularly than in all the others".[22] We are not given any clues as to how we should construe this phrase but it seems that it is here that the relevant causal interractions between mind and body take place. We are then told that the soul exercises its functions by slight movements on the part of this gland, which in turn affects the course of animal spirits (a very fine wind) through cavities in the brain, driving these spirits towards pores of the brain, which then direct them through the nerves to the muscles in various ways so as to make the limbs move in the manner required. And conversely, the gland can be moved by these spirits in as many different ways as there are, for example, perceptible differences in the objects of perception.[23] Of course, to say *where* these causal interractions occur is not to provide a philosophical explanation of how they are possible. The best he can do is to suggest, in effect, that they are *sui generis* and cannot be modelled on causal relations between material things. In the end, however, when pushed on the point in correspondence, Descartes concedes that reason cannot provide an adequate account of the causal interraction between mind and body, though he continues to argue that experience teaches us that it is nevertheless true. Thus, in a famous reply, he suggests "That is why people who never philosophize and use only their senses have no doubt that the soul moves the body and that the body acts on the soul. . . . it is the ordinary course of life and conversation, and abstention from meditation and the study of things which exercise the imagination, that teaches us how to conceive the union of the soul and the body."[24]

Nevertheless, there is a second problem with his interactionism, one which flows partly from the conception of the physical that he initiated: what is commonly known as the over-determination of the physical. Descartes was keen to point out that the foregoing lesson of experience might lead us to assume that all the body's movements were caused by the will, and that this is untrue. As we have said before, an important strand in Descartes' thought was his mechanism. In line with this many, if not most, of the human body's movements can be accounted for simply as the products of its internal material arrangements. Similarly for the movement of body in general. This was the first step towards an understanding of the material world as a closed system which requires nothing more than a mechanical explanation of the events unfolding within it. In this view of the material world, physical causes by themselves are *sufficient* to bring about a physical event. This is now a fundamental assumption underlying modern science and may be termed the completeness of physics principle. The problem with interactionism is that, if this principle is accepted, any bodily event, such as the movement of someone's leg, seems to have *both* a physical cause and a mental cause, both of which may be sufficient in themselves to bring the effect about. In other words, the effect is over-determined.[25] Alternatively, we could say that, at least, it is partly caused by both a physical and mental event and that together the mental plus physical cause is sufficient. Either way, if true, this runs counter to the completeness of physics principle.

The failure of Cartesian interactionism does not, by itself, indicate the failure of psycho-physical dualism. A dualist might conceed the failure of interactionism and instead opt for a form of epiphenominalism where the mind is a non-causally efficacious, non-material by-product of causal events at the physical level: the mind is causally neutral and is itself effected rather than affected by the body. This avoids the problem of saying how the mind controls the body as well as the over-determination of the physical; but it still leaves us unclear how the physical causes this non-material by-product we call the mind. The only way for a dualist to avoid causal problems completely is to follow Leibniz's lead and claim that there is no causal relationship between mind and body at all and that the two run in parallel like two synchronized clocks. There is almost universal agreement among philosophers nowadays that these options are as equally, if not more, unpalatable as Cartesian dualism. Instead they are in broad agreement with the reasons for Descartes' conclusion if not the conclusion itself. Descartes argued that experience teaches us that there is a two-way causal relationship between mind and body and most of us would probably agree with him on that at least. To be cut with a sword would not be a pleasant experience and would, no doubt, result in someone feeling a great deal of pain. We unreflectively believe that is how the pain feels which causes the person's wincing, groaning and avoidance behaviour. What is true for states such as pain is also true for states such as belief and desire: we also think of these as states of a person causally responsible for that person's behaviour. The problem then becomes how to account for the causal relevance of the mind within a framework that rejects the notion of a ghostly immaterial substance yet preserves what is distinctively mental about the mind.

Conclusion

Philosophy is often forgetful of its own history, so the aim of this chapter has been to set our following discussion of the modern debate within an historical context. Many of the problems with which philosophy of mind now grapples have their origin in Descartes' extraordinarily rich and complex work. However, his influence, as we have said, goes beyond providing us with a new puzzle. The very fact that the mind/body relationship is still a puzzle for us itself attests to the way he has shaped our understanding of these notions. As Merleau-Ponty correctly observes, we all stand upon the shoulders of our philosophical predecessors, what he calls the "sedimentation of history", so that, for example, those who reject one or more of Descartes' views usually end up doing so from a standpoint that owes much to one of his other views. As a consequence, he suggests, it is almost impossible to answer the question "Is this author or position Cartesian or not?"[26] Nowhere is this more true than in modern philosophy of mind. Positions that pride themselves on their anti-Cartesianism usually end up being a continuation of Cartesianism by other means: in one way or another, one is tempted to say, we are all Cartesians now.

We must also not forget how his view of the mind was of a piece with the development of his new science and the way he understood the nature of the material world. We should understand this world, he thought, by withdrawing from the perspective of individuals actively engaged with it and, consequently, it should be viewed as something externalized, objectified and governed exhaustively by physical laws. It is a world into which the mind occasionally intrudes in virtue of its union with the human body, and perhaps then only within the localized area of the pineal gland. But, despite his better judgement, he thought that this body too was simply part of the mechanistic realm external to the mind. His dualism was thus motivated by a desire to preserve the distinctive place of the mental within the framework of this new science; but it seems that he could only achieve this by hiving off the mental into a separate realm of "inner" non-material substance. For Descartes, as Gilbert Ryle put it, "Minds are not bits of clockwork, they are just bits of not-clockwork."[27] It is ironic, given the popular view of his contribution to the philosophy of mind, that it was Descartes who also made space for reductive materialist conceptions of human nature – something grasped very quickly by subsequent philosophers.[28] Even though it has lost much of the strictly mechanistic baggage of seventeenth-century science, modern physicalism is in many ways the direct inheritor of Descartes' new science. The recent history of the philosophy of mind can be seen as one side of Descartes' philosophy attempting to swallow up the other: counteracting his immaterialism by privileging the other side of his mental/physical divide.

21

It is with these conceptual resources that modern philosophy of mind operates. However, we cannot arrive at a solution to the mind/body problem by simply ignoring our Cartesian heritage, for it raises substantial issues that cannot be easily ducked. The dominant paradigm in modern philosophy of mind is motivated by some very powerful arguments and a desire to bring the mind within the purview of a single, non-mentalistic causal explanatory schema. This, however, requires us to solve a seemingly intractable conundrum, the very one which, in part, motivated Descartes' own dualism. The mind has certain distinctive features, such as its rationality and subjectivity, which do not allow it to fit neatly with the scientific view of the world we have inherited from Descartes and his contemporaries, and yet it has others, such as its causal efficacy, which suggest that it should. Exploring this question will be our task in the following chapters.

Further reading

The first port of call for students of Descartes' philosophy of mind is his *Meditations on first philosophy*, though it is also worth looking at the *Discourse on the method, Treatise on man, Description of the human body*, and, especially, *The passions of the soul*. All of these (some in abridged form) can be found in the two-volume translation by John Cottingham, Robert Stoothoff and Dugald Murdoch, *The philosophical writings of Descartes* (Cambridge: Cambridge University Press, 1984). John Cottingham has also written an accessible commentary in his *Descartes* (Oxford: Blackwell, 1986) – see especially Chapter 5 – and Anthony Kenny's excellent study is available once again, *Descartes* (Bristol: Thoemmes Press, 1995). For a self-consciously alternative view on Descartes' philosophy of mind and its influence see Gordon Baker and Katherine J. Morris, *Descartes' dualism* (London: Routledge, 1996). The range of literature on the body is now vast, though very little is written from the point of view of the philosophy of mind. One exception is José Luis Bermudez, Anthony Marcel and Naomi Eilan (eds), *The body and the self* (Cambridge, Mass.: MIT Press, 1995). For a general introduction to issues concerning embodiment, see Rom Harré's *Physical being* (Oxford: Blackwell, 1991).

On the Cartesian conception of the body and its alternatives see Drew Leder, "A tale of two bodies: the Cartesian corpse and the lived body", in D. Leder (ed.), *The body in medical thought and practice* (Dordrecht: Kluwer Academic Publishing, 1992); Stuart Spicker (ed.), *The philosophy of the body* (Chicago: Quadrangle Books, 1970); and Donn Welton (ed.), *Body and flesh* (Oxford: Blackwell, 1998).

Chapter 2

Reductionism and the road to functionalism

Causation, scientific realism, and physicalism

Contemporary philosophy of mind is marked by its acceptance of one major strand in Cartesian thinking and its rejection of another. The strand that has been accepted is the causalist one: our psychological states are causally related to our behaviour, and thus they make a difference to what happens in the world of objects. Descartes accepted this and also held, of course, that mental states were states of an immaterial substance. This generated a key problem for him, namely to accommodate the causal interaction between mental and physical states. This is the part of his position which contemporary theorists resolutely reject. For them the only kind of substance is material substance. They therefore have to confront the question, if we abandon dualism, what is a mental state? In some way mental states must be states of a material substance. Different stories of how this can be the case have dominated philosophy of mind for the last fifty years or so.

As we made clear in Chapter 1, Descartes had reasons for his adoption of an immaterialist metaphysic. He was struck by characteristics of the mental, in addition to its causal role, which seemed difficult to reconcile with a simple mechanistic conception of human beings – rationality and subjectivity to name two key ones. Any materialist position therefore has to provide some account of how these features can be accommodated outside of Descartes' dualistic framework. We will address these issues in later chapters. Here our focus will be on the attempts which have been made to put together a causal role for the mental with a materialist metaphysic.

We will begin by considering what concept of causation is informing this task.[1] The central assumption, which has been dominant from the time of Hume,[2] is that to provide a causal explanation of an event is to show that it is the kind or type of thing which generally happens in the circumstances in which it occurs. To point to a particular cause is to point to something which is of a kind or type to regularly bring about the kind of effect in question. If we ask "Why is the window broken?", we may answer "Because a ball hit it." If there is genuine causality here, then this sequence is an example of the kind of thing that generally happens. To spell out the generality would involve references to more than balls and windows. Whether the window breaks depends on more than the ball hitting it; how fragile it was, for example, and how hard it was hit. We often cannot spell out all the conditions relevant to a particular causal sequence when we make a causal claim. According to the account of causation in terms of regularity, however, there will always be a set of conditions present which ensure that the individual causal sequence is an instance of a general law-like generalization.

The account of causation in terms of regularities is interdependent with an account in terms of future conditionals and counterfactuals. Causal claims characteristically support future conditional and counterfactual claims. If the ball hitting the window caused the window to break, then, barring the coincidence of another cause of the window breaking occurring simultaneously, if the ball had not hit the window then the window would not have broken. Moreover, given that the ball hit the window, in those circumstances, then the window would, or probably would, break.[3] Where we point to one phenomenon as causally explaining another we are therefore claiming that in the circumstances the cause was both necessary and sufficient for (or rendered probable) its effect. The grounding of the truth or warranty of conditional and counter-factual claims is a controversial issue in philosophy.[4] However, on most accounts the grounding of such conditionals requires the truth of law-like generalizations of the kind discussed above. The claim that the generalizations are law-like is, after all, the claim that they can be projected, or carried over, to future and counter-factual cases.

In the philosophy of mind, the fact that psychological explanations appear to support conditionals has been an important argument for the claim that psychological states are causally linked to action. For these conditionals seem to parallel those of other causal explanations. If I explain my going to the kitchen by my intention to fetch a drink, then I imply that without such an intention I would not have gone, and also that, other things being equal, if I have such an intention I will go.[5] For most theorists,[6] accepting a causal account of such conditionals requires that individual psychological causal explanations be supported by law-like regularities linking psychological states to each other and behaviour.

The law-like generalizations that are central to such an account of causation are empirical in character.[7] It is generally considered to be the role of scientific investigation to discover such laws. In this way this dominant account of causation brings all causal claims into the domain of science. For some, but not all theorists, such a broadly Humean account of causation needs supplementing. For such theorists each causal interaction must involve something like an underlying mechanism that serves to explain why the regularity holds. For those who hold such a view the basic causal mechanisms are usually regarded as those operating at some fundamental physical level, so that macro causal links are seen as constituted out of causal links between micro-particles.[8] This generates a demand that, whenever we appear to have causal links at some level other than that of physics, we are under some onus to show how they can be grounded in such micro-particulate ones. In terms of the causal links between psychological states and action, the challenge becomes to explain how such interactions can be anchored in fundamental physical ones.

The approach to causal explanation outlined above shows one way in which contemporary philosophy of mind is currently informed by contemporary philosophy of science. Here the positivism dominant earlier in the century has been replaced by what has been termed scientific realist approaches. Within the positivist framework the job of science was to discover regularities which would enable us to make predictions regarding what we could observe. Here there was no commitment to the existence of underlying mechanisms. This difference in the treatment of causality is linked to a difference in the treatment of theoretical entities. On the positivist approach, in our attempt to uncover systematic laws we are led to postulate theoretical states that mediate the law-like relations between observables. These, however, are regarded as heuristic devices, to facilitate predictions between what we can observe: they are treated either as useful fictions or as exhaustively specified in terms of their relation to observables. This is the instrumentalist approach to theoretical entities.[9] However, with the development of increasingly sophisticated observational devices many of these "fictions" came to be observed, and a positivist conception of scientific method proved increasingly problematic. Instead, a "realist" approach to theoretical entities emerged. The theoretical terms in our scientific theory were then interpreted as making references to real entities and properties in our world. Such entities were initially identifiable only by their effects. It was, however, the job of scientific investigation to uncover their essential properties. When this view is put together with the approach to causation above, then such essential properties were expected to provide the underlying causal mechanisms in virtue of which the kinds being investigated fitted into laws.[10]

This approach to theoretical entities fitted an overall approach to scientific method in which scientific kinds were seen as natural kinds. Here the picture is of a nature already divided into kinds which await our discovery ("cutting nature at its joints"[11]). These kinds are those in virtue of which nature instantiates law-like regularities, and are there awaiting our discovery once we hit upon a system of classification that matches the structure of the natural world.

The prevalent approach to philosophy of science influences the account of what is involved in having a mental state. Those who were positivist in their philosophy of science saw psychological states as theoretical entities postulated to explain regularities in behaviour, and their empirical import was exhausted by the implications they carried for such behaviour.[12] On such an account, to desire some end, for example, simply consisted in displaying, or potentially displaying, a certain behaviour pattern. However, such behaviourism fell out of fashion as more realist philosophies of science developed. On this contemporary account our psychological states are being viewed as natural kinds. They feature in causal explanatory generalizations predicting and explaining behaviour and it is up to scientific investigation to find out what their essential characteristics are, in a way which uncovers the causal mechanisms that support such explanations. The assumption of causalism, in the context of a scientific realist ontology, has therefore led to a conception of psychological states as states of a system causally responsible for bringing about behaviour, whose further characteristics are an appropriate object of scientific investigation.

The rejection of immaterial substance, which distinguishes a materialist approach to the question of mental states, has, within the framework of scientific realism, taken on the form of both ontological and explanatory physicalism. Ontologically, material entities and properties find their privileged articulation in the terms of physical science. Any real distinctions in the world, or distinctions with real empirical import, are ones which such physicalist theory can capture. Moreover there is no other comprehensive theory that can do this. From an explanatory perspective any phenomena that can be given a physicalist characterization can be given a complete causal explanation in physical terms. Physical effects have physical causes, supported by law-like generalizations that make reference to only physical kinds whose constitutive features provide us with the requisite causal mechanisms. There is also an additional assumption for the causal realist. All causal explanatory interactions in whatever vocabulary need to be anchored in and vindicated by these fundamental physical causal interactions. The task for contemporary philosophy of mind has, therefore, been taken to be, to give an account of mental states which accommodates the causal role of the mental in a way that is compatible with such ontological and explanatory physicalism.

Reductionism and central state materialism

The simplest way in which these constraints could be satisfied would be if mental states were reduced to physical ones, so this option was explored first. The idea behind reduction is that where we seem to have two entities, properties, or explanations, it turns out that there is only one. Examples from the non-psychological realm of successful reductions include the reduction of lightning to electricity and temperature to mean kinetic energy. Mental states cause behaviour, so, for example, when I go to the buffet for a cup of tea my body moves. These movements of my body are susceptible to physical description. Therefore given the constraint of explanatory physicalism they are susceptible to complete explanation in physical terms, most plausibly by reference to inner bodily states of mine, originating in my central nervous system. How are the psychological causal explanations in terms of my intentions, desires and beliefs to be linked to the physical causal explanations? An obvious move is to regard them as identical; to view our psychological descriptions as picking out physical kinds, just those kinds which also feature in physical causal explanations.[13] The essential characteristics of mental states turn out to be physical ones. Mental states are brain states.

The possibility of making this move rests on a conception of states, events and properties in which the same state, event or property can be picked out by different non-analytically equivalent descriptions. This must be so not only for particular events or states but also for kinds or types. For what is being claimed here is not only that each particular or token mental state, for example my fear of that spider now, is identical with some particular or token brain state. The claim is also the stronger one that being of the type or kind "fear of spiders" is the same as being of some physical type or kind.[14] This stronger claim is needed if we are to accommodate the causal explanatory role of our mental states. For what causally explains my walking towards the buffet is not just that I have a state which happens to be a desire for a drink. Its

29

being a desire for a drink, that is a state of that type, is central to the explanation.[15] Moreover, we are looking for an account of what it is to be a mental state, that is to say to be of a certain psychological kind. A type/type identity theory promises just this. For each psychological kind, it claims, there will be an account, in physical terms, of what is required for a state to be of this kind.

This answer to the mind/body question fitted into an overall model of the way in which different levels of scientific explanations fitted together, the picture of the unity of science.[16] Within this picture, explanations of "higher level sciences" were seen as reducing to those of "lower level sciences", culminating in a reduction to physics, which was seen as articulating in a privileged way the fundamental regularities governing the natural world. Economic and social science were seen as reducing to psychology, psychology to physiology, that to biology and chemistry and these ultimately to physics.

The model of reduction which informed this unity of science picture was given its classical formulation in the work of Ernest Nagel.[17] In Nagel's famous account the reduction of a theory consisted in its derivation from another more fundamental theory. This derivation can only take place if there are "conditions of connectability" relating the terms of the theory to be reduced to terms already present and playing a role in the reducing science. Such a condition is satisfied by means of "bridge laws", biconditionals linking the terms of each theory. Nagel avoided considerations of an ontological kind regarding the status of such bridge laws, but other theorists have in general treated them as claims of reductive identity between the properties or kinds picked out at each level of theory. What could the basis be for asserting such identities? First, the properties up for identification must be found always and only together, in a way that seems to project to future and counterfactual cases (they must be nomologically coextensive). Secondly, the reducing property must explain all the phenomena explainable by the property to be reduced, so that there is no distinct role for the higher property to be playing independently of the lower-level ones. When we discovered that lightning was static electricity our theory of electricity could explain all the effects of lightning. There was no room for the possibility that we might have two coexisting but distinct kinds of entity.

To speak of a theory being reduced is to privilege the descriptions at the reducing level. One reason for this may be the greater generality of the lower-level laws, which might enable, for example, the whole of biology to be derivable from chemistry and physics, but not vice versa. For some, the privileging reflects assumptions concerning the operations of fundamental causal mechanisms. Often it simply reflects the prevailing metaphysical bias favouring certain kinds of entities as less problematic, more comprehensible than others, and attempting to provide explanatory theories in terms of these. When this model was applied to the relations between mental states and physical states the claims made were that law-like generalizations linking psychological kinds and behaviour were derivable from law-like generalizations employing physical kinds as a result of identifications between psychological kinds and physical ones. (See Figure 2.1.)

It is important to notice that the bridge laws express pairings between unique kinds from each level of theory. Crucially the reducing kind can be individuated from within the resources of the lower-level theory and is located within a systematic body of laws there. The asymmetry favours the lower-level physicalist kinds.

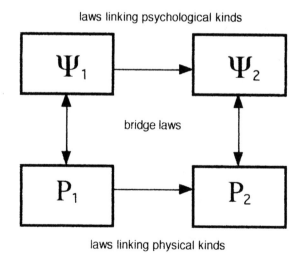

laws linking psychological kinds

bridge laws

laws linking physical kinds

Figure 2.1

31

They are privileged because of our ontological physicalism. In terms of our scientific realist picture such a reduction is a consequence of our supposedly uncovering the intrinsic properties of psychological kinds. The ambition is that we will discover, for example, that pain is the firing of C-fibres, in the way we discovered that water was H_2O, that light is electromagnetic radiation, or that temperature is mean kinetic energy. This type/type identity theory, identifying mental states with internal, usually brain states, of a person was the predominant paradigm in philosophy of mind in the 1950s and much of the 1960s. It is still regarded by many as the only way of ensuring a genuine causal role for the mental in a way compatible with ontological and explanatory physicalism.

Problems with central state materialism

For the classical reductionist picture to fit the relation between mental states and brain states, certain conditions had to be fulfilled. For every psychological kind featuring in a causally explanatory generalization, there had to be some physical kind which was coextensive with it, whose causal properties explained everything we invoked our psychological kind to explain, and which yielded all the identifying characteristics that we associated with the psychological kind (or at least those we regarded as real).

Many of those opposing the reductionist picture have claimed that none of these conditions can be met. They argue that there are distinctive characteristics of the mental which no physicalist identification can accommodate, principally intentional and qualitative content. These are issues for each of the materialist frameworks and will be dealt with in later chapters. Other problems, however, led to the development of other forms of materialist reduction, and will be considered here. The type/type identity theory requires some physical kind which will be coextensive with each psychological kind and will explain all and only what it explains. It became apparent, however, that this was, empirically, wildly implausible. Take the example of an intentional state like wanting to go for a walk. Many different people can be in such a state, and the same person can be in this state on many different occasions and in widely different circumstances: rambling around the moors, being pushed round the block in a wheelchair, and so on. Dogs can also want to go for walks. It does not seem likely that on each of these occasions, when the same kind of psychological state is instantiated, the creatures concerned have brains instantiating exactly the same kind of physical states. Kim makes the point with reference to pain:

> Type physicalism says that pain is C-fibre excitation. But that implies that unless an organism has C-fibres or a brain of an appropriate biological structure it cannot have pain. But aren't there pain-capable organisms like reptiles and molluscs, with brains very different from the human brain? . . . moreover, the neural substrates of certain mental functions can differ from person to person and may change over time even in a single individual, through maturation, learning and injuries to the brain.[18]

One possible response to this line of objection is to attempt to provide organism-specific reductions. We cannot find something to reduce "wanting a walk" to in general, but we can try for humans or maybe for a given individual.[19] The problem with such an approach is that, first, given the considerations which Kim puts forward, this project looks highly problematic even on such a restrictive basis. Secondly, such piecemeal reductions would do away with the generality of the concept. "Pain for H" would be one thing and "pain for D" would be another, and we would have no way of capturing a characteristic that we might share with dogs and reptiles and indeed other people.

This is the "multiple realization" argument against the type/type identity theory which began to emerge in the late 1960s.[20] It is so called because it draws attention to the fact that any single kind of psychological state can have multiple correlates, in different people/organisms or even in the same person at different times. In the face of this problem many theorists tried to satisfy their materialist intuitions by adopting a token/token as opposed to a type/type identity theory.[21] Here the claim was that every particular mental event/state was identical with an event/state characterizable in physical terms. Each mental state had both mental and physical characteristics, but there was no systematic link between the physical kinds of state which on different occasions were identified with one mental kind of state. There are a number of issues arising in relation to such token identity claims. One concerns whether the different principles of classification evident in mental and physical *kinds*, which led to the failure of type/type identity claims, might not also affect particulars or tokens. Secondly and crucially, such token identity theories leave unresolved the question of the relation between mental and physical properties. A dualism of substance has been replaced by a dualism of properties. Such a theory has not therefore answered the question of what is involved in having mental states of certain kinds. This question is not answered simply by the claim that each mental state also has a physical description. Moreover, in retaining a dualism of properties it has retained the dilemma with regard to causal explanation, which provides one of the motivations for reduction in the first place. As we noted above, what causally explains my actions seems to be the fact that I have psychological states of certain kinds. We are therefore left with the question of how the psychological and physical causal properties relate to each other without our behaviour being over-determined.[22]

For some, the failure of classical reduction casts doubts on the legitimacy of our psychological kinds. For such theorists (eliminativists[23]), if properties cited in causal explanations cannot be reduced to underlying physical properties, the reality of such higher-level properties is in question. On this account, explanations that appear to invoke irreducible kinds should be replaced by ones invoking kinds which conform to the reductionist picture. The picture that is being adopted here is one in which everyday explanations, often referred to as "folk psychology", hypothesize the existence of kinds of inner states whose nature it is up to science to investigate. When such an investigation gets underway, however, we discover, for the reasons Kim suggests, that there are no inner kinds whose individuating conditions match those suggested in our folk psychological explanations. The conclusion the eliminativist draws is that this is so much the worse for our everyday explanations. They should be replaced by ones that invoke kinds for which we can find physicalist individuating conditions. Psychological explanations invoking beliefs and desires are, thereby, compared to past explanations that made reference to witches. When we have the replacement theory in place we will recognize that there are no such things as beliefs and desires, in the same way, it is claimed, that we now recognize that there are no witches.

For others, however, to reject our everyday psychological explanations and apparently come to believe, for example, that beliefs do not exist seems scarcely intelligible, and indeed self-defeating.[24] For such theorists, if the model of reduction cannot be satisfied in the mental/physical case then the model needs to be revised, and the constraints of ontological and explanatory physicalism recast in somewhat less demanding terms.

Modified ontological physicalism: supervenience

It has now become common for minimalist ontological physicalist demands to be formulated with the help of the concept of supervenience. The concept of supervenience was first used in the moral sphere, as a means of capturing the relation between moral characteristics of situations and natural ones. Two situations cannot be equivalent in natural properties and yet consistently be judged as morally distinct. If the natural properties are the same then so must be the moral ones. "He hit me and you did not tell him off, so you can't tell me off if I hit him" is a line of defence which is learnt very young![25] The term is now widely used to describe the relation between mental and physical characteristics, to capture the intuition that many people have, that if we were to encounter an atom by atom duplicate of ourselves then we would expect it to have the same kind of psychological characteristics too. (We may need to add the proviso here that they are/have been placed in similar environments, but we are postponing a discussion of that until Chapter 4.)

The concept was introduced into philosophy of mind by Donald Davidson,[26] where, in arguing for a token/token identity theory, he was faced with the question of how the mental and physical characteristics of these token events are related to each other. His answer was that mental characteristics supervene on physical ones. Dualism of properties was thereby supposedly rescued from any dubious metaphysics.

There appears to be an important difference between the moral case and the psychological one. The relation between moral properties and natural ones is built into the grammar of our moral vocabulary. Someone has not grasped the practice of giving moral justifications if they don't accept the requirements of the supervenience relation. If we are to justify a difference in moral judgement we need to come up with some difference in the situation characterized non-morally. "You're bigger than him" might or might not do! In the mental/physical case it is not so clearly a reflection of the grammar of our mental terms that leads to assumptions that physical duplicates will be psychological duplicates also. For most theorists interested in reduction this assumption is a reflection of our metaphysical framework. It is an expression of materialism. Dualists of a Cartesian kind would not hold it. Although we might upbraid them for mystification, we cannot so easily accuse them of not grasping the grammar of our mental terms.

The claim that the mental supervenes on the physical has two strands. First there is the indiscernibility claim: two items that are physically indiscernible must be mentally indiscernible. There can be no mental difference without a physical difference. Crucially, however, there can be physical differences without mental differences and mental indiscernibility does not necessarily yield physical indiscernibility.[27] This indiscernibility claim can be held in a global or local way. At its most global, the relation connects whole families of properties or predicates. Worlds indiscernible in physical respects are indiscernible in mental respects. In this form no attempt would be made to map the mental properties of individuals onto the physical properties of those individuals. At its most local it can be a claim concerning the mental and physical properties of individual events or organisms, and clearly there are a range of possibilities in between.[28] If supervenience is thought of purely as an indiscernibility claim, however, it does not seem to be a relation that is sufficiently strong to capture physicalist intuitions, in particular the ontological priority which many want to give the physical. So a second strand is often invoked, namely the physicalist claim that the mental properties of a thing are *fixed* by its physical properties, which are the fundamental ones. This claim is also sometimes expressed as the claim that the physical facts, those described by the most basic physical theories, are the facts in virtue of which all true descriptions of the world are true. Understanding claims of supervenience to involve both strands, indiscernibility and ontological priority, a commitment to ontological physicalism was recast in terms of the claim that psychological states are supervenient on physical ones.

Once the supervenience relation has been articulated in this way, it becomes clear that there are many examples of it outside of the mental/physical or moral/natural domains. A commitment to the ontological primacy of the physical leads to the claim that all higher-level macro-properties are supervenient on lower-level physical ones. For example, the macro-properties of a room; that it includes tables, chairs, clothes and pictures are supervenient on the micro-particulate properties instantiated in the same spatio-temporal zone (simplifying out for the moment relational properties which might require micro-particulate grounding outside of that space/time zone). Alternatively, the colour of a butterfly's wings supervenes on the biochemical make-up of the wings.

If ontological physicalism is characterized in terms of such dependency claims, however, we need to pay attention to the kind of dependency involved. The supervenience relation is intended to be distinct from that of causality, as that is ordinarily conceived, for the states of affairs concerned are not thought of as being sufficiently distinct for the relation to be a causal one. This has led some theorists[29] to argue that the dependency involved is logical. The presence of the base states *entails* the presence of the higher-level states. However, accepting the entailment claim requires that some account of our mental properties be given which makes clear how such entailments between the physical and the mental can hold. The demand of *entailment*, moreover, seems not to apply to all cases where we might think relations of dependency are present. Consider the case in which our description of a room in terms of macro-objects is supervenient on its descriptions in terms of certain kinds of molecules at certain space/time points. The former description, though dependent on the latter, is not derivable from it. However, once the micro-particulate description has been instantiated the macro-object description has also been satisfied. Crucially, nothing further has to occur for this to be the case. Kim gives an example from the realm of aesthetics:

> Your aim is to create a work with certain expressive qualities ... but the work you do on the slab of marble is laborious physical work, cutting, drilling ... You are giving it a physical shape and texture; that is you are endowing the piece of marble with a set of physical properties. When the physical work has been finished, there is no further aesthetic work to do, no further steps of attaching beauty and other desired aesthetic properties to the object you have created ... [30]

The reformulation of ontological physicalism in terms of a supervenience relation, would seem to involve the following claims. Whenever mental properties or set of properties are instantiated, then some physical properties are instantiated which are sufficient for the mental properties concerned. Such sufficiency claims are supported by law-like generalizations linking physical base properties to higher-level psychological ones. These laws, however, unlike reductive ones, go in only one direction. The mental properties are not in general sufficient for any given set of physical properties, for they may be found with different physical properties on different occasions. The mental, however, cannot float free. If a mental property or set of properties is instantiated, then some physical property or set of properties must be present which is sufficient for it. Nonetheless the mental property remains distinct from each of its many bases. The dependency involved is therefore distinct from that of reductive identification.[31] Such a modified physicalism no longer seeks to give an account of what is involved in having a psychological state in terms of physical essences. It allows a dualism of mental and physical properties so long as the psychological properties are dependent in this way on the physical ones. It therefore appears less demanding in its conditions than the type/type identity theory and able to accommodate the range of physical bases grounding each psychological kind, which proved problematic for this theory.

Although supervenience claims in relation to mental and physical characteristics were introduced to accommodate the issue of property dualism confronting token identity theorists, the two claims are independent. It is possible to accept that mental characteristics supervene on physical characteristics without accepting that mental tokens and physical tokens are identical.[32] Supervenience is less demanding than token/token identity claims. It is a relation between properties and, although it is quite compatible with token/token identity claims, it does not assume that the individuation into token events or states at the psychological level will coincide with such individuation at the physical level.

For some it has seemed that if we accept that mental characteristics supervene on physical ones, then we should be able to make intelligible how it is that our psychological descriptions are made true by physical states, even if this requirement falls short of demanding the kind of entailment favoured by some theorists. Without some account of the mental to suggest how this is *possible*, the relation remains brute and mysterious. Instead of solving the mind/body problem by use of this concept we will instead, it has been argued, simply have reformulated it. Here the case of mental/physical supervenience seems to differ from some of the other cases we have discussed. Although we cannot systematically derive the macro-properties of a room from its micro-properties, we have no difficulty in grasping how it is that, once the base set of properties have been instantiated, no further work has to be done in order for the other set also to be instantiated. But, this is just what does seem puzzling in the mental/physical case. We cannot see how the distinctive character of the mental requires nothing more than the instantiation of physical properties. We will return to the intelligibility condition below, when we consider how it is addressed in contemporary functionalism. But first we need to consider how explanatory physicalism became modified following the failure of classical reduction.

Modified explanatory physicalism: the disunity of science picture

Within the classical reductive picture, outlined above, the causal effectiveness of higher-level properties and laws was a consequence of their respective identification with and derivation from laws at some underlying physical level. If we reject the reductive picture in this form, however, then we need to readdress the issue of how causal explanations and causal generalizations at different levels of description relate to each other. For the explanatory physicalist we need to do this without forfeiting the assumption of the completeness of physics.

Once we accept the multiple realizability thesis then the classical reductive picture seems to require replacement by a model more like that suggested by Jerry Fodor in a paper discussing the status of the special sciences.[33] Here (Figure 2.2) we have a picture in which each instantiation of a higher-level property is dependent on some lower-level property, in line with the model suggested by our modified ontological physicalism. In a given instance the instantiation of the properties at each level are interdependent. So, for example in the psychological case, the necessity and sufficiency

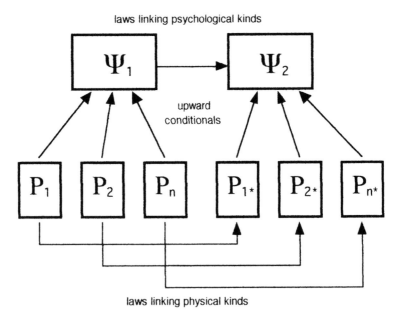

Figure 2.2

of the psychological antecedents of a given act can thereby be made compatible with the existence of physical conditions sufficient for the bodily movement it involves, because of the relation of super-venience between the psychological and physical antecedents. There is, however, a *disjunction* of base properties for each higher-level property, with no suggestion that such a disjunction con-stitutes a unity at the lower level. Consequently there is no way of deducing the higher-level generalizations from the lower-level ones. These higher-level generalizations, therefore, retain a certain autonomy, even though each particular causal interaction involving higher-level properties can be argued to be constituted out of interactions at the micro-particulate level. If we paid atten-tion only to this level, however, we would miss general law-like patterns, which we need attention to higher-level properties to be able to articulate. Fodor suggests that this picture is appropriate for higher-level sciences which are not susceptible to classical reductive procedures.

Such modified explanatory physicalism is much less demanding than that suggested by the unity of science picture. What has been dropped is the requirement that higher-level laws should be deriv-able from lower-level ones. At best, on the modified picture any such derivations will be from a possibly infinite disjunction of lower-level laws, which do not form any unity within their own domain. While rejecting classical reduction, such a model accepts the completeness of physics and rules out causal over-determination by means of the conditional dependencies between the instantiation of the mental and physical properties that follow from the supervenience claims. For some, however, such explana-tory physicalism is not seen as being sufficiently robust. They argue that the higher-level properties are not doing real causal work, for this is taking place at the lower physical level, and on this account the characteristics at each level are not identified. For others, in the absence of classical reduction, the success of the higher-level laws remains mysterious if they are not derivable from lower-level laws. We will investigate each of these criticisms in the following section. It is important to note, however, that these worries would attach to all higher-level causal regularities ("mating cause reproduction") and not just to psychological ones.

Supervenient causation

It has been argued that if we reject the classical reductive picture and replace it with modified ontological and explanatory physicalism then the causal role of higher-level properties is what Kim calls supervenient causation,[34] an offshoot of the nitty-gritty causal processes that are going on at the physical level and the relations of supervenience between this base and the higher-level properties. There therefore turn out to be, for Kim, two kinds of causal relation, causation *per se* and supervenient causation, and the latter is both dependent on and somewhat less robust than the former. Here is how Kim describes Figure 2.3:[35]

> In this diagram "causes$_{sup}$" is to be read "superveniently causes" or "is a supervenient cause of"; the broken arrows represent this relation. As the diagram illustrates, the pain supervenes on N and the wincing supervenes on the contraction of a certain group of muscles.[36]

On this picture the "real" causal work is being done at the physical level with the supervenient base of the pain causing the muscle contraction seen as the base of wincing. The apparent causal link at the psychological level is a consequence of this physical causal link and the relation of supervenience between the physical bases and the higher-level properties. This might seem to bring the causal role of the higher-level properties too close to epiphenomenalism, the theory that the mental, though caused by the physi-

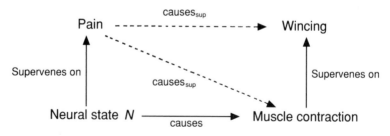

Figure 2.3

cal, has itself no causal impact on the physical. It appears that the causal interactions at the physical level would proceed whether or not there were higher-level properties supervenient on them. Kim replies to this that the higher- and lower-level properties are not sufficiently distinct to make the comparison with epiphenomenalism the apt one. They are rather related "in the way the rigidity of a steel rod relates to its molecular structure". This model of causal explanation also applies to all macro-causal relations, not just those involving mental causes, "which makes supervenient causation as causally robust as . . . the familiar physical phenomena of daily experience".[37] For Kim, therefore, our modified ontological and explanatory physicalism is adequate to accommodate the causal role of the mental within a physicalist framework and therefore to answer the motivations that set us on the road to reductionism. For his opponents, however, this causal role has not been adequately accommodated.[38] If real causation is taking place at the physical level and we wish to ensure a real causal role for the mental, then we need to go back to the classical reductive picture with which we began.

Kim identifies *two* kinds of causal relation by adding to the Humean regularity conditions a causal realism anchored in microparticulate causal interactions. His opponents in accepting such causal realism want a return to classical reductionism. These are not the only options, however. Much hinges on the sets of conditions that are going to be set for genuine causation. For those who rest the legitimacy of causal claims on support from law-like generalizations, the modified explanatory physicalism outlined in the previous section gives the law-like generalizations at the psychological level a certain *autonomy*, which seems to give them some explanatory work to do on their own terms, even if each particular psychological causal interaction is mediated through a physical one.[39] For others, however, this leaves the coincidence of prediction based on generalizations at different levels mysteriously brute. How is it that when the psychological generalizations lead to the prediction of a certain kind of action, the physical generalizations predict bodily movements of a kind to form a supervenient base for such an action?[40] For some writers who regard this as a dilemma we need to return to the classical reductionist view, perhaps with species specific reductions; or find some alternative story, perhaps in evolutionary terms, for the coincidence of predictions emerging from the different levels. Those who think the classical reductive picture is unrealizable, however, and who accept modified onto-logical and explanatory physicalism, must either accept the some-what second-class status of mental causation, as supervenient causation, if they accept a certain kind of causal realism; or remain much more Humean about causation and anchor the causal role of psychological states in the autonomous regularities at the psychological level.

Functionalism

We began this chapter with two tasks which have been informing work in modern philosophy of mind. One was to provide an ac-count of what was involved in having mental states, in a way that respected ontological physicalism. The second was to allow for the causal explanatory role of the mental in a way that respects explanatory physicalism. If we reject classical reduction there is a debate, laid out in the previous section, as to how well the second task has been accomplished. Crucially, however, the first task also remains incomplete. Accepting a supervenience thesis gives us, in itself, no account of what is involved in having a mental state. Moreover, for many it generates an intelligibility condition which needs to be met. It is here that the current paradigm in philosophy of mind, reductive functionalism, comes to the fore. It claims to provide us with an account of what is involved in having mental states of different kinds and to make it intelligible how being in certain physical states can be sufficient, in the way outlined above, for being in certain psychological states. In addition, it explains how it is that a variety of physical states can constitute the same psychological one.

The basic idea informing functionalist accounts of mental states is that the classical reductive picture tried to link mental and physical properties using the wrong level of description of the physical properties. It tried to find physical correlates for mental kinds by attending to physical kinds individuated in terms of their material constituents, neural firings and so forth. Functionalists suggest instead that if we classify our physical states in terms of their relational properties, their overall functional role within the organization of the systems they are part of, then it will be possible to reduce psychological states to them. According to functionalism a mental property is a functional property, that is a property individuated by means of its functional role. The "function" involved here is a causal one, so in this account an agent is in some mental state, for example believing that it will rain, if they are in some state that plays a specified causal role in determining their response to their environment, for example taking an umbrella. Psychological states are thought of as inner states whose identity as distinct psychological states depends on their role in mediating responses to environmental stimuli. The causal relation of states to each other as well as to environmental conditions and behavioural output all form part of their functional role. In this picture functional states, in being causal states, identified by causal role, can feature in causal claims without threat of over-determination. A comparison might help. Consider an explanation of a window breaking in terms of it having the property of being fragile. This is not in competition with an explanation in molecular terms, but more like a promissory note that the molecular explanation redeems. On different occasions, however, the way the note is redeemed may be different.

There is an initial plausibility, for a range of our psychological terms, in viewing these as picking out functional kinds. Behaviourism had initially derived its plausibility from the recognition that there is some kind of constitutive link between the attribution of psychological states and the manifestation or potential manifestation of certain patterns of response. We grasp what is involved in wanting something by grasping that wanting leads us to try to get it. We learn pain vocabulary in the context of damage to the body and displays of crying and wincing. We do not have a grasp of belief if we do not recognize that beliefs tend to generate other beliefs which they directly imply. Functionalism, moreover, in viewing psychological states as inner states causally producing such behaviour, appears to have an advantage over such behaviourism in accommodating the causal role of the mental.

Functionalists, therefore, give an answer to the question of what is involved in having certain mental characteristics. This is to have certain inner states with particular kinds of functional role. In this view psychological kinds can still be viewed as natural kinds, in the sense of carving up the world in a way that enables us to generate law-like causal generalizations. In line with such a natural kinds model we need to give an account of the essential properties of such kinds. The distinctive twist is that such essential properties turn out to be the functional ones allocated to them in causal theories explaining our behavioural outputs in different kinds of environment.

In attempting to give a functionalist characterization of psychological kinds, it is clear that we cannot specify the causal role of one psychological state independently of reference to others. Virtually any belief could yield any behaviour if found with an appropriate set of other beliefs and desires. No one would take an umbrella, for example, on believing it was raining, if she wanted to get wet, or if she found carrying an umbrella too cumbersome. However, if we accept that our psychological states are individuated by their position within a causally explanatory theory, it might be claimed that reference to each of them can be replaced in the theory by a variable. The demand which the theory makes of a system to which it applies can then be expressed as an existential claim to the effect that the system has some set of states related to each other in the way the theory specifies for its variables. It is in such a holistic way that functionalists envisage that we can provide functionalist individuating conditions for our psychological kinds.[41] The upshot of such a method is that we now have a statement that tells us how any creature's states must be related if that creature is to have mental properties.

Although it is possible to be a functionalist and think that the inner states that play these distinctive causal roles are constituted out of soul stuff, in fact most (all?) functionalists are physicalists, for functionalism was designed as a response to physicalist demands that avoided type/type identity. Functionalists assume that the inner states that are needed to make true the functionalist descriptions will be physical states. Our functional characterization tells us that a system must have sets of states causally related in certain kinds of ways if it is to have a psychology. The idea is that we can then establish whether a physical system is of the appropriate kind by seeing if it has sets of states causally related in the way specified. These causal properties are those in virtue of which it exemplifies a functional structure, which is what is required for it to have mental properties. There may, however, be different physical states, in terms of their material constitution, which, on different occasions, instantiate the same functional structure. The functionalist theory therefore recognizes the phenomenon of multiple realization and this provides it with one of its main advantages over the type/type identity theory. We therefore get a model of the relations between the mental and the physical of the following kind: mental kinds are identified with functional kinds. Functional kinds supervene on physical kinds, with the same functional kind being instantiated by (probably) different physical kinds on different occasions. The relation between the mental and the physical therefore becomes comprehensible by the introduction of intermediate levels of description. Once they are given their functional characterization, psychological properties become manifestly ones which physical systems can have. (See Figure 2.4.)

Functionalism, therefore, is a theory that appears to suit the demands of modified ontological physicalism. One of the strongest arguments in its favour is that it makes intelligible the supervenience claims in terms of which such physicalism was articulated. If the psychological classification is in terms of functional role then it is supposed to be clear how a variety of physical states can play the same functional role in different organisms or the same organism at different times. The mystery has disappeared. The functionalist picture also fits into the modified unity of science model, which Fodor suggests. Classification into functional kinds generates lawlike generalizations that can be used for prediction and explanation. These generalizations are not themselves derivable from underlying physical ones; but on each occasion in which we have a causal interaction between states characterized functionally, they supervene on states that can be given a characterization in terms of material constitution and between which micro-particulate causal interactions take place.

A key question arises, however, when we consider how we are to arrive at the functional accounts of our psychological kinds. Here

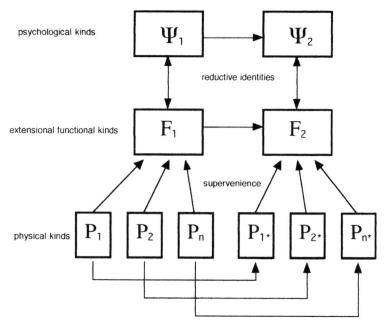

Figure 2.4

functionalists are divided. Some functionalists claim that such descriptions will be available to us simply by reflection on our everyday explanatory practices. Desires for states of affairs produce, other things being equal, behaviour believed to be a way of bringing about those states of affairs. Beliefs produce behaviour consistent with the content of the belief being true, and so on. Pains are produced mostly by damage to the body and bring about avoidance behaviour, requests for sympathy and nursing of the damaged parts. Such definitions can be thought of as *a priori*, in which case the functional descriptions are thought of as analytically derivable from our everyday psychological ones. It is, of course, just such everyday explanatory practices which give the claim that psychological kinds are functional kinds their initial plausibility. Such functional definitions are not reductive, however: they do not identify properties at the psychological level with properties described non-mentalistically. The causal roles of our psychological kinds, which are likely to be available to us from reflecting on our everyday practices, will be articulated utilizing psychological vocabulary. This makes such *anti-reductionist functionalism* of little use within the overall physicalist project. Although it makes the claim that psychological kinds are identifiable with functional kinds easier to defend, it makes the next stage of the process more difficult. It becomes much more difficult to make it manifest how such psychologically characterized properties are ones that physical systems could intelligibly instantiate. If it is to become intelligible how purely physical systems can satisfy our functional descriptions, then the functional roles must not be specified in psychological vocabulary. Rather, the causal properties that are invoked in a functional characterization must be describable in theory-neutral, non-psychological, vocabulary. Then it will be transparent how purely physical states can instantiate such causal roles.

The reductive functionalism that attempts to characterize the functional role of our psychological states in such a non-mentalistic way is of two kinds. Those who defend *commonsense functionalism* argue that even such non-mentalistic definitions will be derivable from our everyday practices.[42] Others, *scientific functionalists*,[43] in accordance with the model of scientific realism outlined at the beginning of the chapter, see the uncovering of the functional definitions as a job for scientific psychology. *Reductionist functionalism*, in one of these forms, constitutes the dominant paradigm in modern philosophy of mind and will be interrogated in later chapters of this book. While such reductive functionalism is viewed as necessary for physicalism, for it provides causal roles that physical states can intelligibly occupy, it is more difficult to make plausible in itself. For it is hard to see how psychological states as we ordinarily think of them can be conceived of simply as states playing such abstractly specified causal roles. For reductive functionalism to work, there must be non-psychologically characterizable functional kinds coextensive with mental kinds, and these must be able to explain and predict what such mental kinds explain and predict, as well as being able to accommodate the characteristics that we consider distinctive of our mental kinds. If such characteristics cannot be accommodated then they must be shown to be in some way illusory. It will be the task of the next few chapters to assess how well functionalists are able to perform these reductive tasks.

Further reading

A number of recent introductions to philosophy of mind lay out the route to the contemporary functionalist paradigm and assess its credibility. See Jaegwon Kim, *Philosophy of mind* (Colorado: Westview Press, 1996); David Braddon-Mitchell and Frank Jackson, *Philosophy of mind and cognition* (Oxford: Blackwell, 1996). Kim's book *Supervenience and mind* (Cambridge: Cambridge University Press, 1993) is the best place to go for a detailed look at that relation.

Chapter 3

Computational models of mind

Intentionality

The current functionalist, materialist paradigm in philosophy of mind resulted from adopting a Cartesian account of the causal relations between mind and action, while dropping mental substance. The causal relation then had to be accommodated within the other half of the Cartesian dualism, a mechanical body. The postulation of immaterial substance was, however, for Descartes, a response to recognizing distinctive characteristics of the mental, which he was unable to accommodate within his mechanistic physical world. The challenge to the contemporary picture is to find a way of accommodating these distinctively psychological phenomena in a way that is compatible with the paradigm outlined in the previous chapter. Such a position, that of reductive functionalism, claimed to show how psychological characteristics can intelligibly arise in a material world whose privileged articulation is given to physical science. In this chapter and the next we will be assessing this naturalizing project with respect to the interconnected characteristics of intentionality and rationality.

> Maureen sets off to her friend Evie's house, remembering her friend's five Barbie dolls, one with a tail like a fish, pleasurably anticipating playing with them away from the discomforting eyes of her mother.

In this story our understanding of Maureen's behaviour rests on the attribution to her of a number of mental states, which possess the feature of intentionality. They are about something or some-one, or some actual or non-actual state of affairs. This is known as their intentional content.[1] Our grasp of what kind of states they are, and their role in making Maureen's behaviour intelligible, requires us to grasp this content. It is not enough to know that she has memories and anticipated pleasures; we also need to know what she remembers and anticipates. Thoughts, beliefs, desires, fears, intentions, perceptions and many other mental states all have this kind of content.

The intentional content of psychological states has several inter-esting features. First, it is captured via descriptions whose mean-ing is anchored in characterizations of objects or states of affairs in the world: Barbie dolls, playing comfortably, going to the house of a friend. This might suggest that our intentional states are rela-tional states, signalling a relation between us and such states of affairs; but this cannot be the whole story. Although Maureen cannot hope to play with Evie's dolls, unless Evie has some, she can hope that Evie has some when, in reality, Evie's mother is as unco-operative in this regard as her own. Our mental states can be directed to a content that does not correspond to any actual state of affairs in the world. The second important point to notice is that it matters how we characterize the intentional content of our psychological states. Maureen may believe her friend Evie has Barbie dolls. Her friend Evie may be the smartest girl in the class, but we cannot thereby claim that Maureen believes that the smartest girl in the class has Barbie dolls. Indeed, Maureen may think she herself is the smartest girl and so believe that the smartest girl in the class has no Barbie dolls at all. This feature of our intentional states, known as their opacity, draws attention to the fact that when we are thinking about objects or states of affairs, we are thinking about them in a particular way.

The question of what kind of relation is required between a subject and states of affairs in the world, if our intentional states are to have the content they do, is an urgent one for the naturalizing project. We will address it in detail in the following chapter. The possibility of thinking about things that do not exist and the opacity of our attributions of intentional content, however, set certain kinds of constraint on what such an account can be like. It cannot simply be the case that the intentional content of our psychological states is fixed by the objects/states of affairs to which we stand in, for example, causal relations. For if that were the case then it would have neither of the above characteristics.[2]

Rationality: the calculative account

Intentional states stand in certain kind of relations to each other, rationalizing relations, in virtue of their intentional content. If someone believes that it will rain tomorrow, and believes that picnics are no fun in the rain, then it is rational for her to also believe that a picnic tomorrow will be no fun. If she believes that it will be raining tomorrow and she does not like to get wet, then she has some reason to plan to stay indoors. If she believes that the dog in front of her might bite, then she has a reason to be scared. Reason-giving links are distinctive. Although they can have causal consequences, to point to a reason-giving relation is not to say that one thing will follow another in accordance with a general law. It is rather to say that one thing *ought* to follow another, or that it would be in some way *appropriate* for it to follow. Of course things sometimes go as they should and sometimes they do not!

It is often said that reason-giving links hold in virtue of logical and conceptual links between the intentional contents of our intentional states. One way of bringing out the nature of this conceptual link is by the construction of reasoning, linking the agents' reason-providing states with the states for which they provide reasons. This suggests a model in which reason-giving links are viewed as essentially calculations based on logical relations between propositions. This is probably the dominant conception of reason-giving relations and we are going to discuss it before amending it later in the chapter. The reasoning envisaged is easiest to construct in the case of beliefs where the content of the reason-providing beliefs inductively or deductively support the content of the rationalized belief.

1. Picnics in the rain are no fun.
2. It will (probably) rain tomorrow.
3. A picnic tomorrow will (probably) be no fun.

Formalization of these processes of reasoning are provided in inductive and deductive logic.

In the case of reasons for actions, constructing the calculations is less straightforward.[3] Classically an agent has a reason to perform a certain kind of action when she has (a) a pro-attitude towards some end or objective, and (b) a belief that an action of that kind will promote this end. The reason-giving link is presented as a process of means/end calculation. The term "pro-attitude" derives from Donald Davidson.[4] It includes "desires, wantings, urges, promptings, and a great variety of moral views and aesthetic principles". It is common to use desire as a generic term for such pro-attitudes. In the case of reasons for actions, we are therefore looking for a relationship between the contents of the agents' intentional states and the descriptions of an action which shows that performing an action of that kind has some chance of promoting the desired goals. Something like the following schema must be instantiated:

Desire	Δ is desirable.
Belief	βing will promote Δ.
Rationalizes	(provides a reason for) βing.

Presenting this in a calculative way makes certain formal demands of the schema that is instantiated. The goal Δ must occur in premise one and two. The course of action, βing, mentioned in premise two must correspond to the description of the action that occurs in the conclusion. In this account we understand Maureen's activities because we can reconstruct a piece of reasoning:

Playing with Barbie dolls is desirable.
Going to Evie's house is a way of playing with Barbie dolls.
Go to Evie's house.

The presence of a reason for believing or acting does not necessarily make it rational for an agent to believe or act in that way.
She may have other beliefs that provide conflicting evidence or
conflicting desires. To establish what it is rational to believe or do
overall we would need, in the calculative account, to establish
principles for assessing competing probabilities and weighing
competing desires. This is formalized in contemporary probability
calculus and decision theory.[5] Of course, we do not always believe
or act in a way that is maximally rational. We accept things on less
than good evidence and often act on impulse or against our better
judgement (for example taking another cigarette). However, beliefs and actions are the kinds of things where it is appropriate to
ask for reasons and justifications, and to discuss and debate
whether our reasons are good enough.

Such a calculative picture of the reason-giving relation was
the one uppermost in Descartes' mind when he conceived of the
mind as the domain of reason, and saw rationalizing links as
systematizable under universal principles and rules. In this account, to grasp the rationality of a response is to see it as instantiating such a general principle.

The computational model of mind

One response by functionalist materialism to the difficulty of accommodating the interconnected features of intentionality and
rationality has been to develop a computational theory of mind.
The computational theory of mind is motivated by a number of
considerations. The general one is that of the reductive functionalist who wishes to make intelligible how a physical system can
manifest mentality. This requires giving an account in extensional
terms of the key features of intentionality and the rationalizing
relations that rest on it. Secondly, the computationist wants to be
able to anchor the causal explanatory work that our intentional
explanations do in causal transitions at the physical level. Such

anchorage needs to vindicate rather than undermine intentional causal explanations.

Most computationists accept that when we explain an agent's action by reference to her reasons we are making a causal claim: reason-giving explanations are a species of causal explanations.[6] Maureen's desire to play with Barbie dolls and her belief that her friend Evie has some provide both a reason for and a cause of her behaviour. The motivation for such a view parallels that for taking psychological explanations in general to be causal explanations. Maureen's reasons seem to make a difference to what happens. Without them she would not be setting off towards her friend's house. Secondly, the causal links here appear to hold in virtue of the rationalizing ones.[7] It is because a desire and belief make the behaviour rational that the behaviour occurs. If we are working on the assumption that the causal links at the intentional level must be vindicated by what happens at the physical level, then there must be some way of capturing such rationalizing inter-dependencies without intentional vocabulary and in such a way that guarantees them a causal role.

These points, it is claimed, can be accommodated within a computational theory of mind. "The Big Idea" as Fodor terms it, is to compare the mind to a computer.[8] There are several stages to the unfolding of this idea and therefore several distinct but necessary claims bound up with it.

(1) The first stage is to see the patterns of connections which constitute reason-giving relations between intentional states as formalizable. They can be spelt out as patterns which hold because of the *structure* or *form* of the propositions that give them expression, rather than the meaning. Such a thought is clearly encouraged by the formalization of inductive and deductive logic, where the pattern of valid inference can apparently be displayed while abstracting from the meanings of the sentences under consideration. It can then appear that the relation of one sentence implying another can be spelt out in terms of something like the shape of the sentences concerned. The structural or formal features of a sentence are called its syntax, whereas features connected to its meaning are called its semantics. The first move, then, is to claim that reason-giving relations are a matter of syntax, structure, or shape rather than semantics.

(2) The second stage is to see that causal transitions between states can result from the structural relations between them. The causal transitions at the psychological level anchored in reason-giving relations are then mirrored in causal transitions at the non-intentional level anchored in syntactic links. The model informing this move is that of the computer. Computers work with symbols that can be assigned semantic interpretations, although clearly the causal processes in the computer only make use of their formal or syntactic properties. For the purposes of these transactions the meaning we assign to the syntactic units are playing no role.[9] The causal transactions are instead dependent on something like their shape.[10]

> When someone reasons to the conclusion Q, from the belief that P ⊃ Q (i.e. if P then Q), and the belief that P, there is inside them a causal process which mirrors the purely formal relation of modus ponens. So the elements in the causal process must have components which mirror the component parts of the inference: that is form must have a causal basis.[11]

(3) The third stage in this computational model is then to view *rationalizing links* between intentional states as reducible to *patterns of causal transitions* between physical states with certain kinds of structural features.

In the most famous version of the computational model, intentional states are thought of as requiring the occurrence of sentence-like structures in the head; a language of thought or Mentalese, in Fodor's terms.[12] Just as to say that it is raining involves the occurrence of some sentence, for example "it is raining", to believe that it is raining involves the occurrence of some mental item analogous to such a sentence. Such states have a structure like a syntax. They include recurring structural types ordered in systematic ways, just as in a language proper. There are other models, however, apart from inner representations having a sentence-like shape. Some philosophers, for example, have argued that the inner structures might function more like a map than a sentence.[13] Here we will concern ourselves primarily with the language of thought model, partly because of its prominence, but also because it illustrates the task facing those who wish to reduce rationality in a particularly clear way. The objections we later raise to the language of thought view, however, apply equally to those who think of inner representations as maps as well as to those who, like Fodor, take them to be sentences.

Fodor's language of thought is a hypothesis. Fodor is a scientific psychologist who thinks that empirical research will explain the workings of the mind. In his view the language of thought hypothesis best accommodates the data. For Fodor, the data requires us to adopt a degree of *intentional realism*, the view that there really are intentional states with genuine intentional properties bearing rationalizing links to each other, which are causally productive in relation to behaviour, and that a scientific psychology will contain laws formulated in terms of such states. Such a view, however, also has to be put together with a physicalism in which, at the most basic level, the world can be described without reference to intentional properties. The solution is to reduce intentional properties to something else.

> I suppose that sooner or later the physicists will complete the catalogue they've been compiling of the ultimate and irreducible properties of things. When they do the likes of *spin, charm and charge* will perhaps appear on the list. But *aboutness* surely won't; intentionality simply doesn't go that deep. It is hard to see, in face of this consideration, how one can be a realist about intentionality without also being, to some extent, a reductionist. If the semantic and the intentional are real properties of things, it must be because of their identity with (or maybe of their supervenience on) properties that are themselves neither intentional nor semantic. If aboutness is real, it must really be something else.[14]

For Fodor, something like inner sentences are the best candidates for such a reduction. They retain at the level of non-intentional realization the surface characteristics in terms of which beliefs and desires are relations to sentence-like entities. This explains how different intentional states can be focused on the same content and the feature of productivity. We are able to think and understand a potentially infinite number of thoughts if the ingredients are systematic combinations of basic ones. It also explains the parallels between intentional contents and spoken and written sentences and can accommodate the opacity mentioned above, since different symbols in the language of thought can have the same referent (on which, more below), but distinct intentional states will be individuated if they involve relations to different symbols. And, of course, such a model respects the rationality constraints, so that the causal interactions between states hold in virtue of formal structures seen as the analogue of logical structures.[15]

If all this works, then the structures of rationality which Descartes took to be the defining features of the mind, requiring the existence of immaterial substance, can be accommodated within the other half of his dualism!

Objections to the language of thought (1)

The first set of problems we will consider for the computational model are internal to the functionalist materialist paradigm, that is to say, to theorists who perceive a need to provide a naturalizing account of intentionality and rationality.

Inside the black box

One line of argument suggests that Fodor has been too strict in what would count as a successful accommodation of intentionality within a physicalist world picture. Daniel Dennett, for example, would argue that all that we require our naturalistic theory to do is to reveal a pattern of behavioural output that can be systematized by the application of intentional descriptions. What is going on inside the "black box", whereby this is done, is something that our intentional descriptions set no constraints upon.[16] (Dennett's version of interpretationism will be discussed in Chapter 5.) Fodor's response is to claim that this fails to treat our intentional descriptions in a sufficiently realist way. Without attention to what is going on inside the black box, we can provide no account of the causal efficacy of our intentional states – an efficacy that is assumed in our highly successful everyday interactions. If our intentional states are to be genuinely causally effective, then they must be demonstrably anchored in fundamental causal interactions at the physical level.

However, many see the kind of anchorage demanded by the language of thought hypothesis as too strong. It is suggested that some form of intentional realism is defensible without the systematic mapping which a language of thought postulates between intentional interconnections and material ones. Here the main challenge is mounted by those who adopt some form of connectionism as a more plausible account of the kind of neural structures that would be needed to form a supervenient base for our intentional states. Connectionists claim that we can accommodate the attribution of intentional content to psychological states without assuming that the structure of our propositional attitudes is mapped at the physical level. A connectionist machine has a large number of simple units (input/output devices) linked to other units with connections of various strengths so as to form a network. Input to some units causes a pattern of activation across the network, all at once and not in a step by step way. Once the network has stabilized, then an output can be read off from the output units. By varying the strength of the connections between the units it is possible to get the machine to produce a certain kind of output from a certain kind of input. For the purposes of comparison with the language of thought hypothesis, the crucial point is that the components of a connectionist architecture do not have any natural interpretation in intentional terms, for they do not map even the formal structure of our propositional states. It is rather the states of the network as a whole which are interpreted as representing them.

> Suppose for simplicity that there is a Mentalese word "dog" which has the same syntactic and semantic features as the English word "dog". Then the defender of Mentalese will say that whenever you have a thought about dogs the same type of syntactic structure occurs in your head . . . Connectionists deny that this need be so; they say that when you have . . . two thoughts [about dogs], the mechanisms in your head need have nothing non-semantic in common . . . In other words thoughts do not have syntax.[17]

Connectionists regard their proposals as more biologically plausible because the networks they are using as models resemble the biological neural networks in the brain more closely than the language of thought model does.

Fodor's reply to such a proposal is that cognition is productive and systematic: that is, we can understand new thoughts and thoughts bear rationalizing links to each other. He argues that these features cannot be accommodated unless the states that instantiate cognition are susceptible to systematic characterization of the kind the language of thought suggests. If they are not so characterizable then it is unintelligible how our intentional representations supervene on them. If they are so characterizable then connectionist architecture is simply a way of implementing Mentalese style computational mechanisms. What then is at issue between the two accounts? The issue becomes that of whether the intelligibility of the supervenience claim requires some intermediate level of syntactic description if rationalizing links are to be intelligibly generated from causal ones. When considering this question, it is important to keep in mind the differences between two projects. One is a purely empirical one considering what kind of physical systems can sustain intentional characterization.[18] A second project is more philosophical, although anchored in empirical work. Its goal is to render intelligible how intentional characteristics can supervene on such a physical system. Fodor's account seems to be anchored in this second kind of project, arguing that an intermediate level of syntactic description is needed which can plausibly reduce rationalizing links and itself be instantiated by a physical system. Here Fodor's strategy seems to be more in line with the functionalist project overall, namely to find some intermediate level of description that can plausibly reduce intentional kinds and that itself can transparently be instantiated by a physical system.

Semantic content

Fodor starts with an account of how to reduce rationalizing links, and accommodates these via considerations of syntax. Nonetheless, intentional states have a semantics as well as a syntax: they are meaningful representations. How are Fodor's computational states to be given a semantics? How can the explanatory role which seems to attach to the semantic content of these states be accommodated within a picture in which the causal transitions are dictated by the formal properties of the instantiating states? This is the problem of providing a naturalizing account of what determines the semantic content of our intentional states. At this point it is enough to point out that Fodor's framework sets constraints on what this kind of account can be like. Within the framework of the language of thought, the intentional content of our psychological states has been given a causal role in virtue of its formal properties. Therefore any aspect of semantic content that we want to claim as causally relevant must be fixed by, or supervene on, such formal, syntactic properties. Furthermore, since such syntactic properties are properties of internal states, brain states in Fodor's view, then the causally relevant aspects of semantic properties must be dependent on the structure of such internal states. These constraints on the allocation of semantic content Fodor calls methodological solipsism.[19] The obstacles to such an account are outlined in the following chapter. If we cannot find an account of the semantic content of our intentional states that is compatible with Fodor's internal computational model, then it will not provide us with an adequate reduction of intentionality and rationality.

Objections to the language of thought (2)

Further objections to the computational model come from those who do not share Fodor's optimism that our intentional kinds and generalizations can be vindicated by means of a reduction into states and patterns of interaction characterized without the use of intentional vocabulary.

Isomorphism

One source of such anti-reductionist arguments is the work of Donald Davidson. Davidson's arguments rest on emphasizing the constitutive role of rationality in the assignment of intentional descriptions. This is the point with which we began this chapter. He puts the matter like this:

beliefs, intentions, and desires are identified by their objects and these are identified by their logical and semantic properties. If attitudes can be identified at all, then they must be found to be largely consistent with one another (because of their logical properties) and in line with the world (because of their semantic properties) . . . if a creature has propositional attitudes then that creature is approximately rational.[20]

Therefore even at the level of spelling out the network of conditional dependencies within which our intentional states are placed, we need to use intentional and semantic vocabulary. Beliefs, for example, tend to produce other beliefs for which they provide reasons. They are not causally stable in the presence of environmental conditions, which counts as evidence against them. In combination with desires they tend to lead to actions that are ways of satisfying those desires. Davidson claims that these reason-giving links that serve to define our intentional kinds "have no echo in physical theory". Without the use of intentional vocabulary such links could not be captured. The consequence of this is to render it highly implausible that any classification in extensional terms could be projectibly coextensive with, and thus mirror, a classification anchored in a network of rationalizing links. This argument is used against Fodor's theory to suggest that *no* set of conditional dependencies characterized without the use of intentional vocabulary can map those which employ such vocabulary.

The computationist will reply that it is just this argument that his theory is designed to undermine. Once these rationalizing links have been formalized, via logic for theoretical reasoning and by decision theory for practical reason, then it is possible to find patterns of purely syntactical transitions that are projectibly isomorphic with them. This makes it clear that a central issue in assessing the Davidsonian argument is whether relations such as "provide evidence for", "gives you some point in pursuing", and so on can be captured in ways that abstract from the semantic content of the intentional states involved and utilize only formal features. This seems dubious. Even where rationalizing links rest on relations of deductive and inductive validity, it is unclear that these can be captured in a purely formal way. John McDowell makes the point about deductive rationality which extends even more powerfully to cases of inductive and practical reasoning:

> Deductive rationality is a capacity . . . to hold beliefs when and because they follow deductively from other beliefs one holds . . . this structure cannot be abstracted away from relations between contents . . . in such a way that we might hope to find the abstracted structure exemplified in the interrelations among a system of items described in non-intentional terms . . . someone who denied the claim would find it hard to explain how his position was consistent with the fact that there is no mechanical test for logical validity in general.[21]

The plausibility of a theory rests on its relation to a network (without rigid boundaries) of other beliefs. It is assessed holistically and with a notion of "fit" which does not seem capturable purely in terms of deductive or inductive implication. For example, consider the adequacy of trials concerning heart disease conducted on only male patients. Their adequacy depends on further, often unstated, assumptions such as that there is no significant difference between men and women in relation to the disease. Even if this assumption is brought to the surface and added as a premise whose truth can itself be tested, other analogous assumptions will underlie such tests, and so on indefinitely. John Searle has also pointed out that the pattern of transitions among our intentional states rests not only on the network of other intentional states but also on sets of background capacities, practices and know-how, all of which inform our responses on a particular occasion.

> Consider, "Sally gave John the key and he opened the door." There is nothing whatever in the literal semantic content of that sentence to block the interpretation "John opened the door with the key by battering the door down, the key was twenty feet long, made of cast iron and weighed two hundred pounds.[22]

What rules out these interpretations, according to Searle, is not formal rules but the background. Similar points could be made in relation to the transitions informing our intentions and actions where the weighing up of alternatives seems to elude capture within the rational consumer model derived from economics.

A computationist could reply to this that if the network of intentional states, together with the background, inform the rationality of our beliefs and intentions, would it not be possible to make these explicit? Then the transitions would become explicitly those which instantiate some formal model. Searle resists such a move, arguing "there is no limit to the number of additions I would have to make to the original ... to block possible misinterpretations ... each of the additions itself subject to different interpretations".[23] If we accept these arguments, which dispute the formal codifiability of rationality constraints, then the first move anchoring Fodor's account is undermined. If rationalizing links cannot be captured syntactically, then we do not have available the causal mechanism to provide the naturalistic reduction.

There is a further point which reinforces scepticism regarding the projectible isomorphism of intentionally and non-intentionally characterized generalizations. The output that our intentional states explain is intentional acts. In the example that we gave at the beginning of the chapter, what we were explaining was Maureen going to her friend's house. The *explanandum* is an intentionally characterized item and not simply a bodily movement. It is characterized in terms of what Maureen takes herself to be doing and there seems to be no projectable way of mapping descriptions in terms of intentional acts onto behavioural descriptions of any other kind.

This crucial lack of isomorphism between the intentional and the extensional functional level is often masked by an ambiguous use of the term "behaviour". This term can be used to characterize *both* intentional actions and mere bodily outputs. Yet once we get beyond "A's arm moving" and "A moving her arm" there is a dramatic lack of correspondance between these two modes of classification.[24] If Maureen's friend is not in, we might expect her to seek another friend to play with, preferably one with Barbie dolls. We are not, however, able to predict what pattern of behaviour characterized non-intentionally this might require, what bodily movements she would need to make to get there. It then becomes wildly implausible to suppose that the conditional dependencies derived from intentional explanations could be captured with only the resources of bodily movement vocabulary, as legs moving in certain trajectories, for example.

Normativity and perspectivity

The problems with the computational account of rationality does not rest solely in the problem of capturing rationalizing links in a purely formal manner. The rejection of such formality is still compatible with seeing rational links as essentially calculations, resting on objective patterns of relations, although these require intentional vocabulary and semantic as well as syntactic content for their articulation. To see rationalizing links solely as instances of such general calculations is, however, to miss something out of the picture. We understand someone's beliefs, responses, actions, by seeing them as appropriate given their other intentional states. Such appropriateness can sometimes be demonstrated by processes of calculation and sometimes not. Nevertheless, even where such calculations are involved, the understanding that results is consequent on seeing that, given these logical connections, this is the thing to believe in this context. The force of inductive/ deductive reasoning is not the mere instantiation of a formal pattern that happens to move us just because we are the kind of creatures who respond causally to these patterns. It is more that, because we recognize that these patterns are truth-preserving, we acknowledge the appropriateness of the conclusions given the premises.

One way of highlighting this is as follows. We do not always do or think what is rational, as the reductionists would seem to imply. Of course, they can accommodate this and accept that the causal generalizations that anchor our intentional terms as a consequence of their rationalizing inter-dependencies are probabilistic instead of deterministic, or accept that there are elements of breakdown in the system. However, what such a picture cannot fit is that, where we fail to act rationally, we *should have* so acted, and that recognizing that we should have is part of grasping what is involved in having the intentional states concerned. When we make a response intelligible, we are doing more than showing that it is an instance of a general pattern, even if that pattern does require intentional notions in its articulation.

We are making the response intelligible by showing that it is the correct (or a correct) response. To emphasize this normativity is to emphasize the distinctiveness of the kind of explanatory projects in which intentional notions are located. This is expressed by McDowell in the following way:

> concepts of the propositional attitudes have their proper home in explanations of a special sort: explanations in which things are made intelligible by being revealed to be, or to approximate to being, as they rationally ought to be. This is to be contrasted with a style of explanation in which one makes things intelligible by representing their coming into being as a particular instance of how things generally tend to happen.[25]

The rationality involved here is not simply a matter of showing that the action or belief conform to some objectively specifiable standard or norm. You do not necessarily make the action of a woman taking her husband's name on marriage intelligible by pointing to a norm; especially if she is a feminist and alert to the context of the norm's emergence. Pointing out that an action conforms to some norm still does not capture the recognition that this, for the agent, was the thing to do. The kind of rationality involved is rather tied up with the essential perspectivity of the mental. When we provide rationalizing explanations we make, for example, an action intelligible by adopting the perspective of an agent deciding how to act. It is from that perspective that courses of action are viewed as being appropriate to the situation. The standpoint of an agent deciding how to act is not that of a detached observer simply predicting the next move or reporting what the norms are. When I find an option attractive and pursue it, I am doing something different from reflecting on my past and concluding what I will do in the future. Anyone understanding my action must appreciate it from my position as an agent deciding how to act.

For McDowell, our intentional notions have their home in this form of explanation. Normativity cannot be grasped without engagement, so we can therefore only grasp our intentional concepts by taking up the perspective of agents engaged in making decisions. Parallel points could be made in relation to reasons for belief, where the recognition that the conclusion is to be accepted given the premises, requires us to adopt the perspective of truth seekers. Let us return to our example of Maureen walking to her friend's house. One model of what is going on here sees her behaviour as an output of a calculation that conforms to a generalizable pattern in virtue of its form. Its instancing of such a pattern allows us to derive certain conditionals and counterfactuals from it and to predict what she would do if certain elements in this pattern changed, for example if she believed that Eleanor had Barbie dolls instead of Evie. At its most ambitious, such a picture claims that the pattern and the conditional claims could be captured without the use of intentional notions: the computational claim. What is missed out from this claim, we have been arguing, is that understanding the behaviour of others as behaviour for which they have reasons requires us to recognize Maureen's behaviour as not only something that we might expect her to do given her desires and beliefs, but also as the thing, or a thing, that was appropriate for her to do, what she should do, given her goals. Such a recognition is perspectival (and not only in the sense that the intentional states concerned must be hers). The rationality cannot be grasped without adopting the standpoint of an agent.

There is moreover a further way in which Maureen's behaviour can be understood as rational or appropriate, which even such a revised formulation fails to capture. Once we know what Maureen wants and believes, then we can recognize the normative appropriateness of her course of action. What this does not necessarily give us, however, is a grasp of what it is about the situation that renders it attractive to her. Maureen is remembering pleasurably Evie's dolls and anticipating playing without the critical eye of her mother. Both of these render the path to her friend's house attractive as she turns out of the gate. For her, at that moment, this seems the path to take. For us to understand how this is the path to take, from her perspective, is not just to recognize that, in the light of some pre-given desires and beliefs, this is what the agent should do (itself a perspectival judgement). It is to grasp that the desires were not pre-formed but became constituted out of the way the world appears to her. This requires an engagement with the specificity of Maureen's perspective onto the world – what McDowell calls "a sensitivity to the specific detail of the subjective stance of another".[26] Let us change perspective and see if we can make intelligible the mother's critical eye, were she to watch the proceedings. The mother sees the parallel between the shape of the dolls and skewed and damaging stereotypes of female beauty. This makes rationally intelligible the snorts and sniffs of disapproval and so makes them appropriate. We cannot, however, attribute to the mother a process of calculation. What would it be? Does she think to herself "If I act disapprovingly my daughter will not admire this kind of shape"? The mother probably does not think this; maybe snorting is counter-productive in such calculative terms – which does not, of course, make it any less appropriate.

The normative and perspectival nature of rationalizing explanations are a reflection of the Heideggerian point that we are creatures who are not only in a world buffeted like objects, but also have a world; creatures to whom the world shows itself.[27] Understanding the appropriateness of our responses requires engagement with the specificity of the world as it appears to us. The kind of sensitivity to the specific subjectivity of others, which these examples suggest if our intentional states and intentional acts are to be seen as rational in this further sense, is one which we will be further addressing in Chapters 5, 7 and 8. Here, however, we have to assess the impact of the perspectival nature of rationalizing explanation on the project of naturalizing, by reducing, rationality. Thomas Nagel[28] has argued that characteristics of the world that are constitutively anchored in a subjective or perspectival view resist capture in the non-perspectival and objective framework of physical science, the project of which is in some sense to capture the world "as it is" rather than how it appears from certain perspectives. What is involved in grasping that certain physical or functional facts pertain does not require the kind of engagement with particular points of view which we have seen as integral to rationality. If we accept such perspectivity, then we have to reject the reductionist demands.

Some writers want to accept elements of the argument for the irreducible normativity and perspectivity attaching to our intentional notions, but nonetheless argue that we need a computational theory to anchor and vindicate our causal claims at the psychological level. Martin Davies argues:

At the personal level of description, we find many notions – subjective, normative – that have no place in science, and we find a distinctive kind of intelligibility. But these personal level descriptions also make use of causal notions, and the correctness of these descriptions is not indifferent to issues about subpersonal level information processing machinery.[29]

In this account our intentional explanations require, but are not exhaustively reducible to computational ones. The main argument motivating such a position is that articulated earlier: the claim that when a thinker performs inferential transitions or acts on her reasons she is doing so because they are reasons. The rationalizing links are the hinge on which the causal transitions work. As we saw at the end of the previous section, if we allow rationality as a whole to escape reduction, then we either give up intentional causal claims or give up the assumption that higher-level causal claims require physicalist grounding. For Davies neither of these options are acceptable and therefore reason-giving explanations must make some demands of the physical system on which the intentional states are supervenient. He concludes that the subvenient states must mirror the rationalizing ones in the way suggested by the computational model. The suggestion seems to be that subjectivity and normativity together with the distinctive intelligibility they carry evade the causal net, and therefore the need for such vindication.

Such a position, however, does not escape the problems attaching to the formal codifiability of rationality which we raised above: it still requires an isomorphism which is wildly implausible. Moreover it splits the explanatory work of our intentional notions in an unacceptable way so that the normativity becomes separated from the instantiation of certain objectively characterizable patterns – these doing different explanatory jobs. But this does not seem quite right. It is not the case that recognition of a formally characterizable pattern causes me to form a new belief, while its normative appropriateness makes it intelligible in some other way.[30] The normative and causal notions are interdependent. The causal explanation of my response has to be that "that was the thing to believe" or "that was a desirable thing to do". If, however, there is an intertwining of such normativity with whatever causal notions are in play here, then accepting Davies's initial argument for a computational model would seem to require that *normativity* is mirrored at the physical level, and that, he accepts, is not possible.

Conclusion

The computational model of mind has been offered by functionalists as a way of accommodating the interconnected features of intentionality and rationality that are characteristic of our mental life. Such a model requires that the rationalizing links between intentional states be capturable as objective patterns of transitions between formal features of such states. This runs into the difficulty that even calculative patterns of rationality cannot be captured in a purely formal way and without the use of intentional vocabulary. More radically, however, the kind of intelligibility that rationalizing links bestow on our intentional states and our intentional acts outruns what can be captured in such objectively characterized patterns. Such intelligibility involves engagement with the perspectives of the agents concerned. This perspectival form of intelligibility is at odds with a naturalizing project aiming for a characterization of the world *per se*, rather than one anchored in particular perspectives within it.

Whether or not bodies who are intentional agents must have brain states that are systematizable in terms of computational functionalism is a question for empirical science to investigate. What we must conclude from the deliberations of this chapter, however, is that such a model cannot fulfil the philosophical task of reducing and thereby naturalizing the rationalizing and normative features that are the markers of our mental life. If, however, we cannot capture rationalizing relations in a topic-neutral functional vocabulary, as the computational model hoped to do, what are the consequences for the naturalizing project? One move might be to claim that rationalizing patterns, on which justifications rest, are simply a descriptive device useful for everyday purposes but not featuring in any scientific account of the world (any more than patterns I detect in my wall paper might do). We might find a certain comforting intelligibility in their articulation; but that does not necessitate that the physicalist integrate them into her picture. We will have some sympathy with such thoughts, as will be evident in later chapters, but here it is important to note how substantially they retract on the naturalist project. For in this view we have no account of mentality in physicalist terms and no account that makes supervenience intelligible. Secondly, such a view either requires giving up on the causal explanatory role of the mental or it requires the admission that there are causal links that cannot be vindicated by mapping onto lower-level causal links (the rejection of which formed the cornerstone of explanatory physicalism). We return to these points in Chapter 5.

Further reading

The "Big Idea" of a computational theory of mind is captured by Fodor in the *Times Literary Supplement*, July 1992. His *Language of thought* (Hassocks: Harvester Press, 1976) is the place to go for a defence of his view. Computational models, including the debates with connectionism, are well discussed in Tim Crane's *The mechanical mind* (London: Penguin, 1995). John McDowell's "Functionalism and anomolous monism", in E. LePore and B. McLaughlin (eds), *Actions and events* (Oxford: Blackwells, 1985) brought into Anglo-American work on rationality the perspectival nature of normativity.

Chapter 4

The content of thought

The internalist picture

The Cartesian picture of the mind draws a sharp distinction between its contents and the contents of the world outside. The
contents of the mind could be as they are whatever the contents of
the world outside might be. Descartes himself notoriously believed
that we could be totally deluded about the world, so that what we
thought about had no correlates outside. We can call the doctrine
that draws this sort of distinction *internalism*.[1] It is not confined to
the Cartesian picture, but surfaces in the classic functionalist one
as well.[2] Here, too, the contents of belief (and other intentional
states) are taken to be independent of the external world they are
beliefs about, in the sense that a belief could in principle be the
belief it is even if that world which it concerns was quite different
from the way it is.

The classic functionalist defence of internalism is, however, different from the Cartesian one, to which we shall return shortly.
It is a defence resulting from the adoption of *methodological*

solipsism, which, as we noticed in the previous chapter, sets constraints upon the attribution of content to thought. Methodological solipsism enjoins us not to assume the existence of anything other than the subject to whom a psychological state is ascribed. In contrast to the Cartesian position, we are permitted to assume the existence of the subject's body with its sense organs and its limbs, but we are not to assume the existence of anything beyond them. Then when we seek to explain the movements of those limbs in terms of the subject's psychological states we should do so on the basis of the way the sense organs are stimulated and the interactions of the states they produce with others. We should not do so, for example, by saying what objects in the subject's environment caused the sensory stimulation. The reason for this is clear: different objects might produce the same stimulation, and *which* object does this will be irrelevant to its effects within the subject. If we are explaining the effects by reference to her psychological states then these states cannot essentially involve those objects. We should therefore view them along internalist lines.

The internalist account of a subject's psychological states makes them supervene solely upon the state of her body. The state of the world beyond it is irrelevant to them, so that whatever state the world is in, two subjects in the same bodily state will enjoy the same psychological state. Slightly more radically, if we can regard the rest of the body as merely providing a receptor, motor and support system for the brain, then we can view psychological states conceived internalistically as supervening solely upon brain states. A brain kept alive in a vat[3] could in principle be the subject of the same psychological states as someone playing with her child. For though the brain is detached from a body, it could exhibit the same causal processes as would produce bodily movements like those of the mother. The internalist assumes that it is only insofar as a psychological state involves such causal processes that it plays a part in explaining behaviour.

What we should notice here is that a functionalist's use of internalism again displays his Cartesian conception of the body. It is but a piece of machinery whose movements are to be explained by internal goings-on. If psychological states explain them, then they too can have nothing to do with what goes on outside it. It is for this reason that a functionalist can, if he wishes, share with

Descartes a further argument for internalism, namely that our psychological states can make no essential reference to the world without, or we could not have the introspective knowledge of them that we do. For if what thoughts we had depended on how the world was (depended, say, on our not being brains in a vat), then we would need to know how the world was in those respects to know what our thoughts were. But in the Cartesian picture our thoughts are open to our inspection precisely because we do not need to know anything about the world (for example whether we are brains in a vat or not) in order to know what our thoughts are.

Indeed, it may seem that we can go further than this, and say that certain sorts of mistakes about the world are possible precisely because, although we know what our thoughts are, the identity of these thoughts is quite independent of the way the world is. Consider Saul Kripke's example of Pierre, who learns from French informants, "Londres est jolie".[4] On coming later to London he asserts, "London is not pretty", not realizing that the two names stand for the same place. Now clearly Pierre takes himself to have beliefs about two quite separate places, while we know that there is just one place to which he attributes inconsistent properties. Does Pierre have, then, inconsistent beliefs without realizing it? If we were to say that in each case his thought involved the same content we would have to attribute inconsistent beliefs to him. But surely *inconsistency* is in principle detectable by Pierre and removable by him by reflection upon his thoughts alone. That in this case the mistake is *not* so correctable shows, the internalist will argue, that Pierre's thoughts can be identified as the thoughts they are independently of their relation to a particular place in the outside world. While we may report people's thoughts by reference to such items in the world, the example of Pierre shows how misleading this can be. For the internalist, Pierre's thoughts are not inconsistent. They simply appear to be so when we report them in terms of his relationship to objects outside of him.

An internalist functionalism would hold, then, that the semantic content of psychological states can be accounted for simply in terms of those properties of the internal states which constitute them that are independent of the way in which such states relate the subject to her environment. We shall not pursue the question of how this might be attempted. It may be helpful, however, to keep in mind the Cartesian picture of thought as involving, with the exception of the idea of the self, only ideas of general, world-independent properties. In this picture, then, thoughts can be individuated by specifying these properties. Pierre, for example, will presumably associate different properties with the place he picks out as "Londres" from those involved in "London", even though we do not know what these different properties are.

Externalism

Yet we *do* report thoughts and other psychological states in just the way that generated the paradox about Pierre's beliefs. And there are powerful arguments to show that we should. If they succeed, then internalism is false and psychological states are not independent of the world external to their subject because their content can only be specified by reference to items in that world. This doctrine is, unsurprisingly, *externalism*. The most celebrated argument for its truth derives from a thought experiment devised by Hilary Putnam.[5] Imagine, he says, two subjects who are atom for atom replicas of each other, but who inhabit different worlds. One of them, myself, lives on Earth and has thoughts about the water on it – I want to drink some water, say. The other, my *doppelgänger*, lives on Twin Earth, where no water is to be found. Instead there is a chemically distinct substance, superficially similar to water and playing the same role in the Twin Earthians' lives: call it "twater". Then my *doppelgänger* will have a thought analogous to mine, but she will want to drink some twater, not some water. The thoughts of my *doppelgänger* and myself are different, Putnam claims, precisely because we inhabit different worlds. They do not supervene, therefore, merely upon our inner bodily states, which are ex hypothesis identical. "Meanings", as Putnam's dictum has it, "just aren't in the head".[6]

The obvious response to the Twin Earth example is to assert that I and my *doppelgänger do* share a psychological state, namely one about a colourless, tasteless, refreshing liquid, which is what water and twater both are. But, the externalist replies, this is not what I want. Were I to be transported surreptitiously to Twin Earth then, even though I could not tell the difference between water and twater, if I were given the latter I would not get what I wanted: it is water that I want and my concept of water is not just the concept of a liquid with certain apparent properties.

Putnam gives what amount to two distinct reasons for this. One is that my concept of water is the concept of a certain sort of substance, namely the substance in fact identified by certain chemical properties which are not readily apparent to sense. Water is in fact identified as H_2O, and twater, hypothetically, as xyz. I may not be able to tell the difference, nor know wherein the difference lies, but I can trust the experts to do so. My concept of water is employed in a way that is answerable to their judgement. Yet so far this need not worry the internalist. Granted, it is a certain substance that I want, one I have been accustomed to imbibing and not some seriously indistinguishable substitute. But my thought may be the same as my *doppelgänger*'s: we both want a certain substance that we pick out fallibly by its apparent properties, but which is definitively identified as the normal bearer of those properties by the experts.

Putnam's claim that terms like "water" involve a "division of linguistic labour"[7] applies only to concepts that are essentially linguistic in the way they are employed. The same can be said of some other examples produced in support of externalism by Tyler Burge. The most celebrated concerns a patient who believes his arthritis is now affecting his thigh.[8] His belief must be false, for by definition arthritis is a disease of the joints. Nevertheless, argues Burge, the patient shares our concept of arthritis, since that concept is constituted by the way people in our society use the term. In a different society, where it was used to cover disease in the muscles as well, an atom for atom replica of the patient would have a different belief when he said "Arthritis is affecting my thigh", namely a belief not about arthritis but about another disease – call it "tharthritis". In this second Twin Earth type of example, beliefs do not supervene upon their subject's bodily states because their contents are differently constructed as a result of different linguistic usages in the subjects' respective societies. The internalist will reply, however, that in each case the patient has the same belief, namely that his thigh is affected by what in his society is called "arthritis". In our society the patient's belief is false, in the other, it is true.

Putnam has, however, a second sort of reason for insisting that the subjects on Earth and Twin Earth have different beliefs which is not susceptible to the kind of reply we have noted above. It is that the concept of water, say, has an irreducibly *indexical* component: "there is a 'property' which people have long associated with pure water and which distinguishes it from Twin Earth water, and that is the property *of behaving like any other sample of pure water from* our *environment*".[9] That water comes from *our* environment can be stated only by *pointing out* the environment in which it is found. If the concept of water involves such an indexical component, then a belief involving it cannot supervene solely upon its subject's bodily state. For two subjects could be in the same state but different environments, and their beliefs differ simply in virtue of what would have to be pointed out in indicating to what their concepts apply. Furthermore the indexicality argument provides a response to the internalist replies to Putnam's other argument and to Burge's noted above. It is that when I defer in my usage of "water" to the experts, or to society in general in my use of "arthritis", it is to *these* experts and to *my* society that I defer. Although I and my *doppelgänger* appear to share our concepts, the indexical components involved point to different items, and for that reason our beliefs have different contents.

Singular thoughts

The indexicality concealed in concepts like water is an overt feature in another range of cases cited in support of externalism, namely thoughts about particular objects pointed out as this or that thing. If someone wants a drink of water, then in order to explain why they drink some water we need to attribute to them the belief that *that* is water. And, the externalist continues, it is precisely such interactions with the environment that we do wish to explain in understanding behaviour, rather than simply bodily movements that are blind to the environment in which they occur. Now it is evident again that otherwise identical subjects in two distinct environments will differ in their psychological states.

For the states of one will be directed towards just *these* objects on which she is to act, and the states of the other upon just *those*.

Let us grant that the externalist account of what requires explanation has force and that indexical beliefs are required for it. We do not yet, however, reach the externalist's conclusion. For that, we need to show, first, that indexicality cannot be understood in terms simply of the subject's internal states, and, second, that indexical thoughts require the existence of the objects they are directed towards. John Searle has denied the first of these claims.[10] If I believe of that man over there that he is wearing a red cap, says Searle, what I believe is that the man causing *this* visual experience is so hatted. Obviously this is an account of indexicality in terms of the subject's internal states alone. But it is not clear that it works; for if you also believe of that man over there that he is wearing a red cap you would ordinarily be taken to have the same belief as me. On Searle's account, however, you have a different one, since yours is directed at your visual experience and mine at mine.[11]

The second claim, which would be fatal to internalism, is that indexical thoughts concerning particular objects in the external world require the existence of those objects in order to exist themselves. They are, that is to say, *singular* or *Russellian* thoughts. Bertrand Russell famously distinguished thoughts involving definite descriptions which were false if the objects we tried to pick out by means of them did not exist, from thoughts which relate us directly to an object.[12] In the case of these – Russellian – thoughts the non-existence of an object for us to pick out implies the non-existence of any thought at all: there is simply nothing for us to have a thought about in such a case. Russell himself believed that singular thoughts related us only to sense data and the like, not to objects in the material world, but that is not a scruple which need concern us here: his notion has been given a wider application by contemporary externalists. The point, then, is whether indexical thoughts with respect to the particular things around us are Russellian thoughts, thoughts whose identities are constituted out of the objects they involve.

The objection that they are not might well stem from reflecting that someone who is hallucinating a glass of water before her might have the same thought, "That's water", as someone really seeing a glass. After all, in each case her hand goes out for a glass, and in each case its doing so manifests a capacity she has to move her hand to a certain spatial position where action is to occur. This capacity, it might be said, is what is exercised in indexical thought. Its exercise is sufficient for such thoughts, just as the exercise of conceptual capacities is in general sufficient for thought. The existence of things for them to be exercised upon is not required.[13] And this line of thought could be backed up by an appeal to introspection: surely the hallucinator knows what she is thinking, which she would not do if hallucination robbed her of thought as well as water.

It should by now be clear that under externalism introspective knowledge of our psychological states is problematic. But we should not too readily assume that this is a failing. Certainly the hallucinator and the veridical perceiver would both report their thoughts in the same way at the time by saying, "That's a glass of water." But later, when the hallucinator realizes her mistake, she cannot say, "I thought that *that* was a glass of water", since the demonstrative pronoun has nothing to refer to. Her earlier report of her thought, unlike that of the veridical perceiver, was in *some* way incorrect.

The central thrust of the objection to indexical thoughts being Russellian derives, however, from the claim that hallucinator and perceiver act in the same way. But the externalist denies this. The fact that in one case a glass is successfully grasped and in the other it is not is important, for it is just such successful interactions that need to be explained. Nor are they explainable simply by the happy accident that a glass is there in the one case and not the other.

We have a kind of explanation for our successful behaviour quite different from the normal one in cases where we hallucinate objects and the world just happens to provide us with objects like those hallucinated, so that we fortuitously succeed in satisfying our desires. It is behaviour of the normal sort in which we intentionally act upon the objects we actually perceive that indexical thoughts are routinely relied upon to explain. For it is because I believed of *this* object that it was an umbrella that I successfully went out with some protection against the rain. An indexical thought of this kind is, the externalist insists, indispensable to the explanation of our ordinary behaviour.[14]

The point is reinforced if we consider the case of someone for whom hallucinations of everyday objects around her are commonplace but still compelling. She acts on them just as from her veridical perceptions and quite often the objects required for successful action are there and get moved around. But when she does pick up a glass because she saw rather than hallucinated it this is indeed a happy accident. The normal case is quite unlike this, for while here we would attribute her success to her thought that that was a glass, where hallucinations are an ever present possibility we would not. Although there *happens* to be a glass before her, she is not in the right relation to it to have indexical thoughts about it. Her capacity for locating the part of space to be acted upon will not, however, be routinely successful in getting her what she wants. Sometimes the circumstances will be propitious, sometimes not. It is not just the capacity but the circumstances in which it can be exercised successfully that are required for indexical thought, and these are circumstances in which it is not just accidental that the object required is present. But then indexical thoughts are Russellian, and the externalist argument is complete.

Dual component theories

We have reached, then, an important crux in the argument. We have seen how the constraints of methodological solipsism lead scientific functionalists to internalism about semantic content. But we have also seen that such an internalism does not do justice to the role that thoughts with these contents play in explaining our behaviour.

These externalist arguments pose considerable problems for classic functionalism. On the one hand, such functionalists are likely to accept that the explanation of behaviour proceeds in terms of the rationalizing links between the agent's beliefs and desires and her actions. But these actions are characteristically described in terms of interaction with external objects so that her relevant beliefs and desires will also allude to these. An

81

externalist account of her thoughts may then seem inescapable. On the other hand, classic functionalists will also insist that atom for atom identical agents must have the same causal powers and that these causal powers are what we allude to in the explanation of their behaviour. There are two strategies for combining these positions. One, which we shall look at next, is to concede a role to our relations to external things while retaining an internalist picture of psychological causes. The other, which we shall come to later, is to give an account of the causal powers implicated in psychological explanation that is compatible with an exclusively externalist picture of the content of thought as involved in psychological explanation.

Dual component accounts of content attribute to subjects two kinds of content, *narrow content* which causes bodily movements along internalist lines, and *wide content* which figures in rationalizing explanations and can involve relations to external objects. Thus I and my Twin Earth *doppelgänger* will share our narrow thought content but differ as to its wide content. The moves that we noticed the internalist making against the conclusions the externalist draws from such examples can now be recognized as attempts to specify this shared narrow content. Whether the attempts are successful is, as indicated earlier, very doubtful. But what is the place of wide content? This depends upon how narrow content itself is viewed.

In one approach[15] narrow content is taken to be given by the functional or conceptual role that the thought which it figures in has in the psychological economy of the subject. That is to say, the narrow content of a thought is determined by what other thoughts it is causally related to, and, ultimately, by what perceptual inputs and behavioural outputs give rise to or are produced by it, when these inputs and outputs are specified independently of the particular environment the subject inhabits. Then the wide content of the thought is given through referring to those objects in her environment which have the properties its narrow content concerns, and which thus, in that environment, are what the thought uniquely relates the subject to. Yet wide content is here simply a device for attributing thoughts essentially constituted by their narrow content. All the subject's thought properly refers to are properties common to different possible environments. Picking it out in terms of its wide content is just a shorthand way of specifying these properties through their instantiation in the environment she occupies. So, for example, a thought is a thought about water, if it is triggered by wet, colourless stuff, interacts with general thoughts about liquids, gives rise to drinking behaviour in appropriate circumstances and so on. This narrow content is shared with a twater drinking *doppelgänger*. The two subjects' wide contents differ simply because we use their relations to different substances to *identify* their narrow content, which is the same.

The second approach[16] attempts to reproduce one aspect of the indexicality of the content of thought through the relation it posits between wide and narrow content. Narrow content is viewed as essentially incomplete, requiring a context to supply a reference for its terms. Thus I and my *doppelgänger*'s narrow thought contents coincide, but our wide contents differ because the contexts in which they occur supply different references for them. Narrow content captures the conceptual capacities we bring to bear in thinking about the world, but *what* we thereby think about is something only the world that we are in can determine. It is the exercise of these capacities that gives rise to behaviour, but what that behaviour amounts to in terms of action upon objects is determined by the world, just as the wide content of our thinking is.

Each of these approaches has its advantages and disadvantages. In the first, narrow contents are complete intentional entities and thus themselves bearers of truth and falsity. They are true if their subject's world instantiates the general properties they concern. The price of this is that the subject's relation to the external objects in her world plays no part in explaining her behaviour. Instead, it is a relation drawn upon simply to attribute the narrow contents which do explain her behaviour; and these, as we have seen, concern only general properties common to different possible worlds.[17] The second approach does not substitute some generalized properties for the thought-contents we ordinarily take to explain behaviour in the world. But it does thereby rob narrow content of any *intentional* role. Psychological states thus become causally efficacious independently of their *being* intentional states. In that case, thoughts with a narrow content for which the context provides *no* reference could be as causally efficacious as others, even though there is now no way of specifying *what* thoughts they are. This mysteriously severs the causal efficacy of thoughts from their role in intentional explanation. Indeed, the dual component strategy in both its forms leaves it a mystery why the world should conspire with the narrow content thoughts it posits to make the behaviour which they cause as successful in its environment as it is. For neither dual component view can properly account for the indexical thoughts which, as we saw in the last section, are necessary to explain this.

Naturalistic externalism

The second strategy for combining the insights of externalism with a causal explanatory framework for psychological explanation along functionalist lines involves a quite different view of content. On the one hand, it denies a duality of content. Insofar as an agent's psychological state provides her with certain causal powers that supervene upon her physical state, it does so not because it has a mysterious narrow content, but because having an exclusively wide content gives rise to such powers. On the other hand, the wide content of her state is ascribed in virtue of the way that having those powers adapts her to the environment she is in. Whereas for dual aspect theories of content scientific explanation stops at the boundaries of the body, under what we shall call *naturalistic externalism* it goes beyond them to identify the items in her environment to which the subject is related in virtue of her biological nature and the perceptual encounters it makes possible. It is these items which figure in the content of her thought, because they explain her causal powers. They are not mentioned in attributing wide content simply as a means to identify those causal powers, or as what a context picks out as the object they are directed upon.

There are several different ways in which the naturalistic externalist programme may be carried through, though they share a common starting point. It lies in an analogy between the way natural signs mean things and the way certain psychological states might have the content they do. Distinctive tracks mean deer, because the passing of deer causes such tracks. Might not our beliefs as to the presence of certain items have the content they do, namely mean that such and such an item is present, precisely because they too are caused by these items? This naturalistically externalist approach to semantic content gives rise to a number of problems,[18] the answers to which distinguish the various sophisticated theories which build on the suggestion one from another.

The first problem – sometimes called the *misrepresentation problem* – is how to account for error. If certain distinctive tracks are present then deer really have passed by: natural signs do not lie. By contrast, someone's belief as to the presence of deer may be mistaken, and indeed it is crucial to its status as a *belief* that it can be. What is taken for a deer may be a large dog seen in poor light. So why do we say someone has a false belief about the presence of deer, rather than a true one as to dogs? How can he be misrepresenting a deer rather than be correctly representing a dog, if his belief is, indeed, caused by a dog and not by a deer? But now it is evident that the belief that a deer is present may be caused *either* by deer *or* by a dog in poor light. In that case, why is his belief not itself disjunctive in form, namely the belief that either a deer or a dog in poor light is present? This is the *disjunction problem*. This problem is closely related to another, namely why is it an animal conceived of as *a deer* that he believes is present, rather than one conceived of more generally as a deer-like animal? This is the *qua problem*, so called because it challenges us to explain why it is *qua* deer (that is under the description "deer") that someone believes that the thing in front of him is present. For what causes his belief might just as well be described as a deer-like animal; better in fact, since this description may apply equally to the dog, which we are supposing he is mistaking for a deer. And lastly, it might be suggested that what leads to his mistake is that his retinal stimuli are the same in both cases. Then why not say that he has a belief as to the presence of such stimulation rather than of the creature which gives rise to it. This is the so-called *depth problem* because it raises the question at what level of the causal chain leading to a belief is its content to be specified. But unless it can be answered it threatens to be fatal to the naturalist's attempt to offer an *externalist* account of such content.

It will be apparent from these problems that we cannot just say that a thought is a belief in the presence of deer because it reliably indicates deer, since its occurrence co-varies with their presence. Nature has not made us as reliable as that. One theory[19] suggests that a thought is a deer-belief when it reliably indicates deer in ideal conditions. There are two difficulties with this. First, we sometimes make mistakes even in ideal conditions. But second, if we don't, is that because ideal conditions have been specified in a circular way as those in which deer-beliefs do indicate deer? If the theory is to provide us with a criterion for the content of belief, however, the conditions in which the belief is reliable must be specified non-circularly. We will not know what item in the world a thought is sensitive to unless we know under what conditions the mechanisms that produce it are functioning optimally. For that we need to know what the function of these thought-producing mechanisms is. The natural answer – to detect deer – just takes us back full circle to the problem of content ascription with which we started.

Another influential theory of content which exploits its causal links to the environment seeks to escape these difficulties. Jerry Fodor's theory[20] of an "asymmetric dependence" of content upon environmental items holds that my thought is a deer-belief, rather than a deer-or-dog-belief say, because it can be caused by dogs only because it is caused by deer, and not vice versa. This captures our intuition that I might believe a deer is present when I see a dog because the dog looks like a deer; but deer would look the way they do and give rise to deer-beliefs whether they looked like dogs or not. This deals with the disjunction problem, but it is no help with the qua problem and is inapplicable to the depth problem. The contents of our thoughts may need to satisfy Fodor's asymmetric dependence condition, but his theory does not go far towards telling us what it is for them to be thought-contents. Indeed Fodor himself supplements it with a theory of narrow content. Nonetheless it points in the direction of a model of mental content as consisting in the exercise of capacities set to discriminate various sorts of items and actuated by these items or derivatively by others. Thus the reason I might mistakenly believe a deer is present when a dog runs across my shadowy path is that I have a capacity set to discriminate deer and which is actuated by dogs only in virtue of this. It is a small step to see such capacities as innate, or built up from innate capacities, so that attributing content involves discovering what sort of items such innate capacities might be attuned to.

Teleological theories

Following this line of thought brings us to what are called *teleological* theories of content.[21] Such theories are so called because they give an account of deer-beliefs, say, in terms of their purpose. Their purpose is to occur, we may suppose, just when deer are present. But teleological theories offer a criterion for the purposes of beliefs. It is that the purpose of some organism's state is what it has been evolutionarily selected for. The purpose of having eyes is to see things because light-sensitive organs that resulted in their owners' responding to the things which activated them are, in most species, favoured over those which did not result in sight. Similarly the purpose of a deer-belief is to provide information on the presence of deer because the development of such beliefs was evolutionarily advantageous. We can imagine it to have been more so than the development of less discriminating deer-or-dog-beliefs, say. The content of the belief is thus given by referring to the items responses to which had survival value in the evolutionary past of the species of which the subject is a member. Or, the teleologist can say, less rigidly, it is given by referring to items a capacity to learn to respond to which was evolutionarily advantageous, so that specific conceptual capacities need not be innate.

This is an ingenious type of theory which arguably yields the right intuitions in Twin Earth type cases. I and my *doppelgänger* will be members of species with different evolutionary histories such that appropriate water-beliefs and twater-beliefs respectively have conferred survival value. It was water my forbears needed to discriminate, and twater my *doppelgänger*'s: that is why my belief concerns water and hers twater. But the mechanisms we have developed for making these discriminations have been remarkably similar. In both of us our beliefs are triggered by the same sensory cues and lead to the same bodily movements for taking in the relevant fluid. Yet the similarity stops there.

There is no need to identify an identical *psychological* state in the two cases, for the common state's psychological character depends upon its purpose, and that, as we have seen, is different in each.

We have already hinted at how teleological theories cope with the disjunction problem. Although both deer and dogs in a poor light might trigger a deer-belief, it is a *deer*-belief because it is responses to deer alone that confer evolutionary advantage (which occasional responses to dogs do not outweigh). If it had not been so, then its content might have been that a deer or dog was present. Similarly with the qua problem. It is not qua animal of a certain appearance, say, that deer are discriminated, but precisely because it is this family of animals that our ancestors gained evolutionary advantage from identifying, as against some similar looking creatures. And this deals with the depth problem as well. For what benefited our ancestors was discriminating deer, not responding to a certain class of retinal stimuli. But surely the latter did too, it will be replied, for they indicated deer. Not necessarily, for even now we can be misled by our senses as to the presence of deer, and we may suppose that in the course of evolution the class of stimuli responded to was progressively refined by natural selection. The purpose of our belief is to indicate deer and the response to certain retinal stimuli is just part of the mechanism whereby this purpose is fulfilled.

This exposition of teleological theory is necessarily over simple. The processes involved in acquiring beliefs with given contents may be considerably more complex than these, possibly including learning, as mentioned earlier. Indeed, it is one of the criticisms of teleological theories that they owe us an account of how concepts are acquired which go beyond those whose deployment has an immediate survival value. For most of our thinking goes well beyond such imperatives. We are owed some account of how it can; of how, for example, the basic materials furnished by evolution can be put together in the complex ways required in our diverse beliefs. Maybe it will be forthcoming. The principal objection commonly offered against teleological theories, however, is this: if the content of our thoughts derives from our evolutionary antecedents, then a subject who had no such antecedents would lack any thoughts. But suppose that a subject – call him Swampman[22] –

arose just like us, though through quite different processes. Would we not want to credit Swampman with the same thoughts as us whatever his history, and just because of the fact that he acts like us?

One possible response is simply to deny that we would. In the absence of an evolutionary history, the response goes, we do not know what, if anything, in his environment Swampman is responding to, and, however he is responding, it is not in a way that justifies the ascription of thoughts with environmental content. All we can say is that he has the same internal mechanisms as we do. But this, as we have seen, does not justify the attribution of the same *psychological* states. This may not convince, for Swampman seems as well *adapted* to his environment as we are, whatever the processes that gave rise to this. We can judge this without knowing anything about his antecedents. Yet what does it mean to say that he is well adapted? Presumably that he is able to adjust his behaviour to his environment in such a way as to ensure a reasonable degree of success in his actions. And success must mean here success in getting what he desires. At this point the teleology theorist has her comeback. How, she asks, do we know that Swampman is getting what he desires? To know that, again requires the attribution of content. The objector to teleology must give the grounds for this attribution, but the teleologist already has them: the content of a desire is what is its evolved purpose to bring about. We can only think of Swampman as well adapted by a tacit assumption of the same desires as us. But it is begging the question against the teleologist to assume this, since teleology will deny Swampman desires for the same reason as it denies him beliefs. Yet, in the light of Swampman's behaviour, the denial of desires to Swampman may seem even less plausible than the denial of beliefs.

Finally, in assessing the success of the teleological approach to content, we need to consider the constraints on naturalizing accounts and how such externalism fares in relation to them. As with the physicalist project in general, there are both ontological and explanatory constraints. To satisfy ontological physicalism we need to provide an account of what it is for an agent to be in an intentional state which makes reference only to extensional characteristics that physical systems could unproblematically possess.

This condition the teleological account of content, if successful, would appear to satisfy.[23]

The explanatory constraint, however, seems to raise problems. If the intentional content of our intentional states is to be causally relevant to the effects that they produce (as Fodor for example believes), then the naturalizing account which we offer must be one which yields such causal relevance to intentional properties. It is just this which led to the demand for internalist theories of content, as we saw above. How do teleological theories fare in this regard? Well, for them, what fixes the intentional content of an agent's states are facts in her evolutionary history. The causal role given to these facts is to ensure the survival of creatures with certain kinds of functional organization. Those distant historical facts have no causal role to play in relation to the behaviour which states with such intentional content currently produce. So the fact that in the past a certain kind of structure was linked in the appropriate way to the presence of deer, and this is part of the explanation for its survival, means that currently such a structure can be said to represent deer. Such past considerations, however, have no bearing on what behaviour such structures will now produce. This will be the same whatever the history of such structures, as the example of Swampman shows. For the same structures will produce the same behaviour whatever the causal history behind their production. But the teleological approach links the representational properties of these structures to their distant causal histories, not to their present relation to behaviour. That an agent has beliefs about deer is, then, causally unrelated to her engaging in current deer-directed activities. This seems counter-intuitive by anyone's lights!

Teleological theories of content identify *kinds* of item in the world beyond the subject as what she thinks or desires. But they do not draw on the indexicality of terms like "water", which we argued earlier was such an important feature of their use in locating kinds of items in the external world as those items that our thoughts concerned; and this has important repercussions. We can dramatize these by imagining that a scientist extracts the brains of human foetuses and keeps them in a vat, subjecting them to stimuli equivalent to those they would receive had their owners grown up normally. What thought-contents do they have? Teleology seems to deliver the wrong answer to this question. For according to it, they will have thoughts about the kinds of item their evolutionary ancestors came to discriminate, even though they currently have no perceptual or interactional contact with them. This seems to concede too much to internalism,[24] and it does so because it has no account to offer of a subject's singular thoughts about the particular things in her environment. But it is ascription of such thoughts as essential to the subject's psychology that marks the crucial break with the picture inherited from Descartes. Teleological externalism does not make it. Indeed, it seems unlikely that any naturalistic theory of the sorts we have looked at can give an adequate account of indexicality.

Conclusion

How, then, we might ask, should we? What we can perhaps do is abandon the assumption which, as we have seen, dual component and teleological theories both make that the bodily movement involved in action upon the environment is something for which psychological explanation should account, so that the causal powers shared by atom for atom identical twins in different environments are similarly implicated in the explanation of their actions. But why should we suppose that? We are usually not at all interested in what bodily movements occur, only in what their effects on the environment are in virtue of which the agent is performing the action she does. To assume otherwise is to be captivated by the Cartesian picture of the body as a physical thing just like any other in the world, whose motions require explanation as part of a causal chain in which other objects get moved around. Yet that is not how we – owners of such bodies ourselves – routinely see them. What this leaves out is seeing them as expressive of the desires and thoughts which explain our actions.

In this model the point of psychological explanation is to account for the way an agent negotiates her environment, usually successfully but with occasional lapses that need accounting for. There is a conception of success at work here, but it does not need to be analyzed in terms of what is conducive to the fulfilment of biological purposes. This is again to treat the behaviour under investiga-

tion as simply one more phenomenon in the physical world requiring a scientific explanation, albeit a complex diachronic one. In
practice we usually know when others are successful in their
everyday actions and when they are not. In virtue of our common
human condition we can read the signs of success and satisfaction
or failure and frustration. This is one aspect of the way in which
we find the behaviour of our fellows intelligible, and, when we do
not, require some information on their desires or beliefs which
make it so. Pierre, for example, whom we met at the beginning of
the chapter, may puzzle us for a while. But once we grasp that he
attaches different *names* to the same place, and is therefore able to
attribute inconsistent properties to it, our puzzlement disappears.
He *does* have inconsistent beliefs which he is unable to recognize
as such until he grasps that it is the same place about which he is
thinking, that the names he uses apply to the one place and not to
two. And this requires him to see his beliefs, just as we see them,
as relating him to the environment in which he moves.

The acceptability of an explanation for action depends, in this
model, on whether it succeeds in making it intelligible to us.
Crucial to this is that it should attribute thoughts that relate the
agent to her environment along the lines of an externalism which
stresses the importance of indexical links. For what we want to
know is why the agent acts as she does in *our* world; in the world
whose occupants we pick out indexically as that man in a red cap,
say, and which she can pick out similarly, so that we focus on the
same individual and can compare our thoughts about him. We
attribute to each other the beliefs that are needed to make our
actions intelligible. Confronted with an agent whose identifications we could not share, we would be mystified, however con-
tented he seemed to be and however much information about his
world he purported to supply us with. The particular items in the
world that all of us cohabit need to enter into the content of our
beliefs if they are to make our actions mutually intelligible. And
that is because other beliefs not making reference to these items,
could not explain our interactions with them. The scientific naturalism we have looked at in these last two chapters fails to account
for the way that our intentional states provide the kind of explanation of behaviour that they do. Intent on locating these states
within the causal nexus of the body, it fails to show how they relate

us to the world outside. Dropping this demand allows us to be externalists about the content of our thoughts without providing any special account of how our thoughts can reach out to a world which is, as it were, outside of them. For dropping the demand to identify those thoughts as internal states gets rid of the assumption which generates this problematic picture, and replaces it with one in which our thoughts are as much a part of our commerce with the world as our actions in it are.[25]

Further reading

Introductory books that cover intentional content include Colin McGinn, *The character of mind* (Oxford: Oxford University Press, 1982) (2nd edn), Chapters 4 and 5, and Jaegwon Kim, *Philosophy of mind* (Colorado: Westview Press, 1996), Chapter 8 (which has a particularly comprehensive bibliography). David Braddon Mitchell and Frank Jackson, *Philosophy of mind and cognition* (Oxford: Blackwell, 1996), Part 3, and Tim Crane, *The mechanical mind* (London: Penguin, 1995) are particularly good on teleological theories, while Gregory McCulloch's *The mind and its world* (London: Routledge, 1995), Chapters 7–8 is rather more iconoclastic. Somewhat more advanced is Georges Rey, *Contemporary philosophy of mind* (Oxford: Blackwell, 1997), Chapter 9, which offers an internalist approach, while Akeed Bilgrami's *Belief and meaning* (Oxford: Blackwell, 1992) is a sophisticated defence of externalism and Hilary Putnam's *Representation and reality* (Cambridge, Mass.: MIT Press, 1991) places his externalism in a broader metaphysical framework. Useful collections are Stephen P. Stich and Ted A. Warfield (eds), *Mental representations* (Oxford: Blackwell, 1994) and Barry Loewer and Georges Rey (eds), *Meaning in mind* (London: Routledge, 1991).

Chapter 5

Anti-reductionist alternatives

Interpretationalism

In the preceding two chapters we have been discussing character-istics of our intentional states which raise particular difficulties for the contemporary project of reducing such intentional idioms to non-intentional functional ones. In Chapter 3 we concentrated on the anchorage of intentional kinds in normative, rationalizing patterns of explanation which, in Davidson's words, seem "to have no echo in physical theory".[1] In Chapter 4 we concentrated on the issue of the semantic content of our intentional states. Such content seems to be constituted out of the relationships in which we stand to states of affairs in our environment and moreover to our situatedness within certain social practices in ways that seem to elude capture in internalist or externalist functionalist terms. From both chapters it became clear that what we invoked our intentional states to explain were facts quite distinct from, though having implications for, bodily movements. What we invoke our intentional states to explain are intentional engagements in our world and expressive interactions with it. There seems no chance of finding projectible classifications in non-intentional terms for such *explananda*. In this chapter we will explore approaches to the question of what is involved in having intentional states and the nature of intentional explanations which seek to avoid the difficulties that beset reductive functionalism.

One approach that appears to avoid this set of problems is that of interpretationism. The best known exponents of this position are Donald Davidson and Daniel Dennett.[2] The central idea underlying this approach is that intentional patterns of classification provide us with an interpretive framework which we can apply to the behaviour of others on the basis of what we can observe of their interactions with their environment. Our grasp of what is involved in having intentional states requires us to grasp their position in such a pattern of interpretation. The application of this framework of interpretation does not have implications for what is going on "inside the head" of the agent. Nothing of this sort is required to vindicate the attribution of intentional states.

Davidson draws attention to the constraining features of such a scheme by envisioning the situation of radical interpretation, a situation in which we are trying to make sense of people without knowing their language, or having an interpreter. In this situation if we are to see the people concerned as intentional agents, then we must undertake a project of interpretation that is holistic. We must assign meaning to their words, provide interpretations of their actions, and attribute motives to them which all hang together. Such a project is constrained by overarching principles of rationality.

> Individual beliefs, intentions, doubts, and desires owe their identities in part to their position in a larger network of further attitudes; the character of a given belief depends on endless other beliefs; beliefs have the role they do because of their relation to desires, intentions and perceptions. These relations among the attitudes are essentially logical; the content of the attitude cannot be divorced from what it entails and what is entailed by it. This places a normative constraint on the correct attribution of attitudes ... the pattern of attitudes in an individual must exhibit a large degree of coherence. This does not,

of course, mean that people may not be irrational, but the possibility of irrationality depends on a background of rationality; to imagine a totally irrational animal is to imagine an animal without thoughts.[3]

The issue here is not simply the internal coherence of the package of thought envisaged. We are in the business of interpreting creatures in given environments to make sense of their behaviour in such environments. We therefore attribute content to their thoughts on the basis of the objects to which they are related, and ascribe objectives which appear to make sense in that context. "In our need to make him make sense, we will try for a theory that finds him consistent, a believer of truths, and a lover of the good (all by our own lights, it goes without saying)."[4] The parenthetical phrase "all by our own lights" is also important here. As interpreters we are searching for ways of describing the environment and the agents' intentional acts which inform the intentional content we ascribe to their states. For Davidson this can only be the case if we hit on patterns of characterization that could, for us, be ascribable to the world that they are in. Where this is not possible, then we cannot make these creatures intelligible and therefore cannot see them as intentional creatures at all.

For Davidson the situation of radical interpretation captures the features of the situation we are in whenever we use intentional descriptions; although we do not become explicitly aware of the process or the principles we employ in cases where we ascribe states to others in the same language community. The constitutive principles of rationality provide us with an account of what it is to be an intentional agent. In this account people do not have minds, thought of in terms of underlying inner processes. Rather, psychological predicates are true of them, when they are susceptible to such intentional patterns of description. "Having an attitude is just being in a certain state; it is a modification of a person. There need not be any 'object' in or before the mind for the person to be thinking, doubting, intending or calculating." Instead, the intentional objects in terms of which our thoughts are individuated are thought about as ways of picking out whole states:

Such objects serve much the same function as numbers serve in keeping track of temperature or weight. There are no such things as weights or temperatures, "this box weighs 9 pounds" relates the box to a number on the pound scale, but the number is an abstract object unknown to the box.[5]

Consequently the attribution of states with intentional content requires no set of inner states with syntactic structures mapping those of our propositional attitudes.

Daniel Dennett has reached a position very close to Davidson, but from rather a different starting point. Dennett expresses his position in terms of the "intentional stance". He discusses the example of the chess-playing computer and explores three levels at which we can make sense of its behaviour and predict what it will do.[6] At one level, the physical, we will be concerned with the causal interactions of its hardware. But the complexity of organization would make this difficult and time-consuming to adopt. The next level is that of the design stance where we try to predict and explain the behaviour of the system in terms of functions its component parts are designed to serve. The highest level is the intentional stance in which we treat the system as if it had beliefs and desires and predict and explain its moves by treating it as a rational agent intent on winning the game of chess. For the chess-playing computer, when we wish to predict its move this is the most successful stance to adopt. The point of this story for Dennett, however, is to do away with the distinction between as if intentionality and real intentionality. We understand what is involved in being an intentional system once we grasp what it is to successfully adopt the intentional stance towards a system. The difference between us and the chess-playing computer is simply in the levels of our complexity. As with Davidson, central to the intentional stance is the assumption of rationality. We assume the computer/person will do what they rationally ought to do. This is not always successful as a strategy, but it is successful often enough to make it worthwhile.

The approach of interpretationalists such as Davidson and Dennett is compatible with the materialist metaphysics that inform most current philosophy of mind, in that, for them, the existence of minds does not involve the existence of any non-material substance. Davidson attaches his interpretationalism to a claim of token identity between intentional states and physical states.[7] This is a move designed to rescue the causal implications of our intentional descriptions, given his claim that there are no supporting laws at the intentional level. However, the intentional descriptions of these physical states are fixed by a process of interpretation. Davidson also accepts a supervenience claim for intentional types or properties (see Chapter 2) so that the intentional descriptions to which a system is susceptible are fixed by its physical characteristics and its environment. Where Davidson differs from most contemporary materialists, however, is in resisting any systematic links between the physical and intentional levels of description. The intentional realm has an autonomy which should mean that we do not expect to make sense in physical terms of our susceptibility to intentional characterizations. It seems to be simply a given about the kind of creatures we are that we can understand each other in this way.

Dennett's concerns are closer to the functionalist materialists' than those of Davidson. Like them, he is anxious to naturalize our mentality and anxious to explain scientifically "how a physical structure could accomplish what the mind does".[8] He does this, not by expecting the brain to replicate our rationality, but rather by starting with the assumption that the evolutionary process has ensured, over a period of time, that at the macro-level we are approximately rational, in terms of our overall negotiation of our environment. For Dennett this can be achieved without any assumption of processes at the sub-personal level with structural parallels to our propositional attitudes. It does mean, however, that Dennett has a concern with the "how" question (how does it come about that we can be interpreted intentionally?) that does not enter into Davidson's picture. For Dennett this "how" question has two strands. First, how can a physical system be such as to be interpreted intentionally? He thus concerns himself with making supervenience intelligible; a concern which prompted reductive functionalism. His response is to point to work in artificial intelligence and to argue that "the way to explain the miraculous seeming powers of an intelligent intentional system is to decompose it into a hierarchically structured team of ever more stupid intentional systems, ultimately discharging all intelligence debts in a fabric of stupid mechanisms".[9] The other strand of the "how" question is different. It is more like, "how come there are intentional systems about?" Where artifacts are designed, this question is answered by reference to the designer. In the case of living creatures, such as ourselves, the place of designer has to be taken by what Dennett often refers to as "Mother Nature".[10] Our intentionality is a product of evolution. This appears to set some additional constraint on the intentional interpretations available to us. For the objectives ascribable would seem to need to be those which have evolutionary advantage or those which could have arisen on the back of such advantageous objectives. (There are obvious parallels here with the teleological account of content discussed in the previous chapter.)

The positions of both Davidson and Dennett are examples of what we shall call constitutive interpretationalism. For both, what is involved in having intentional states is just to be interpretable by some observer as having intentional states. Such a position seems to accommodate the problematic features that we raised for the functionalist reductionist programme in preceding chapters. Interpretationalists insist on the central role of rationality in the anchorage of our intentional understanding. Normative notions thus remain at the forefront of our intentional ascriptions. Their standpoint is also resolutely externalist. They are engaged in interpreting a creature/system in its environment and characteristics of that environment dictate the content of the intentional attitudes that we ascribe to them. This also spills over into the characterization of the actions that we interpret them as performing, which are transformations of that environment to yield desirable goals. There is no necessity that these transformations be classified in terms of bodily movements. For Davidson, however, these classifications must be ones that would be recognizable to an interpreter, and for Dennett there appears to be an added condition that they involve patterns of behaviour which could have emerged on the back of those that are to our evolutionary advantage.[11]

Real patterns

The most commonly voiced objection to interpretationalism is that it is not sufficiently realist about mental states. Our intentional descriptions seem to end up as mere ways of talking and thereby, it is claimed, they are not viewed as sufficiently robust constituents of the world. Dennett fuelled this criticism, as in early writings he accepted a characterization of his view as instrumentalism. This is a concept derived from philosophy of science where we postulate unobserved entities in an attempt to formulate useful predictions regarding what we can observe.[12] We then have an option of being realist or instrumentalist about such entities. If we are realist, we assume they exist, have the characteristics we attribute to them, and that improved observational techniques might deliver them up to observation. If we are instrumentalist, we treat them as useful fictions that aid us in making predictions about what we can observe.

For Dennett, to accept a label of instrumentalism for interpretationalism was, however, to invite a misreading of this position. Unlike other forms of contemporary materialism, it does not view mental states as inner entities which we postulate to explain observable behaviour, and which we then have an option of being realist or instrumentalist about. As the quote from Davidson makes clear, psychological states are states of persons as a whole. Far from being hidden from view, they exist only if they are available to interpreters. They do not have the kind of existence as inner processes envisaged by Cartesians or their materialist successors. It nonetheless seems inappropriate to designate them fictions. Consequently, in later papers, Dennett has referred to the intentionality we attribute to systems as a "real pattern", detectable in their responses to their environment, making it possible to say that our intentional descriptions are true of them.[13] If this is not enough to be a realist about the intentional, it must be because some additional requirement is being sneaked in. This would seem to be the case, for example, with Fodor, who sees his intentional realism as requiring an isomorphism between our intentional characteristics and physicalist ones. Yet, as we have seen, it is not clear why we should accept this constraint.

A connected and more telling criticism which is often brought, in particular against Dennett, is that he makes no distinction between "as if" intentionality and "real" intentionality. Consequently, we have to attribute genuine intentionality to whole ranges of artefacts in a way that we find quite counter-intuitive;

for example, computers and, possibly, thermostats as well.[14] One response to the problem of there being too wide a category of intentional systems is to suggest that intentional characterizations should be employed only when we cannot satisfactorily explain the behaviour by adopting one of the other stances. Where this becomes too complex, then we have an intentional system. Such a response, however, seems to be insufficiently principled. Whether something is intentional could vary according to whether its interpreters work easily with long calculations and this does seem to undermine the previous claims that intentional characterizations pick out "real patterns". A second response simply accepts the generous consequences of the approach: yes there are intentional systems of many kinds, some much more complex than others, and the difference between ourselves and thermostats is simply a matter of complexity. We shall turn to the reason why this seems so deeply unsatisfactory in the following section.

Davidson, as we saw, attempts to establish his realist credentials by adopting a token identity between intentional states and brain states. This, however, does not answer the claim that the intentional characteristics of such states do not pick out genuine characteristics, real features of the world. In Davidson's case this accusation might seem to be supported by his explicit adoption of the indeterminacy thesis. One consequence of interpretationalism seems to be that there might be more than one interpretation which respects the principles of rationality. Davidson accepts this, resisting any thought that there must be anything beyond interpretability which could serve to fix what states we are really in. "There is no further court of appeal, no impersonal objective standard against which to measure our own best judgments of the rational and the true."[15] One way of seeing this is to acknowledge that future occurrences can lead to our modifying intentional characteristics that we applied to earlier states, rather as, in seeing more and more of a roll of wall paper the pattern we detect may change. At no moment, therefore, are the intentional characterizations determinate, although distinct intentional characterizations nonetheless have predictive differences. Davidson, however, seems to view intentional descriptions as indeterminate in a more radical way. He claims that different intentional characterizations of the same physical setups are merely notational variants of each other. The concept of a "notational variant" here suggests that the same empirical import is captured by conceptualizations that are nonetheless distinct from each other. Such conceptual distinctions, however, do not reflect "real" distinctions in the world. Such an admission is seen by some as a recognition that the reality attaching to our intentional characteristics is in some sense secondary to that attaching to our physical ones. The empirical import here appears to be captured by the physical characterizations of the world. If two intentional descriptions, though intentionally distinct, reflect no empirical distinctions, this fuels the objection that in the interpretationalist view intentional characteristics are not real features of the world.

This consequence of Davidson's account is connected to another, common to both him and Dennett. Their presentation of interpretationalism suggests a two-stage process. We observe people's behaviour in their environment and then interpret it intentionally. "We wonder why a man raises his arm; an explanation might be that he wanted to attract the attention of a friend . . . [This] explains what is relatively apparent – an arm raising – by appeal to factors that are far more problematic – desires and beliefs."[16] This suggests that we are aware of the behaviour prior to its intentional characterization at a more fundamental level of observation (as something like a bodily movement). The intentional stance involves an interpretation of this bodily movement. Such a picture would then serve to reinforce the secondary status of the intentional description.

Direct interpretationalism

Neither the indeterminacy which Davidson attributes to intentional descriptions nor the suggested two-stage epistemological process, with its associated privileging of physicalist modes of characterization, are essential to interpretationist approaches.[17] In that two-stage process we encounter certain observable patterns of behaviour, perhaps directly characterizable as movements of a person's body, which we then have the project of interpreting, utilizing our principles of rationality. Here the physicalist descriptions play a foundational role and form the bedrock to which our intentional characterizations are applied and to which they are answerable. They remain determinate when our intentional characterizations may be indeterminate. This picture, of course, fuels the feeling which surfaced above that the reality of our intentional characterizations is somewhat second class.

In the alternative account our intentional modes of characterization do not require grounding in some more basic observation concepts and do not require vindication by them. Intentional modes of description directly pick out interrelated phenomena – actions, speech, mental states and modes of characterizing the environment in which the agent is placed. Here we can make a comparison between understanding language and understanding intentional acts. Reading or listening to a language we understand, we do not first become aware of the signs and then move to interpret them. We see or hear the meaning directly, as an aspect of that to which we are attending. It is, in general, only when we do not understand, that the shapes and sounds of words become the objects of attention. Similarly we do not first pick out a bodily movement and then consider what intentional act it could be. The identification of speech and intentional acts are immediate and direct.

For an interpretationism of this kind, intentional modes of characterization are simply learnt along with our everyday characterizations of objects. The teachability and projectibility of such patterns of conceptualization and explanation seem to vindicate the claim that here we are dealing with real patterns, features of the world whose ontological status seems no less robust than the categories picked out by physical science.[18] For interpretationalists, then, our grasp of what is involved in having intentional states is given by grasping this interconnected pattern of conceptualization. To be an intentional agent is to be susceptible to such conceptualization. Intentional explanation is thus of a *sui generis* kind. It depends on uncovering a pattern of rationality in the agent's overall behaviour, a pattern that makes the behaviour intelligible to us and enables us to respond appropriately and make predictions as to how others might act and respond on future occasions. Such explanations are not of a causal kind and therefore they escape the reductionist demand that they seek vindication in internal physical structures.[19]

Psychological causalism

Interpretationalism avoids the problems that beset reductive functionalism by giving up the assumption that psychological kinds are natural kinds partially individuated, at least, by their role in causal explanatory generalizations. Other anti-reductionists, however, wish to hang on to the assumption that our psychological states are embedded in causal explanations; but to do so without accepting the reductive functionalist picture. According to what we shall term *psychological causalism*, intentional classifications are autonomous and irreducible to, because not isomorphic with, classifications made by non-intentional science. They adopt a system of classification of intentional acts, speech and environment of the kind utilized by interpretationalism, and accept that within this system the intentionally characterized phenomena bear rationalizing links to each other. These rationalizing links, however, form the basis for generating *causal explanatory generalizations* governing the transitions which the system undergoes. Crucially these causal generalizations can only be articulated by making use of the rationalizing links. Without the use of intentional vocabulary there would be sets of causal and law-like relations in the world that we would be unable to recognize; for example, that, *ceteris paribus*, people do and believe what they have reason to do and believe because such actions and beliefs are rational. Without such generalizations we would be unable to explain and predict their behaviour. Therefore the generalizations, which for interpretationalists are constitutive principles constraining our interpretations, are, for causalists, empirical causal generalizations. Any apparent constitutive link between beliefs, desires and intentional acts is explained as a result of their position within a theory that at least partially defines its core notions.[20]

Psychological causalists can adopt several of the naturalizing assumptions that motivated the reductionist picture. Psychological states can be seen as inner states, mediating input–output relations, in line with the scientific realist picture. What is denied is that the essential characteristics of such states can be captured using non-intentional vocabulary. If their identifying conditions are thought of as being exhausted by their role in such a causal explanatory theory, then the view is equivalent to the anti-reductionist functionalism discussed at the end of Chapter 2. It therefore remains possible to see psychological kinds as natural kinds, ways of classifying the world which enable generalizations, predictions and the support of conditionals. The key difference from reductionist accounts of natural kinds is that there is no assumption that natural kinds at one level will be isomorphic with those elsewhere. It is nevertheless possible for such theorists to acknowledge the pull of modified explanatory physicalism (see Chapter 2). They can accept that each of the causal transitions which are picked out intentionally be grounded in causal transitions at the micro-particulate level. This could be done by accepting that the psychological states causing actions supervene on the physical states causing movements. In such a way each intentional causal transition supervenes on a physical causal transition. The necessity of the intentional states for both bodily movements and intentional acts then follows from the causal relations at the physical level and the dependency and determination of the intentional level by the physical level. There is then no threat of over-determination, as the intentional and physical determining conditions are not independent.

Despite this, to attempt to marry anti-reductionist psychological causalism with scientific naturalism is to generate some uncomfortable tensions. First, in accepting the need to ground intentional causal transactions in micro-particulate ones, and thereby accepting the causal realism that motivates such a move, they lay themselves open to the charge that intentional causation is only supervenient causation (see Chapter 2). Secondly, the attempt to link intentional causes of action with inner physical causes of movements looks impossible, given the robust and essential externalism of our intentional classificatory scheme and the quite disparate classifications into intentional acts and bodily movements. Even at a token level, the suggestion that intentional acts could supervene on bodily movements or intentional states on the physical causes of such movements cannot be sustained. Thirdly, the suggestion that intentional and other psychological kinds should be viewed as *theoretical entities*, postulated to explain our response to our environment, does not seem reconcilable with the insight that we gained from the discussion of direct interpretationalism above. Here it became clear that intentional descriptions of ourselves are ones that we learn to apply directly, and not as a result of a two-stage process.

Modified psychological causalism

A modified psychological causalism wishes to accept the causal explanatory role of intentional explanation without modelling the intentional case on that of scientific natural kinds. It therefore does not feel the pull of explanatory physicalism and the need to ground all causal transactions in micro-particulate physical ones. It also accepts most of the picture of direct interpretationalism, whereby psychological states are not viewed as inner theoretical entities postulated to explain observable behaviour, but as "modifications of a person" which we learn to perceive directly.[21] The difference from such direct interpretationalism lies in accepting the causal implications of intentional explanations, shown in the use of causal language and the conditional implications that they carry. Such intentional causal explanations are, however, compared to causal explanations of an everyday rather than scientific kind. Although they may be supported by rough generalizations, there is no assumption that empirical work will tighten these into strict laws. Intentional causal claims are justified not by being anchored in scientific ones of a physical kind, but rather by the intelligibility they bestow on the actions they explain and the successful interactions and predictions they facilitate. Such modified explanatory physicalism is close to the direct interpretationalism discussed above: it has simply added causal claims to the interpretive framework.[22]

Third-personalism and perspectivity

How satisfactory a package is this? There are many important virtues of this position anchored in its recognition that intentionality is anchored in a distinctive *sui generis* pattern of conceptualization and explanation, which does not require vindication or anchorage in some more foundational level of description.

This is its major strength, in virtue of which it avoids many of the problems attaching to reductive functionalism. What remains problematic, however, is that our grasp of what it is to be an intentional agent remains anchored in the position of a third person making sense of the behaviour of others. What is playing no role here is how such intentionality appears from the perspective or point of view of the subject who is intentionally interacting with the world. It is the omission of this key factor which made Dennett's replies with regard to the intentionality of artefacts so unsatisfactory. It is possible, it has been argued, that we could interpret the behaviour of a system in terms of an intentional schema even when, in the words of Charles Taylor, the behaviour had no *significance or meaning* to the system itself and when the system lacked a point of view or perspective onto the world.[23]

The point here is not simply the familiar one that, in addition to intentional mental states, there are also those which are differentiated in terms of their experiential content. The particular issues arising out of such content will be addressed in the following two chapters. The point is more general and directly applicable to issues of intentionality and rationality. As pointed out in Chapter 3, our intentional states are invoked in bestowing rational intelligibility on other intentional states and intentional acts. Such intelligibility, however, is anchored in the point of view of an agent engaging intentionally in her environment. This is the perspective that we need to adopt if we are to provide rationalizing explanations. It is just such a perspective which is missing from the interpretive picture.

Charles Taylor often makes such points in terms of the claim that we are *self-interpreting animals*.[24] By this he means, not that we observe ourselves and reach judgements concerning our intentional states, for that would be absurd. We evidently do not normally come to say what we believe, for example, by discovering what makes sense of our behaviour. We are simply able to avow our beliefs. What Taylor means here is that the articulations we provide of our own feelings, beliefs, desires and emotions are constitutive of these being the kind of states they are.

> This means ... that there is no adequate description of how it is with a human being ... which does not incorporate his self

understanding, that is the descriptions he or she is inclined to give of his emotions, aspirations, desires . . . etc. What we are at any moment is, one might say, partly constituted by such self understandings.[25]

Taylor is insisting that the world in which the agent is placed appears to her in a certain kind of way, as also does her response to it. If we are to have an understanding of an agent and her intentional states, then we need to grasp how the world shows itself to her. We need to engage with it from her perspective. Reverting to the example from Chapter 3, we understand Maureen setting off to her friend's house when we grasp how that option strikes *her*. This is crucially distinct from the position of inter-pretationalism, where the conceptualization of the environment and the behaviour is that provided by the interpreter. It is such perspectivalism that needs to be added to the package of direct interpretationalism and modified psychological causalism.

The role of perspectivity alluded to here as constitutive of our mental life was, of course, recognized by Descartes and seen by him as rendering untenable a physicalism about mind. His ac-count of it, however, was profoundly unsatisfactory. He offered the mind as an inner arena to which we had privileged and incorrigi-ble access. In this picture our relationship to our own intentional acts involves a process of introspecting our beliefs, desires, inten-tions, and so forth, to all of which we have privileged access. Such inner states then issue in movements of our physical bodies, in relation to which we have no privileged epistemic status. But, as Greg McCulloch points out, this picture fails to accommodate how our intentional interactions do actually appear to us:

> introspection . . . just delivers up the world again. What intro-spection delivers is an awareness of existing in the midst of surroundings, moving and intervening . . . the separation of the strictly introspectible from the rest is simply a product of the Cartesian model of experience.[26]

It became clear in the previous chapter that such an intro-spectionist model makes the intentional content of our psycho-logical states utterly mysterious. It cuts us off from the world.

What perspectivity allows us access to, in contrast, is the world in which we live our lives, but from a particular perspective within it.

The world from the point of view of the subject

What picture of our relation to the world does direct inter-pretationalism and modified psychological causalism yield when married to perspectivalism? There are a number of interconnected features.

(a) We experience ourselves as embodied agents, within the world, as able to manipulate and respond to our environment. Such awareness of our bodies does not experience them as physical objects external to our mind, but rather as intentional entities engaged in active transformations of our environment. This has consequences which we will explore more fully in later chapters; but one of them is to unsettle the mind/body dualism that we inherit from Cartesianism. From the perspective of the intentional subject the body is not a material object to which our intentional states are either causally related or reductively identified. Rather the body is experienced as that through which we act and suffer.

(b) The world that is presented from the point of view of the subject is what Heidegger calls the familiar world, the world of everyday objects, tables, chairs, and trees.[27] What perspectivalism adds to this insight of interpretationalism is that such a world is experienced as *salient* to us, making certain kinds of response apt or appropriate. This is of crucial importance. We do not add value to a world experienced neutrally, in accordance with how it matches up to our independently constituted desires. Instead the content of such desires is constituted from a world experienced as being significant to us:

> we do not, so to speak, throw a "signification" over some naked thing which is present to hand, we do not stick a value on it; but when something within-the-world is encountered as such, the thing in question already has an involvement which is disclosed in our understanding of the world.[28]

It is, in Heidegger's phrase, an object "ready to hand". Our intentional acts are meaningful activities, purposive interventions into an already salient environment.

(c) This has consequences for the nature of rationalizing explanation, which we noted in Chapter 3. Within both interpretationalism and psychological causalism rationalizing links are a distinctive and *sui generis* pattern of conceptualization which bestow a distinctive kind of intelligibility on the phenomena which they explain. Rationalizing patterns, however, remain *objective* patterns and the force of the normative *ought* remains unaccommodated. With attention to perspectivalism, however, it becomes clear that rational explanations require engagement with the perspective of the agent. This delivers a view of the world as salient to her, a world in which certain responses are appropriate or required. Grasping the rationality of the response requires grasping the appearance of the world which renders it appropriate. This is not an objective characterization but a perspectival one.

(d) The patterns of conceptualization of our intentional states are in most cases immediate. They are transparent to us and do not require anchoring in more primitive observational terms. This is not to say that they are incorrigible: we do, of course, often revise them. The kind of transparency here is not necessarily self-reflective in the way that that is true of introspection. In being aware of the earth around the seedlings we are planting as requiring firming, and pressing in and down accordingly, we do not need to be aware of ourselves as experiencing the earth in that way. Such self-reflective aspects are additional elements and not always present.

(e) This transparency also attaches to the way other people appear to us. In McCulloch's terms we see them as "minded".[29] People are experienced as having points of view and engaging in intentional acts, for many of which we can provide an immediate intentional characterization. Of course, the behaviour of others is not always transparent to us in this way and there are times when we need to decipher it. In such cases we need engagement with their point of view and the way the world appears from it. The conditions for such engagement will be considered in the following section.

Context and culture

We have been insisting that an adequate account of intentionality requires recognition of the interdependent rationalizing and perspectival nature of intentional explanation. This, in turn, requires recognition of a mode of conceptualizing our interactions with our world which is *sui generis* and does not require vindication by integration into the classificatory schemas of science.

For writers with the naturalizing impulses which inform present-day philosophy of mind this is a profoundly anti-naturalizing move. Our intentionality is not to be captured within the net of scientific explanation and this appears to make it mysterious. John McDowell, however, in recent work challenges the account of naturalism that is offered within these accounts. What is natural about us, he argues, is not exhausted by what can be captured within the domain of scientific law. It is an entirely natural fact about us that we are the kind of creatures for whom the world presents itself in meaningful and significant ways, ways which give us reasons to judge and act. Such natural facts do not require anchorage within the framework of scientific explanation. This is quite compatible with the recognition that in order to be such creatures we need to have certain kinds of physical bodies with certain kinds of functional organization.

> To reassure ourselves that our responsiveness to reasons is not supernatural, we should dwell on the thought that it is our lives that are shaped by spontaneity, patterned in ways that come into view only within a framework of an inquiry framed by what Davidson calls "the constitutive ideal of rationality". Exercises of spontaneity belong to our way of living. And our mode of living is our way of naturalising ourselves as animals.[30]

For McDowell, following Wittgenstein, human beings are initiated into the space of reasons by upbringing: "initiation into conceptual capacities, which include responsiveness to . . . rational demands. Such an initiation is a normal part of what it is for a human being to come to maturity . . . The resulting habits of thought and action are second nature."[31]

The possibility of intentional agency may well rest on entirely general features of our intentional embodiment. It is also a general characteristic that we are the kind of creatures for whom the world can take on significance or salience. The specific kind of significance or salience, however, is learnt in a social context and anchored in shared practices, so that some judgements or some emotional responses are only possible in certain contexts or cultural settings. Charles Taylor illustrates this through the example of shame.

> I may be ashamed of my shrill voice, or my effeminate hands. But of course it only makes sense to see these as objects of shame if they have for me or my culture an expressive dimension: a shrill voice is . . . something unmanly . . . not something strong, solid . . . macho self contained . . . Effeminate hands are effeminate.[32]

The way of conceptualizing reality and the salience it carries is highly specific. Such an emotion is usually available only to certain subjects, men (although a woman might be ashamed of her partner or son for being unmanly), in certain quite specific cultural settings.

These patterns of conceptualization are not fixed and unalterable. Naomi Scheman has discussed the example of the role of consciousness-raising groups in providing a context in which women became able to conceptualize their situation in a way that allowed them to feel anger about it.[33] Here it is not the case that there were prior determinate feelings which were discovered to be anger. The conceptualization made possible by the groups made it possible for this to be the emotion experienced. The kind of salience that our world takes on is anchored in shared contexts and practices. The important fact is that such patterns of conceptualization underpinning our intentional states are ones that can be learnt and into which others can be initiated.

Where the behaviour of others is not transparent to us, we need to engage with their perspective if its meaning is to become available to us. Engaging with a perspective is not like entry into some hidden realm. We rather need initiation into the context and practices in relation to which their patterns of conceptualization and response make sense, finding our way around their cultural and personal worlds.[34]

Wittgenstein pointed out that communicable meaning rests on agreement in judgements and the possibility of this rests on what he calls shared "natural history".[35] This shared history can be extended to incorporate social as well as biological elements, as our examples have made clear. But we must be wary of regarding perspectives as closed and self-contained boxes. Between people there will be a patchwork of shared and overlapping perspectives; a patchwork of shared and overlapping similarities and differences in judgements. Moreover our histories are constantly changing, often by encounters with others, yielding the possibility of agreement in new types of judgement. Understanding others is not an all or nothing affair. It is rarely impossible and rarely complete. In contrast to the Cartesian picture, however, it is not a matter of entering into some inner realm hidden behind their behaviour.[36]

Conclusion

In the account of understanding others which is offered by many causal explanatory theorists, we observe people's behaviour, and then, in the light of the general law-like regularities with which we are familiar, we frame hypotheses regarding the kinds of inner states that might have brought about this behaviour. Of course this is helped if they speak to us and tell us what they want or believe, but even in this case we have to form hypotheses about the inner intentions that may have produced their utterances. Our grasp of what is involved in having intentional states requires regarding them as such inner causes. In its reductionist guise, such inner causes can be mapped onto the scientific physicalist ones.

In the interpretationalist's view, we observe people's behaviour and seek an interpretation of this in relation to which we can plausibly attribute intentional states that would make such behaviour, over a period of time, appear as reasonable. In this we are constrained to attribute beliefs that could reasonably be held in the environment they find themselves in and objectives that we could plausibly view as desirable. Here the overriding principles are not empirical causal laws but principles of rationality. Our grasp of what is involved in having intentional states requires seeing the way in which our behaviour is systematizable into such objective patterns.

In the view which we have been developing in this chapter, which takes the perspectivity of intentional action as being central to understanding others, we are required to engage with the point of view of others and to appreciate the way the world appears from it. Doing so means that we can grasp the meaning which their acts have for them and so view these acts as in various ways appropriate. This also requires us to recognize intentional modes of description of a system of classification that applies to ourselves and our world in a different way from scientific modes of classification. It is a system that is anchored in our practical engagements with the world, mediated by the culture and context in which it is learnt. If we want to grasp what is involved in being an agent with intentional psychological states, then we need to grasp the distinctiveness of such intentional modes of classification, and the projects of understanding others in which they are located. This requires us to recognize the perspectively anchored, rationalizing nature of these projects.

Further reading

For interpretationalism read Daniel Dennett, "Intentional systems", *Journal of Philosophy* **68**, 1971, pp. 87–106 and "Real patterns", *Journal of Philosophy* **89**, 1991, pp. 27–51; and Donald Davidson, "Radical interpretation", in *Inquiries into truth and interpretation* (Oxford: Oxford University Press, 1984). For psychological causalism see K. Lennon, *Explaining human action* (London: Duckworth, 1990). For direct interpretationalism married to a modified causalism see W. Child, *Causality interpretation and the mind* (Oxford: Clarendon Press, 1994); J. Hornsby, *Simple mindedness* (Cambridge, Mass. and London: Harvard University Press, 1997); and L. Rudder Baker, *Explaining* *attitudes* (Cambridge: Cambridge University Press, 1995). On Heidegger, try M. Inwood, *Heidegger* (Oxford: Oxford University Press, 1997) and R. Polt, *Heidegger* (London: UCL Press, forthcoming).

Chapter 6

The content of experience

Consciousness

Descartes believed that the mark of the mental was that a mental state should be a conscious state. That view is now seldom espoused.[1] Following Freud, unconscious desires and beliefs are recognized, and, at a less esoteric level, ordinary everyday desires and beliefs can be seen to guide our actions without being brought to consciousness in the shape of felt cravings or reflective thoughts. But what is a conscious state? The phrase is at least ambiguous. In one sense it is a state of consciousness, of being conscious of something, as in perceptual experience whether veridical or hallucinatory. In another, it is a state of which we are conscious, as when we turn our attention inwards upon our own experiences. Descartes seems to have thought that *all* conscious states were conscious in both senses, perhaps because to be conscious of something was for one's mind to have a certain content whose intrinsic properties were both necessary and sufficient for one to be aware of the possession of that content. The occurrence of a mental image might be an example of this.

Let us, however, keep these two senses of "conscious state" apart and leave consideration of the latter – reflexive consciousness – until later. What states are conscious in the former sense? They are, it has been usefully suggested, those states of which we can ask "What is it like to be in that state?".[2] If, for example, someone has a peculiar sensation, what we want to know is what it is like to have such a sensation: that is to say, what it is like to be in that state of consciousness. If, however, someone reports that a strange thought has suddenly struck them we do not naturally ask what it is like to have it, for to think a strange thought is not to be conscious of something strange, in the sense that to have a peculiar feeling is to be conscious of something peculiar.[3] Following established usage we shall term the states in which we are thus conscious of something, phenomenal states, and call the consciousness they exemplify, phenomenal consciousness. We shall call what it is like to be in such states the *qualia*, or qualitative character of these states. By this we may understand the distinctive feel of them – the sort of feel our experiences have and in which they differ one from another. What, though, are such qualia?

It is important here to keep two questions quite distinct, though often they are confused. One is the question of how we *define* qualia, for evidently it is a technical term. The other is the question of the philosophical account we give of them. We have defined it in terms of what it is like to be in a phenomenal state. The quale of a burning pain, say, is the distinctive way such a sensation feels; the quale of hearing a bumble bee, the particular character of that auditory sensation. This is a very modest definition. Under it, to deny the existence of qualia is possible only if one doubts that there are *facts* as to how things feel – one is attempting to point towards a class of facts by means of the sort of examples given, but one fails to hit a target. The general motive for such a denial and its further development will soon be evident. A specific motive may, however, be that there is something mysterious about such facts. In the Cartesian picture they are facts about mental states construed as occupants of a non-physical realm. But if on physicalist grounds one does not recognize such a class of states, then one will wonder what on earth such facts could be about, and perhaps incline to denying their existence. But notice that this is a different position from that of *defining* qualia as non-physical features of the world and immediately denying their existence from an adherence to physicalism. Confusingly this sort of definition is sometimes offered (as when those who hold to the existence of non-physical qualia are described as qualia freaks). Here we shall stick to the modest definition and explore the difficulties that the supposed existence of qualia so defined pose for physicalism.

We can put the principal difficulty like this: how can the features of what it is like to have a burning pain or hear a buzzing sound be explained in terms of the physical features of the state I am in when I have these experiences? On the face of it, it seems unintelligible that qualitative characteristics like these should arise simply from the workings of the brain. The fact that certain neurones are firing may be able to explain how messages are transmitted to get muscles to move, say, in accordance with some comprehensible mechanism. But it is quite unclear what mechanism (or other explanatory model) could account for the occurrence of qualia. Indeed, on the basis of the physical facts alone, it is apparently mysterious why such phenomena should exist at all. Yet if qualia cannot be explained in terms of physical facts, the so-called "explanatory gap" argument runs, then they must be regarded as non-physical features of the world, contrary to physicalism. What reasons are there for supposing there must be the sort of gap postulated here?

The knowledge argument

One line of reasoning to the effect that facts about qualia are radically different from physical facts, and thus not derivable from them as they would be if our qualia could be explained physicalistically, is Frank Jackson's celebrated *knowledge argument*.[4] We are to imagine Mary, a scientist who has always been confined in a black and white environment and never seen colours. She has, however, a complete knowledge of all physical science relevant to colour vision. Would she, asks Jackson, thereby know *what it is like* to see colours? No, for that is something she learns only when she is released into the polychromatic world. When she steps out into that world she learns something she would never have been able to derive from her scientific knowledge of the physical world, complete as that was. The conclusion to be drawn is that qualia are not physical features of the world, but something over and above them.

There are a number of possible replies to the knowledge argument. One response[5] – congenial to eliminativists about qualia – is to deny that Mary acquires any *factual* knowledge when she steps into a multicoloured world. Instead she acquires a knowledge of how to recognize colours which she previously lacked, and a knowledge of how to imagine others' experiences of colour which she must formerly have been without. It is these knowings-how, these abilities, that constitute knowing what it is like to have a certain experience. What it is like is something that can be known, but no *fact* over and above the physical is thereby known. It is a misconstrual of our discourse about what it is like to have an experience which leads to the assumption that there are such facts. Now no-one need doubt that the knowings-how referred to in this response to the knowledge argument are involved in knowing what it is like to have an experience. But it does not follow from this that they are *all* that is acquired. Indeed it seems natural to say that the knowings-how are acquired precisely *because* some factual knowledge is acquired: Mary knows how to imagine another's experience because she knows what it is like to see colours; and that is knowledge of a fact, a fact about an experience of a certain sort that makes imagining it or recognizing it possible.

There is, however, another kind of response to the knowledge argument which can concede this point.[6] It is to say that the state of experiencing a red quale, say, is something that monochromatically confined Mary does know all about: she knows all the properties that hold of this state, and no additional properties are revealed to her by confrontation with the colour red. Yet while monochromatically confined Mary can only bring these properties under physicalistically conceptualized properties, polychromatically free Mary can bring them under concepts of a sort available only to those who already have experiences of the sort in question. What she learns are, that is to say, new *concepts*. Whether we say she learns new *facts* here depends on how we individuate facts. If we individuate them in terms of the *properties* instantiated in them, then she learns no new facts, for the same property can be brought under different concepts, for example "water" and "H_2O". However, if we individuate facts in terms of the *concepts* whereby they are articulated, then Mary does learn new facts because she deploys new concepts. It is our proneness to do the latter which accounts, so this response runs, for our intuition that she has learnt new facts which account for her new abilities, abilities which stem from her acquisition of new concepts. It does not follow, however, that she has learnt about new properties.

This response to the knowledge argument does not, of course, establish that qualia are *not* non-physical properties of experiences. But it does suggest a way in which they might not be. Yet the suggestion still leaves unresolved problems for the physicalist. Why should we suppose that our ability to classify our experience in terms of concepts acquired from it – phenomenal concepts, as we shall call them – picks out properties which *could* be characterized physicalistically, as is required by this position? The explanatory gap originally discerned between physical properties and qualia now opens up between physicalistic concepts and the phenomenal ones under which qualia are brought. For it is not evident why there should be any unity at the physical level to explain the unity at the phenomenal level presupposed in our application of the concept of redness, say, to what we experience. Yet if there is not such a unity, then we shall have no physical explanation for why our experience is covered by such concepts. We shall not be able to derive the differences and affinities that our concepts of experience pick out from any differences and affinities detectable in terms of physical concepts. And therefore there will be differences and affinities which monochromatically confined Mary will not be able to learn on the basis of her physical knowledge.

The preferred method for bridging this explanatory gap is to offer a functionalist account of experiences in terms of their usual antecedents, connections and upshots, and to regard the deployment of phenomenal concepts in characterizing these experiences as itself an aspect of their functional role. For example, a pain in the big toe may be thought of as the usual result of stubbing one's toe, leading one to grimace, hop about on the other foot and also, importantly, believe that one is in agony. The motivation for making this move in response to the knowledge argument is that it serves to explain the difference that does exist between monochromatically confined and polychromatically liberated Mary. For this is not *just* a difference between the deprivation and possession of colour qualia, but between lacking and having colour beliefs, and the latter must be dependent upon the former. The functional account aims to explain the possession of qualia in terms of, among other things, beliefs involving experiential concepts. But will this do the task of securing the required correspondence between qualia and functional states, including those aspects of functional states which involve bringing the qualia under concepts? Two sorts of argument suggest that it will not, and it is to these that we turn next.

Absent qualia and inverted spectra

The *absent qualia* argument[7] invites us to imagine a functional system exactly like our own in the responses it produces to environmental stimuli but such that there is nothing it is like to be in that system; in other words a system functionally equivalent to ourselves but with absent qualia. One way of running the example involves thinking of this as the functional system of a zombie, externally identical to ourselves but lacking an inner life. Another, designed to stimulate assent to the conclusion that functional organization is not necessarily sufficient for qualia, is to conceive of the system as instantiated by the sort of mechanism beloved by comic book artists, in which the interior of the head is populated by little men whose activities mimic those of the brain. This so-called homunculi-headed system, we are meant to suppose, cannot itself be conscious. But there are two problems with this. First, the existence of little men as part of the mechanism should be irrelevant to our intuitions about the system. Leibniz supposed that if we entered an enlarged mechanical mind we would find nothing to explain its consciousness.[8] But by the same token if we imagined scanning our own brain's interior architecture, then neither would we. Presumably the discovery of little men within it would not shake our confidence that we were conscious. Secondly, though, if the little men are responsible for the system's behaviour through their *own* planning processes, then the system as a whole is not conscious, for, although it functions *like* us, it does so as a result of *their* decisions and not because it is hard-wired to do so. Although superficially similar, it is not a functionally equivalent system.[9] Let us return, then, to our zombie counterpart.

The difficulty is that if the zombie really is functionally equivalent to us, then he will share our beliefs as to the experience he shares with us as well as his behavioural reactions. He will believe, for example, that his hearing a bumble bee involves a certain buzzing quale. But it is natural to say that our beliefs derive from our actually having such a quale. Ex hypothesi this is not the case with the zombie. He makes the same judgements of this sort – call them phenomenal judgements – that we do, and they arise from functionally equivalent physical states: yet in his case they are systematically false. In that case, however, we may wonder whether we *ourselves* are zombies, for if we share our phenomenal judgements with them and theirs are false, then what reason do we have for supposing that ours are not? If there is none, then either we abandon our belief in the qualia of our experience or we deny the possible existence of zombies. The only alternative is to suppose that we can tell that our beliefs are justified from an introspective consciousness of which the zombie is incapable. But now introspective consciousness too has broken free from the formation of beliefs about our experience in a way that seems quite arbitrary and mysterious. We may prefer to suppose that an experience's possession of *some* phenomenal character is assured by its giving rise to such beliefs.

Unfortunately, however, this does not finish the matter. It is one thing to give an account of a mental state as having *some* phenomenal character in virtue of how it functions, and quite another to give such an account of *what* phenomenal character it has.[10] The *inverted spectrum* argument[11] is intended to suggest that the latter cannot be done. It asks us to engage in the familiar fantasy of imagining someone who behaves just like us but whose colour experiences are systematically different from our own. When we see green he has an experience with the same qualia as our experience of red and so on. Now if this is possible, then clearly no functionalist account can be given of such qualia. One immediate reply might be that inversion of the kind imagined does not work. Red is a vibrant colour, for example, while green is a calming one, and this will show up in different behavioural responses. We cannot, runs the reply, imagine someone having the same quale that we have when we see green but being excited by it, as the inverted spectrum subject is supposed to be when, just like us, he covets a shiny red sports car.

But the inverted spectrum argument's proponent can, if required, accept this point. The example, she may insist, is not to be taken too literally. It is intended only to suggest that there is a possibility of *different* qualia from our own occurring in the same behavioural context. It is not intended to identify the character of these qualia, which may well be unimaginable to those who have not shared them. Thus she need not present the argument as envisaging that someone may see *as green*, what we see as red,[12] though this is, indeed, a common – if misleading – way of presenting it. Let us review some of the options available to the functionalist for dealing with the inverted spectrum argument.

Functionalist responses

A robust functionalist rejoinder is simply to deny that the fantasy situation envisaged is really imaginable. In imagining another responding just as we do we *are* imagining them having the same experiences: the *picture* of an internal screen simultaneously registering quite different qualia simply fails to capture what it is to imagine an experience, for crucially that does depend on imagining classificatory and behavioural responses. If these are not different, then nothing is. The proponent of the inverted spectrum argument has a reply to this. Suppose, she says, that an operation was performed on us as a result of which we see colours quite differently. Gradually, however, we adapt to our new circumstances and come to behave in them just as we previously did. Are *we* not now functionally equivalent to the way we were, even though our qualia are different? If we are, the functionalist can still respond that we have come to *see* things after the operation just as we did before: our qualia are the same. If, however, we insist that our qualia are different, then functionally we are not the same, for someone in the same functional state will judge their experiences to be similar.

A different possible rejoinder is motivated by the supposition that the inverted spectrum subject may have a different brain process from ourselves. It seems possible to imagine that this should be so, whether or not it is empirically possible. For a different brain process might still preserve the subject's functional equivalence to us. Now it may seem plausible to suggest that the qualia of experience are correlated to types of brain process rather than to functional role, which accounts for all other aspects of experience. A functionalist might relax sufficiently to agree to this. The fundamental physicalism of his position is retained, but the awkward problem of qualia is resolved by reliance on an application of type/type identity theory for just this sort of case.[13]

This stratagem, however, is very dubious. If a functionalist account cannot fill the explanatory gap between physical state and phenomenal content, then it seems even less likely that a physiological account will. For what features of our experience could facts about our brain processes explain in a way that made it evident why their occurrence should issue in just *these* qualia? The type/type identity theory simply does not address the problem of the explanatory gap. Nor does it face up to the challenge of the knowledge argument. Secondly, the addition of a type/type identity component to a functionalist account is undesirably *ad hoc*, since functional systems are intended to be independent of their hardware realizations. We can see this graphically by imagining that our ageing brains had their parts successively replaced while their overall functional organization remained unchanged. Conceivably this could leave us with brain processes not like those we started with, but like those of the inverted spectrum subject. Yet there seems no reason to have to imagine a qualia change. The theorist who wishes to apply type/type identity at this point to individuate qualia will reply that what we can *imagine* is not relevant to what is empirically the case. If the inverted spectrum subject's brain processes account for her qualia, then our qualia *would* change if we acquired her brain processes. But if this change is to be empirically detectable, then there must be, at least temporarily, some functional difference, and the supposition of undetectable differences dependent upon different brain processes is scientifically intolerable.

A further functionalist response to the inverted spectrum argument which tolerates hybridity, yet recognizes this last point, is to resort to eliminativism with respect to qualia. This may be motivated by the reflection that in the supposed case in which our own qualia are inverted by an operation, there is nothing to choose between the hypotheses that our experience has changed and that our *responses* have. We may simply have lost, for the time being, our power to recognize the colours of things, which we gradually regain. Compare this with Dan Dennett's fable of two coffee tasters, one of whom claims he no longer likes Maxwell House coffee, the other that the way it tastes to him has changed.[14] One way to react to such examples is to claim that it is not that one hypothesis is to be *preferred* to the other. It is just that it redescribes the *same* facts in a different way. But if this is the case, then there are no facts about qualia to be described. There are only facts about our behavioural responses, including our inclination to say that it is our experiences that have changed.

Most people will find this, like other versions of eliminativism, just too radical. The judgements that people make about their experiences do not hang unsupported, so to speak, by the facts that they describe. We can put ourselves in the position of those who make them and imagine what they describe – imagine, that is to say, what it is like for them. To deny this is to gain a victory for a modified functionalism too easily. However, the relationship between experience and judgements about them has suggested a popular functionalist strategy for dealing with qualia, at which we must now look.

Internal monitoring

The strategy in question is one that we have in fact already seen in operation, but have not specifically identified. It is to take what we earlier called "reflexive consciousness" as a functional state and give an account of qualia in terms of it. At its simplest it is to say that the qualitative character of an experience consists in our being conscious of our experiential state as having certain properties. In functional terms what is happening is that mechanisms are operating whereby the sort of states that occur in perception are monitored internally in such a way that judgements arise with respect to these states. The content of these judgements is the ascription of qualitative character to them. But whereas in the Cartesian picture reflexive consciousness involves the scanning of irreducible phenomenal properties, in its functionalist counterpart what are scanned are functional properties, though these are reported in terms of the qualitative character they present to reflexive consciousness.[15]

This functionalist story departs from the traditional one in a consequential way. Reflexive consciousness is normally thought of as involving *incorrigible* judgements: if I believe that I am in pain then I am in pain; I cannot be mistaken. The functionalist view allows for the possibility of error. Through malfunctions in the scanning system I might come to believe I was in pain when I was not. All that this means, however, is that I can be in a state that *feels* like pain, but which lacks its other functional roles. By the same token my reflexive consciousness is not necessarily triggered by states that have the other functional roles of pain. If we regard them as constitutive of it then it will not be the case that if I am in pain I necessarily believe that I am. But we may be better to regard pain as constituted by its total role, including that of giving rise to the reflexive consciousness in virtue of which it has a qualitative character.

These features may themselves seem counter-intuitive, but there are other problems. First, it is not clear why reflexive consciousness as manifest in judgements about experience should render those experiential states conscious states in the required sense. Either it does so because these judgements themselves are conscious or they are not. The former cannot be right, since we often have pains without consciously *thinking* about them, even though we feel them. But if the latter, then how can beliefs that are not conscious confer consciousness on their subject matter? No doubt I have beliefs as to what I believe, but fortunately this does not make all the first-order beliefs they concern conscious ones. The same surely goes for experiences. This objection tells even more strongly against a diluted version of the theory, namely that experiences are states "whose content is *available* to be consciously thought about"[16] (our italics).

A further difficulty is that higher-order thought must involve some conceptualization of experiential states. But it is quite unclear why *having* experiences should require abilities to conceptualize them in even a primitive way. The sort of behaviour that goes with such conceptualization has a complexity and flexibility quite different from the immediate and rigid reactions that characterize experiences of bodily and perceptual sensation. If the latter are thought to be insufficient for attributing experience, then it must be denied to many animals and young children which may be taken to possess it. There are several possible responses to this. One response involves denying that the object of our higher-order thought whose existence makes the experience a conscious one is the fact that the experience has occurred. All that is required, it may be suggested, is that the content of the experience – what we experience – should be the object of our thought. This is the view that conscious experience requires *access* to what we experience, that is to say that when an experience is conscious we are able to bring what we experience into our thinking. But, as its proponents could admit, such access might be possible even though there is nothing it is like to have the experience – perhaps as when we operate efficiently in a familiar environment with our minds on something else. Here, what we are seeing, touching and so forth may be registered in such a way that, if asked to explain what I am doing, I mention these features of my experienced environment as reasons for my actions. They enter my judgements about the situation. But they need not be attended to, for a complete account of what I am consciously experiencing might be provided by describing the music that is playing on the radio. Access consciousness in this case *contrasts* with experience that has qualitative character, as we have introduced it in terms of what it is like for one.

Another response to the criticism that reflexive consciousness requires too much conceptualization to provide a plausible account of experience, is to treat reflexive consciousness not as higher-order *thought*, as we have previously assumed, but as a *perception*-like state, directed inwards upon the experiences we have in, for example, outer perception. Then just as outer perception may not involve sophisticated conceptualization of its object, nor need inner perception. Indeed, Descartes' own account of reflexive consciousness seems to have elements of this conception, though in its materialist version what this reflexive consciousness is trained upon is some functional or physical state, albeit not one perceived as such in inner perception. Yet this inner perception view encounters the problem that the outer perception to which it is supposedly analogous does, of course, involve experience. If inner perception also does, then *its* qualitative character would have to be explained, quite implausibly, by a further, third-order, perceptual capacity. If it does not, there is no warrant for regarding reflexive consciousness as perceptual rather than judgemental.

In either case, the classic objection to regarding introspection as providing knowledge of its objects can be trained upon this kind of account of experience, namely that it *changes* what it scans. What it is like to be beside oneself with rage is very different from what it is like to attend to one's state as one of anger. Indeed this counts as a very general objection to trying to account for conscious experience in terms of some reflexive consciousness. There is no reason to think that to be conscious of something, as in phenomenal consciousness, will be the same as to be conscious of that state, as in reflexive consciousness. What it is like to have the two sorts of consciousness may well, on any pre-theoretic understanding of them, be different. In which case the latter cannot provide an adequate explanation of the former.[17]

Intentionalism

The two types of theory of consciousness we have just looked at illustrate an important difference in treatments of qualitative content. In order to escape the objection to the second-order judgement theory that it involves too much conceptualization, the inner perception theory most naturally views qualitative content in accordance with a Cartesian picture of qualia which persists in much modern physicalistically inclined philosophy. It is a picture of qualia as a special sort of *property* of our experiences, such that when we discriminate our experiences from each other reflectively we do so by attending to these properties in much the same way that when we discriminate different coloured beads we do so by attending to theirs. These phenomenal properties, as we may call them, are thus thought of as directly discriminable and seemingly intrinsic to the experience they characterize, in the sense that they appear to characterize it independently of its relation to other states. What is more, they supposedly underlie the *intentional* content of the experience – its being an experience as of a tomato, say; for that it is an experience in which such an outer object, real or imaginary, is presented is held to be possible only in virtue of the phenomenal properties the experience has. We see in this last feature the Cartesian internalist paradigm reassert itself: experiences could in principle be as they are whatever the world outside was like.[18] Such phenomenal properties are evidently quite mysterious, even if inner perception appears to deliver them up to us. For though materialists will identify them with physical or functional properties of mental states which appear to inner perception in this guise, it is still unclear why they should so appear. No naturalistic explanation of this fact has been given.

Reflexive theories of consciousness that appeal to second-order judgements can escape the difficulties involved in accepting this picture of qualia as phenomenal properties whose seemingly intrinsic character is inexplicable. For since they hold that qualia are constituted by judgements about experiential states, they can hold that the content of these judgements picks those states out only by their *intentional* content. My perceptual experience has the qualitative character it has, for example, just because it is as of a tomato, and that is how a second-order judgement judges it to be. Second-order theories can, that is to say, be a species of those theories that aim to lay the Cartesian ghost by treating experiences as having no properties available to their subjects except their intentional content. Then an experience's having the property of being as of a tomato does not require it to *instantiate* some property of redness or the like. Phenomenal properties are avoided because the only properties needed to specify the content of an experience are the properties that figure in its intentional content. But these are properties, real or imagined, of what in the world it is an experience of. The red tomato one seems to see may or may not exist, but its properties are those of things in the world, not of mental contents.

In such intentionalist views the problem of qualia breaks down into the problem of how we can view some intentional states as conscious, on the one hand (to which one answer, which we have already sketched, is given in terms of second-order judgements), and, on the other hand, of how such states can have the content they do. Typically a functionalist answer will be attempted for the latter, though, as we saw in earlier chapters, the prospects for such an answer are not rosy.

Yet is intentionalism plausible as a strategy for treating qualia? The answer turns on whether there is a good case for saying that there are non-intentional – or as they are often called, non-representational – properties of experience, in virtue of which it is the experience it is. This depends upon whether there are properties that pick it out otherwise than in terms of how it represents the world as being. It would be too quick to reply immediately that obviously there are, since bodily sensations like pain do not represent the world as having any particular proper-ties, by contrast, say, with visual sensations. Pain does present a part of the body, perhaps a "phantom" part, as affected in a certain way – in very general terms as adversely affected, as in injury or disease. That we cannot specify a property the body seems to have independently of our reaction to it need be no more troubling than in the case of tastes or sounds. For the fact that they are nauseating or deafening does not prevent them being features of the world.

Proponents of non-representational properties have typically offered examples of experiences that have a certain intentional content but supposedly also something else besides. In one of Christopher Peacocke's examples,[19] I see two trees at different distances as having the same height, but one takes up more of my visual field and this, unlike their height, is not an intentional property. Yet the example is in fact wrongly described. What takes up more of my visual field is the *shape* of the tree and I can see the scene before me as an array of such shapes. This *is* to ascribe a certain intentional content to my experience, albeit a different one. A similar move could be made in response to another of Peacocke's examples, that of the allegedly non-intentional similarity between our switching experiences of some double aspect figure. It is true that the change of aspect can be explained in terms of different intentional contents. But arguably so too can what remains the same, namely the outline viewed as a *two-dimensional* array. Obviously proponents of non-representational properties will take issue with these accounts. The challenge for intentionalists is to make plausible such redescriptions of allegedly non-representational content. We shall defer until the following chapter any further consideration of whether experiences of a given type have qualitative characteristics that cannot be worked out in terms of their intentional content, and, if so, whether a functionalist account of them can be successful.

Form and content

Intentionalism is a strategy for avoiding having to admit phenomenal properties as naturalistically inexplicable features of our experience. For if we concede that our experience has non-representational content, then it may seem that it must be thought of in terms of inexplicable phenomenal properties. Yet this may be denied. It may be claimed that the character of our experiences can be accounted for naturalistically, without resorting to intentionalism. The explanatory gap can be closed, it may be claimed, by revealing their non-representational properties as the inevitable outcome of the physical properties that typically give rise to them.

An experience of white, say, is typically caused by something with the property of whiteness. So it has, for example, been claimed that the character of this experience, the way white *looks*, can be explained in terms of what whiteness is, namely the high diffuse reflectance of a surface.[20] It is claimed that white does actually look like the high diffuse reflecting of light by a surface, insofar as we have any prior expectation about how such a thing would look. White's high diffuse reflectance ensures, for example, that it is always the lightest colour, can be dazzling and so forth. Obviously the difficulties already alluded to in discussing spectrum inversion might be adduced in opposition to this strategy: could not what has the qualia we associate with black occupy a corresponding place in the colour system to that of white and have the effects associated with dazzle? We shall not pursue this immediately, as there is a more specific objection. An account of white must be an account of a visual feature of a thing. But high diffuse reflectance is not a visual feature, for it is not attributed on the basis of a thing's appearance. Rather if a thing looks highly diffusely reflective it does so *because* it looks white, so that its looking the former way *cannot* explain its looking the latter. Indeed, the high diffuse reflecting of a surface does not have any *looks* at all. That some surface is reflecting light is *inferred* from its looks, not seen in them, as white is seen.

The criticism to be made of these attempts to explain qualia naturalistically is that they treat qualia as phenomena to be attended to and investigated, so that their properties can be identified and, it is hoped, systematically correlated to some set of physical properties. This presupposes the existence of seemingly intrinsic phenomenal properties, but tries to render them unmysterious by deriving their character from features of their typical causes. But what it is like to see white, say, cannot be explained in terms of its causes since we could always imagine these causes being different. What needs to be explained is, for example, that while there can be dazzling white we cannot *imagine* what it would be like to be dazzled by black. This is not because of the limitations of our own experience, but because the description of an experience as one of dazzling black does not make sense. The concepts of blackness and dazzle cannot intelligibly be applied to the same thing in the required way. We can sum the point up by saying, in Wittgenstein's phrase, that what colours look like is a matter of *logical grammar*, not a matter of the physical nature of colour, which supposedly explains the qualitative character of our experiences of colour.

Even if an account of colour experiences cannot be given in terms of the *physical* nature of colour, still, it may be insisted, they do differ one from another in virtue of their intrinsic phenomenal properties, however mysterious these are, and this is true for qualia generally. We need to recognize such properties because all that logical grammar can tell us about is the conceptual scheme we have for describing our experience. Certainly that scheme requires us to preserve certain relationships between different qualitative characteristics that experience may have. Whatever feature we describe as black, say, cannot be combined with some feature we refer to as dazzling. But this is consistent, it is claimed, with the qualia involved being different from the way we would expect them to be from our own experience. That they are just *this* way, and not some other which could support the same system of concepts for describing them, is not something that an elucidation of this system alone can seek to explain.

The move is sometimes phrased in terms of Moritz Schlick's celebrated distinction between the *form* of our experience and its *content*.[21] The form, Schlick believed, could be communicated through a shared conceptual system, since every normal person's experience had the same structure. But the content was incommunicable, since only the subject of experience could be directly aware of it. In principle, it was possible for it to differ between individuals as in spectrum inversion cases, but for the difference to be undetectable. This feature of the theory is still very much alive. Qualia, it is often said, are strictly speaking ineffable. We can only talk about the surroundings and behavioural concomitants of experience: what it is like to have it cannot be described. We can know this from our own experience, but it makes no difference to what others can observe and investigate.

It is evident that this position makes a functionalist account of qualia impossible. It is consistent with a physicalist one only if we adopt the view we earlier dismissed as scientifically intolerable, namely that of linking different qualia associated with equivalent functional roles with different brain processes, but allowing that the difference in qualia was otherwise undetectable. This type/type identity move is intolerable since it simply stipulates a difference where it cannot observe one. Few physicalists would want to make it. Indeed the only enthusiasts for the position reached here are so-called "qualia freaks": those who hold that there are qualitative characteristics of experience, construed as seemingly intrinsic phenomenal properties, but that these are brute and physically irreducible. We are back to a dualist theory, but is there, apart from a general reluctance to embrace dualism, any reason to reject the qualia freak's account of qualia?

The private language argument

Qualia on the freaks' account are private in the sense that Wittgenstein has in mind when he mounts his celebrated private language argument. In such an hypothesized language the words "refer to what can only be known to the person speaking; to his immediate private sensations. So another person cannot understand the language."[22] It is important to grasp here that Wittgenstein is imagining that sensations actually *were* as some philosophers claim they are, namely individuated in part by qualitative characteristics of which only the subject can be directly aware. He is not saying that our sensations *are* like this, so that, if his argument against a private language is correct, we cannot describe them even to ourselves. His argument is designed to show that since we can describe our sensations, then they are *not* like this. The consequences of regarding them like this are intolerable, because it is not just that we cannot *communicate* our sensations to others, we cannot describe them to ourselves or even *think* about them. But if we cannot think about them on the supposition that they are in the required sense private, then on that supposition we cannot even frame the hypothesis that they are private.

The details of Wittgenstein's argument are the subject of a variety of interpretations which it would be inappropriate to discuss here. But the essence of the argument lies in hypothesizing a private language user who tries to keep a record of one of his sensations by writing down "S" in his diary whenever it occurs. Now obviously for this to be possible "S" must be used in the same way on each occasion. But, Wittgenstein points out, on the supposition that sensations are private in the required sense, there is nothing to guarantee that this will happen: "whatever is going to seem to me right is right. And that only means that here we can't talk about 'right'".[23] To put this differently, whether I am using "S" correctly or incorrectly has to make a difference. But if "S" is meant to apply to a purely private experience then this is not the case. Suppose, for example, that the diarist tried to check whether his current use of "S" was correct by recalling a previous experience he classified as "S". This will only work if he identifies it as the correct experience to be so classified. But his capacity to do this is precisely what is in question. In order for there to be a criterion of correctness to be observed, there must be a logical grammar[24] governing the use of "S" – in particular a grammar determining how one putative use of "S" is to count as the same sensation as another. Yet ex hypothesi there is no such grammar, for *what* the supposed sensation is is knowable only to its subject. But the grammar of a word is something we learn publicly. So either the diarist must utilize the ordinary grammar of the word "sensation" for recognizing examples of S, in which case he must give up the idea that S is private since now others could in principle understand his language, or else he must accept that what he is trying to record is not capturable in any coherent thought at all.

A defender of qualia conceived of as private phenomenal properties might try to fight a rearguard action against the private language argument by maintaining that all it shows is that there must be behavioural expressions of our experiences of a regular and shared sort, but that what it is like to have them might have been different, either for all or some of us. It may be suggested that in those circumstances we would have been *referring* to different properties in alluding to our experiences, even though there is no way of filtering these properties out from the ensemble that constitutes experience and developing a private language for describing them. Wittgenstein's reply to this is that "if we construe the grammar of the expression of sensation on the model of 'object and designation' the object drops out of consideration as irrelevant".[25] If the grammar that determines what is to count as the same experience leaves no room for supposedly ineffable differences in what it is like, then the notion that we might be referring to such different items becomes incoherent. The insistence that there *are* such items revealed to introspection is, in this account, a misunderstanding of what the qualitative character of experience really consists in. And it is a misunderstanding that makes that character quite unintelligible and the puzzles it gives rise to insoluble.

The private language argument is a powerful weapon. If it is sound then the insistence by qualia freaks that the qualitative character of experience is to be found in features of experience that are publicly undetectable, yet directly discriminatable by their subject, becomes untenable. As we indicated at the end of the previous section, the argument also disposes of the type/type identity account of qualia which was there described as scientifically intolerable. For the conception of qualia as they are then identified with brain processes is precisely that of phenomenal properties private to the subject who discriminates them.[26]

It is the failure of functionalist accounts of the qualitative character of experience (with the possible exception of intentionalism at which we shall look again) that gives rise to these current conceptions of qualia which get caught in the private language argument's net. But if functionalism fails here then, as noted earlier, there is no physicalist defence against the knowledge argument. Yet the conception of qualia that this argument delivers *is* that of the qualia freaks, namely a conception of them as intrinsic and irreducible properties of experience, and as such publicly undetectable. It delivers this conception, though, only because it assumes that the sole alternative to a physicalist reduction of qualia is their admission as mysterious mental properties. If the private language argument rules this conception out, then there must be a way of conceiving of qualia that slips between the horns of this dilemma, and that will be the task of the following chapter.

Further reading

Most introductions to philosophy of mind cover the puzzles about experience discussed in this chapter, for example by Jaegwon Kim, *Philosophy of mind* (Colorado: Westview Press, 1996), Chapter 7 and David Braddon-Mitchell and Frank Jackson, *Philosophy of mind and cognition* (Oxford: Blackwell, 1996), Chapter 8. David Chalmers in *The conscious mind* (Oxford: Oxford University Press, 1996) is the foremost contemporary "qualia freak", while other anti-functionalist positions are occupied by Galen Strawson, *Mental reality* (Cambridge, Mass.: MIT Press, 1994) and John Searle, *The rediscovery of mind* (Cambridge, Mass.: MIT Press, 1992) – the former offering a "naturalized Cartesianism", the latter a picture of the brain as intrinsically mental. More orthodox are Robert Kirk's defence of a broadly functionalist approach in *Raw feeling* (Oxford: Oxford University Press, 1994), and William Lycan's *Consciousness* (Cambridge, Mass.: MIT Press, 1987) and *Consciousness and experience* (Cambridge, Mass.: MIT Press,

1996). The Wittgensteinian account is perhaps best approached via Marie McGinn's *Wittgenstein and the "Philosophical investigations"* (London: Routledge, 1997), Chapters 4–5. Useful collections are Martin Davies and Glyn W. Humphreys (eds), *Consciousness* (Oxford: Blackwell, 1993) and Ned Block, Owen Flanagan and Güven Güzeldere (eds), *The nature of consciousness* (Cambridge, Mass.: MIT Press, 1997).

Chapter 7

Subjects of experience

Subjectivity

We have characterized the qualitative character of experience in terms of what it is like for its subject to have the experience. This formulation is due to Thomas Nagel,[1] who employs it to introduce a strikingly different conception of qualitative character – or what he calls "subjective character" – from those we have encountered so far. Nagel raises the question, "What is it like to be a bat?" in the light of the fact that bats experience their environment through a system of echo-location whereby the echoes of their high-pitched shrieks are picked up and processed to provide information about the objects around them. Since we have nothing corresponding to this sensory system, Nagel concludes that we do not know what it is like to have the experiences generated by it. He uses this as an argument against physicalism, for the physical facts about bats can be known even though we do not know what it is like to be them. Thus, he argues, the character of their experiences cannot be revealed by such facts.

So far the argument is analogous to Jackson's knowledge argument. But Nagel places his on a different footing. The reason, he maintains, that we cannot grasp the bat's experiences is that we cannot adopt their point of view. But this point of view is essential to these experiences having the character they do, since "every subjective phenomenon is essentially connected with a single point of view".[2] This feature, of subjectivity, is what makes experiences accessible only to creatures with the same point of view. It is not, as in Jackson's picture, that our sensory experience limits *what* we can apprehend, but that it limits *how* we can apprehend it – how things can become the content of our experience, and hence what facts we can learn.

Nagel uses this notion of a subjective point of view to fend off the response which might be made to Jackson, that what each of us knows through experience of colours, say, is the same as what we know through a grasp of physical theory about them, though it is brought under different concepts. His reply is that this would be possible only if what we thereby knew had an *objective* character, such that it could be "comprehended from other points of view also, either by the same organism or by others".[3] But an experience lacks such an objective character. "What would be left of what it was like to be a bat if one removed the viewpoint of the bat?" If it were replied that its functional role would be left, then Nagel would respond that this is to "substitute an objective concept of mind for the real thing".[4] What is essential to experience, the point of view its subject occupies, is not something that can be brought under concepts other than those which only a subject of the same sort can deploy. It cannot be brought under the concepts of physical science since these are only objective concepts.

Now it may be thought that this last point begs the question against physicalism, and cannot be used as part of an argument against it. This would be a little unfair, for what Nagel is offering us is an alternative framework for thinking about experience to the one which the physicalist shares with the Cartesian, namely one in which experiences are items whose nature – or *objective* character, as Nagel would see it – is somehow to be determined. Instead Nagel, like Wittgenstein, sees the character of experiences as something that needs to be accounted for in terms of the concepts we have of them, which, he insists, are subjective concepts in the sense of being graspable only from a certain point of view. Nagel seeks to undermine the motivation for insisting that experiences are items to which subjective and objective concepts might both apply, so that the familiar problem arises of explaining how something that falls under such and such objective concepts must also fall under so and so subjective ones. To maintain this insistence would only be justified if it could be shown that there were no facts accessible only from certain points of view. This is hard to do in a non-question-begging way. For if it is maintained that a fact about an experience consists in some property holding of its subject, independent of the way the property is conceived, then one simply falls back into the "objective" characterization of properties which Nagel repudiates.

The subjective viewpoint

What reason do we have, though, for *accepting* Nagel's framework? To answer this we need to see that his contention that we can only have access to experiences from a certain point of view involves a quite specific conception of experience, namely as something which itself embodies a point of view on the world. Experience is not to be thought of, as by qualia freaks, as the instantiation of an irreducible phenomenal property; nor, as by some functionalists, as the instantiation of some reducible one. *Either* of these conceptions is in fact an objective one, even though in the former case the potential investigator of an experience's objective character is restricted to being its subject in a brute and inexplicable way. Rather, experience is to be thought of as presenting the world to us from a certain point of view. We cannot adopt different points of view towards the same experience, precisely because to have an experience is to take up a certain point of view towards the world. What we are trying to appreciate in grasping what it is like to have an experience is what it is like to look at something, as it were, from a particular angle. It is only from this angle that the experience involved can be appreciated. It is not a further item which can be viewed from different angles. That is why Nagel can harmlessly, if misleadingly, speak interchangeably about taking a subjective viewpoint towards our experience and taking a subjective viewpoint in virtue of having it.

In the light of this conception of experience, we can reformulate the question of what it is like to have a bat's echolocation experiences in terms of what it is like for the environment to appear as it appears to a bat. This is not to try to imagine something that could in principle pertain even if there were no outside world to be experienced, so that our problem is just that our inner world does not contain the necessary ingredients for imagination to succeed. It is to try to imagine how what we bring under the concepts acquired from our own point of view would appear from another point of view. And this presents a quite different kind of difficulty. It is the difficulty of knowing how *our* world, the world we bring under our experiential concepts, could ever be the object of another kind of experience. We may characterize the world to be so experienced *objectively*, but as so characterized the world is precisely *not* an object of our experience.

This throws light on what it is like to have the kinds of experience we have. It is to be a certain sort of subject of experience, which is to say, to have a certain sort of viewpoint on the world. An adequate account of experience must therefore reveal its relation to the world. This is precisely what the standard picture of experience as instantiating phenomenal properties fails to do. For in that picture an agent can supposedly interact with the world just as we do, while having no qualitative experience at all or a radically different one. On this supposition there can be no essential connection between the world in which she moves and the character of her experience.

It is this consequence which the intentionalism encountered in the last chapter seeks to avoid. But it is important to see how Nagel's account differs from it. First, however, for the affinity. Both Nagel and the intentionalist see experience as a site where the world presents itself to us in a certain way. Yet for the intentionalist the character of experience is exhausted by the way in which its objects are represented as being. This comes out most strikingly in a view of perceptual experience[5] as consisting simply in a disposition to *believe* something of the objects of experience, where what is believed is thought of as their instantiating concepts applied directly on the basis of experience. In having an experience of red, say, we are inclined to believe that there is something red, other things being equal, and redness is a property we typically apply just because of this inclination. This certainly brings out the way the content of experience can depend upon certain sensory modalities. What it fails to bring out is how such content has an essentially subjective character. On Nagel's account experience does not just represent objects as being a certain way, it represents them as being that way from a certain sort of viewpoint. To understand what it is like to experience something must involve grasping from what sort of viewpoint the beliefs it leads to arise. It must, in other words, comprehend the kind of subjectivity that they express.

The view of perceptual experience criticized here is, of course, another version of the intentionalist accounts of qualitative character we looked at in the last chapter. The criticism can be generalized to them as well. They fail to show in a non-question-begging way how the intentional content of an experience could reveal the viewpoint from which the world, as it presents itself in that content, appears. For if a light is seen as red, say, then that tells us about the experience only if redness is already regarded as a concept available solely to those with certain sorts of experience. But then this aspect of the experience's intentional content needs unpacking in terms of its qualitative character, and cannot give an account of it.

Intersubjectivity

This may well seem to lead us back to the ineffable qualities of experience that fall foul of Wittgenstein's private language argument. This is not the case. Nagel accepts the force of Wittgenstein's argument and denies that what is subjective is thereby private. Indeed he goes further. Speaking of sensations, he remarks that "only if we acknowledge their subjectivity – the fact that each is essentially an appearance *to* someone – can we understand the special way in which sensations are publicly comparable and not private".[6] If experience consisted in the instantiation of phenomenal properties whose similarities and dissimilarities were the sole measure of the similarities and dissimilarities of experiences, and the basis for judgements of the similarity and dissimilarity of other objects, then indeed it would be private, though conceived of objectively. For we would be conceiving of these phenomenal properties as if they *could* be viewed from different standpoints, only to discover to our chagrin that they were accessible solely to their subjects. Similarities in our experiences are, by contrast, similarities in the way things appear to us, and normally these will be outer things. Our talk of the way things look, for example, is public, even though it is the outer things that look this way towards which we can share a viewpoint, not some inner "look" of these things.

If we think of subjectivity in terms of the occupancy of a certain sort of viewpoint, then we have no reason to think of the experiences which embody such a viewpoint as being private to their individual subjects. We can think of them as understandable by all subjects who share the same *sort* of viewpoint. Nagel conceives this shareability in terms of membership of the same species. Given the same sensory system and the same biological make-up that renders the same items in our environments salient for us, we will share the same sort of viewpoint and understand each other's experience in a way unavailable to us if we differ from others as we differ from bats, for example. But there is a continuum of similarity and shareability here. Some life forms seem more alien to us than others, and their experiences less imaginable. The criteria involved here are obscure. More tractable perhaps are differences within our species, which Nagel's talk of a continuum of understanding calls to mind. As we saw in Chapter 5 cultural affinities and differences affect our understanding of others in general. So here might there not be *cultural* similarities, as well as biological ones, which render the experiences of those in our immediate circle more comprehensible than those from very different environments and ways of life?

To answer in the affirmative is to see that it is not such things as shared sensory systems themselves that make others' experience comprehensible. Such things are rather what make possible the shared way of life that does so. In themselves they are assumed rather than corroborated when we set about trying to understand others. What does strike us as a possible impediment is a difference in the way creatures live their lives. Radically different reactions from our own, whether stemming from biology or culture, are what make the experiences from which they arise hard or impossible to imagine. For then we will not know what to imagine to render those reactions appropriate. We will not be able to put ourselves in the other's position and see her reaction as the sort of reaction we would have had ourselves. But this is what it is to understand another's experience, and for it to be possible the practices and patterns of behaviour that the other exhibits must be ones that come, or at least can come, spontaneously to us as well.

Notice here that the sort of imagination that understanding another's experience requires is not to be thought of in terms of having a faint image of that experience. This is the model that is suggested by the picture of experience as the instantiation of phenomenal properties. For what else *could* imagining and experience as so conceived consist in, except entertaining an image of them? They are, after all, disconnected from any necessary relation to circumstances and behavioural reactions. The model is, however, a tenacious one. We may, for example, if normally sighted, feel that we cannot imagine the experiences of the colour blind, since to imagine a monochromatic world is necessarily to imagine it as having *some* colour – black and white, say – when for the colour blind we are to suppose that it has none. But if there are problems in this act of imagination it is not our incapacity to form an appropriate image. They are the difficulties of imagining ourselves reacting to the environment we find ourselves in without reacting to its colours – being gladdened by the blue of the sky, refreshed by the green of new foliage and so forth. Yet these reactions themselves are likely to be specific to certain environments and cultures, however inescapable they may be for us.

Simulation theory

The idea that we come to understand the experiences of others by imagining ourselves in their position and seeing how we would be inclined to react has been developed into a physicalist strategy designed to accommodate perspectivity.[7] Simulation theory, as it is called, supposes that the fact that we *do* function similarly to our fellows gives us a way of understanding them that does not depend upon our utilizing a *theory* about their behaviour. Rather we rely on the similarity of our psychological processes, which we are able to run "off line", that is to say, disconnected from inputs from our own environment and from the behavioural outputs they would produce. Instead, information about the input to another triggers a process simulating her, and gives rise to behavioural inclinations that may be expected to mirror her own. It is obvious that no such process will be available to enable us to understand creatures that function differently from ourselves. Is this kind of simulation what enables us to understand those that do?

The mere fact that we *can* simulate the inner life of another does not show that we do so by setting in motion physical processes like those that take place in her. Indeed, "theory theory" is generally contrasted with "simulation theory" as giving an alternative account of our knowledge of psychological states. It holds that our psychological concepts are theoretical and are attributed on the basis of our acceptance, albeit tacit, of the empirical theory they figure in. On theory theory our ability to simulate the states of another is explained not by our running through the same processes, but by our using our tacit theory to prompt our imaginative reliving of her situation. The contrast can be seen if we consider the case of explaining another's beliefs. In theory theory we deploy an empirical theory of belief formation. In simulation theory we engage in the same processes as would lead to the formation of those beliefs in us, were we to share the input. It is less clear how a satisfactory theory theory alternative could be offered, however, to simulation theory's account of understanding another's experience, if experience, perhaps unlike belief, is, as Nagel holds, subjective and hence not something of which an objective theory can gain an adequate characterization.

There is, however, an alternative to both simulation and theory theory in the case of belief explanation, which may shed some light on understanding experience without resort to simulation. Arguably, what we do in explaining another's beliefs requires us to grasp what, in her circumstances, it would be *reasonable* to think. It is not simply that we have a way of predicting what they will do without resort to a theory. We have a grasp of what they *should* do, and this, moreover, is a grasp we are sometime able to achieve even when they operate differently from ourselves; see the discussion in Chapter 3. But this is neither to deploy an empirical theory nor, necessarily, to reproduce her internal processing, especially if this is thought of, as physicalists are disposed to think of it, in terms of the operation of fixed biological mechanisms.

The cultural norms alluded to in the last section are what shape at least a very good many inclinations to find some belief reasonable in certain circumstances, or not, as the case may be. It is plausible to suppose that our sharing of such norms with others, on a wider or narrower scale, is what enables us to imagine ourselves in the position of another and to conceive of the way her beliefs unfold. And this may be regarded as a more general account of what happens in the specific instance of our finding some belief reasonable because it complies with maximally wide-ranging canons of rationality. What is more, it is an account that can be readily adapted to the case of experience as well as of belief. For to know what it is reasonable to believe in a certain perceptual situation is, to that extent, to grasp what the experience is like. But this is characteristically dependent upon occupancy of a particular environment and a particular culture for dealing with it. What the taste of orange juice is like, say, depends in part upon having a reason to believe one is drinking orange juice in enjoying that taste. Unfamiliar tastes are experienced quite differently from familiar ones like this. Indeed there is a sense in which one is sometimes not sure oneself what it is like to experience them.

None of this, we suggest, sits easily with the physicalist account of understanding experiences offered by simulation theory. For it is our ability to see our experiences as normatively related to environment and behaviour, not their merely functional relations, however grasped, which allows us to understand them.

Normativity and normality

To know what another's experience is like is, in a view that emphasizes its subjective character, to know how the world appears to them, and to know this not just in terms of the intentional content of their "seeming glimpse" of the world, but in terms of how this intentional content is made available through the character of this glimpse. Here, we have suggested, knowledge arises from seeing the others' reactions to the world they glimpse as appropriate or expected reactions. It is useful, though, to contrast two ways in which their reactions can seem appropriate. One relates solely to the intentional content of what is experienced. Someone brakes while driving because they see, or seem to see, a red light. This gives them a reason for thinking there is a red light in front of them and thus for braking. The other way in which their reaction can seem appropriate is different. They brake *sharply*, because they are *alarmed* by the flashing into view, or what is taken for a view, of the light. The sharpness of their reaction is a normal reaction we expect to what is glimpsed suddenly and startlingly, whether or not it is reasonable as measured by its appropriateness to the state of affairs signalled by the experience. Indeed, often the spontaneous reaction is one there are good reasons *not* to make, and which we must be trained to avoid.

We can distinguish, then, between two ways in which our experience can provide a reason for belief and action. The former sort of reason pertains in virtue of the reasonableness of belief or action, given the experience. It fits the Cartesian pattern of psychological states as connected through their adherence to rational norms. The latter sort, however, is not explicable in terms of reasonableness as gauged by conformity to norms of correctness, but in terms of what we, as human beings or members of a certain sort of society, simply do. The notion of what it is normal to do here is not an empirical one, but one grasped through our capacity for fellow feeling with creatures like ourselves. It is the normality of responses as so understood that can reveal the qualitative character of their subject's experience. Indeed these responses are recognized as normal – as specific human reactions or social attitudes – only because they are readable as expressing just such understandable experiences.

In order to know what a given experience is like – for example, the alarming appearance of a red light to an over-relaxed motorist – we usually need to grasp how it makes certain beliefs and reactions appropriate in both of the ways distinguished in the preceding paragraph. For it is characteristic of the way an experience explains such beliefs and reactions, by contrast with a judgement, that they are not only more or less reasonable in the light of it, but understandable: the subject has a reason for them, but not something to be assessed as a good or a bad reason, because their relation to experience is not to be assessed solely along this dimension. An action arising from experience is not only well or ill judged, it is, say, a frank or ill-concealed *expression* of feeling: what it is like to have the feeling comes out more or less clearly in it.

While behaviour that is appropriate to the way the world is seemingly glimpsed in an experience, in the sense of being *reasonable* in the light of it, is appropriate primarily because that way of behaving is conducive to dealing with the environment successfully, behaviour that is *normal* in these circumstances has no evident role in being conducive to success. If it does, for complex evolutionary or social reasons, this fact plays no part in our recognition of it as appropriate. This is accomplished simply through our grasp of what comes naturally to subjects like ourselves, which is often manifest in a capacity to simulate it. Wittgenstein notes this connection:

> Think of the recognition of *facial expressions*. Or of the description of facial expressions – which does not consist in giving the measurements of the face! Think, too, how one can imitate a man's face without seeing one's own in a mirror.[8]

The simulation that thus makes possible an understanding of the qualitative character of another's experience arises from our sharing a repertoire of expressions of experience. What makes it possible to read another's expression is often that we employ the same ourselves, and do so, not, as it were, as a second language that requires interpretation, but as our first.

Examples like this pick up on an inadequacy in certain of the interpretationalist accounts of understanding others, as discussed in Chapter 5. For they bring out what, in some cases, makes certain bits or stretches of behaviour *transparent* to observers equipped with the relevant sympathies. Whereas for key interpretationalists we must bring the behaviour to be accounted for psychologically under some description prior to seeking its meaning, the transparency of behaviour makes it, in a certain sense, *invisible* in its own right. One sees, for example, the joy in another's face, but one does not see what facial configuration it is that registers this joy. One recognizes a reaction to the sudden appearance of danger in an attitude of alarm visible in someone's movements, but one does not usually notice precisely what those movements are.[9]

Expression

We can see again now how the puzzle of understanding another's experience arises from the Cartesian conception of the body as a mere machine which the soul inhabits. The puzzle is then that of inferring from the movements of the body how the soul is affected. But the movements of the body seem arbitrary. That a happy person's face composes itself in the way it does rather than in another, or that a person who is alarmed moves jerkily rather than sinuously, seem the merest accidents of physiology, so that we should be able to imagine that things had been otherwise – or even that, in some cases, they actually are. But this is, as we have seen, mistaken. For to imagine a joyful experience is, among other things, to imagine a certain sort of expression for it, and there is no way in which we, as the kind of creatures we are, are able to imagine having a different expression that we could *use* as an expression of joy. What makes the echo-location experiences of bats mysterious is not least that their *movements* are not ones that we can imagine making as part of our ordinary negotiation of a stable environment. *Their* bodies do seem to be merely mechanical, precisely because we cannot read in them the character of how their world appears.

It should now go without saying that what we need in order to understand others is similar bodies. But the sense in which they need to be similar is not given by the requirements of simulation theory. Rather it is given by the fact that our bodies must be usable for much the same range of expressive possibilities. Some of this is no doubt a matter of natural history, but some is a matter of acculturation too. Our bodies are shaped by the pieces of behaviour we are taught to perform, the specific types of smile or cry that are made part of our repertoire, because they are recognized and responded to in our society. And, as new expressive possibilities are learnt, new emotions are added to our repertoire. A radical anti-Cartesian conclusion can be drawn from this, and one that counts equally against functionalist positions that retain the Cartesian conception of the body. It is that the specific experiences we have are themselves available only because their specific bodily expressions are. For if the qualitative character of an experience is constituted by its providing a reason for such an expression, then to ascribe that experience to a subject unequipped for this expression (and not, say, temporarily incapable of it) can make no sense. In this model, our experience cannot outrun its physical expression any more than thought can outrun its linguistic one, and for much the same reason.

This may, however, seem too radical. Though it is a model that is perhaps plausible for the emotional aspects of experience, it may seem hard to see how it can cope with the complex manifold of sensory experience. Two points need to be made here. One is that sensory experience provides us with a wealth of intentional content whose expression is not to be thought of along these lines, but which can, it could be argued, be made public to any degree of detail required in words, pictures or the like. Not, one might add, that a sharp line is to be discerned here between intentional content and qualitative character – the appearance of a particular colour or combination of colours, for example, partaking of both. The second point is that it is principally insofar as it gives a reason for desires or evaluative beliefs that experience has a *direct* bodily expression – a cry of alarm, say – rather than as providing reasons for beliefs about the contents of the environment. The distinction is not sharp, and it is because the things in our environment have a shared salience for us that we can grasp what it is like to seem to glimpse them. This salience is, in its turn, manifest when appropriate in the character of our dealings with them. We handle what is familiar and well loved differently, for example, from what is new and threatening, and all this is readily apparent in our bodily behaviour.

This model of the body as a text in which our experiences are inscribed threatens to omit an important feature of what it is to recognize these experiences from our behaviour, though it need not do so. The feature in question consists in our propensity as observers of others to *experience* their behaviour in a certain way and react to it spontaneously. We are not, that is to say, dispassionate readers of their expressions. Another's smile elicits, normally, a reciprocal response, another's alarm, a sympathetic concern. Our having these reactions is an important aspect of our capacity to read another's behaviour as being expressive of their experience. The Cartesian body is unexpressive precisely because it fails to elicit them. Or, rather, we choose to suppress these reactions for what we take to be a more clear-sighted view of the body. Yet we thereby suppress the very features of our relationships with others that make the body intelligible as, in Wittgenstein's phrase, a picture of the human soul.[10]

To see a body like this is to see how it expresses a way the world appears. The paradigm of this is to see the world the *same* way, through adopting, perhaps quite literally, the same posture towards it. But a shared apprehension of the world does not require the same bodily response. It can evoke complementary ones, as in dancing with another one responds appropriately to her because both of us experience the music in the same way. One can also *imagine* being moved by it as she is, and still dance appropriately. But now I am not experiencing the world in the *same* way as her, though to respond to her, to join in as I do, is the measure of my understanding the way she does experience it.

Self-knowledge

So far we have looked at what makes possible a grasp of another's experience. It consists in certain sorts of similarity that imply that one will commonly have the same sort of experience in the same circumstances, and is thus able to imagine having it if one is not in those circumstances but, say, you are. That one *does* imagine it in response to your behaviour is, we have just suggested, founded upon a spontaneous human reaction which often betokens a propensity to *share* your experience. But though your experience may rub off on me, to imagine your experience is, of course, quite different from sharing it. For in the former case I am attributing the experience to you, while in the latter it is to be attributed to me as well. To attribute an experience to another is a sophisticated performance, since it requires us to view it, as we have repeatedly insisted, as the way the world *appears* to another. This necessitates a distinction between the way the world is and the way it seems to be from a particular position within it. The distinction here is not that between an objective characterization of the world accessible to a variety of types of viewpoint and a subjective one available only to a certain type. It is between the way the world actually is, as accessed from a certain type of viewpoint, and the way it presents itself to a particular individual's gaze. It is the distinction we need in order to spell out what it is to be a particular subject, rather then merely a specific type of subject. For in order to grasp that it is *another's* experience we are imagining, I have to appreciate that her experience can be *different* from mine, not just in presenting parts of the world not presented to me, but in presenting the same parts otherwise than as they are to me.

This requires the distinction between the way the world is and the way that it appears to be, for the following reason. I grasp what experience someone is having by appreciating what view of the world would make their response appropriate. But this presupposes a notion of the appropriateness of responses to the way the world actually is. Braking is appropriate to a red light's actually coming on, and that is why it is a response appropriate for one who takes a red light to come on, whether their experience of a red light is veridical or not.

Once we have the distinction between the way the world is and the way it appears in experience, we can apply it not only to the experience of others but to our own. In reflecting upon my own experience I see it not as a revelation but as an appearance too, a seeming glimpse only, which gives us a reason for responses that may not be well suited to the way things actually are. To know what I am experiencing provides us with a range of responses different from the immediate ones that are criterial of experience. If I feel hot I may spontaneously act to cool down by throwing off some clothes. I do not need to reflect on the fact that I feel hot in order to act in this way. But if I do reflect, I may utilize such bits of knowledge as that if I *feel* hot, but there is no other reason to believe that it actually *is* hot, then perhaps I have a temperature and should take an aspirin. To take one is then appropriate to feeling hot, but to the fact that I *feel* hot, not to the heat that appears in our experience.

It is important to reiterate that experience does not consist in a reflexive awareness of the state in which we do react spontaneously to the way we take the world to be. Our experience itself does not require this; only a judgement about our experience does. For, in general, to experience the world does not require one to grasp that what one experiences is indeed the content of an experience, rather than the way the world is *simpliciter*. I need to grasp that only when I can counterpoise to our experience other reasons for belief as to how it is, including the way others experience it. For then I am representing the experience as mine, as a glimpse of the world from *my* standpoint, which may fail to capture the way it actually is. The experience itself requires no such sophistication. This is one reason, as we saw earlier, why accounts of conscious experience in terms of higher-order consciousness are unsatisfactory. Having a conscious experience involves the world giving me, through it, a reason for certain reactions. This is a very different thing from my experience, as an event in the world, giving me a reason for certain judgements about it, as the second-order judgement view of consciousness supposes.

In the account of experience suggested here my beliefs about experience are beliefs as to what I have a reason to believe or to desire just on the basis of being in this experiential state. To form them is to grasp my particular viewpoint on the world and how my behaviour relates me to it in a way fraught with uncertainties. This gap between the way the world is and the way it appears to me is precisely what fuels the Cartesian picture of an inner world of experience with phenomenal properties peculiar to it. But the picture is quite unjustified, for my descriptions of my experience are classifications of things in an outer world. That the outer world may not contain them does nothing to show that another world contains their correlates. It shows only that the reasons *I* have for belief in them may yet fall short of establishing that they exist.

The Cartesian picture of our knowledge of our own experience is correspondingly flawed. There are no phenomenal properties to be observed, and thus no physical correlates of them that might be scanned, with all the possibilities of *mis-scanning* which that would involve. There are only appearances, and appearances cannot have some second-order appearance. There is, it is true, a richness and complexity in our experience which eludes a complete specification. But this is to say that it provides reasons for an enormous variety of beliefs and desires, most of which will have no bearing on my current preoccupations. Part of what is involved in reflecting upon one's experiences is, indeed, detaching oneself from the ordinary flow of behaviour in which one reacts quite naturally to them, and producing an impression of the world which could be put to the service of a myriad imaginary projects.

There is no reason, however, to abandon the traditional view of reflexive consciousness as providing us with incorrigible judgements as to our experience, that is, judgements which cannot be mistaken. Indeed the traditional view becomes compulsory, for if experience is not to be thought of either as the instantiation of phenomenal properties or as a state disposing us to certain behaviours, then there is nothing about which we *could* be mistaken. What we take our experience to be will consist in the way that we conceptualize it. To suppose that we could misapply these concepts is to fall victim to the so-called "myth of the given", the notion that what is presented in experience is grasped in a form prior to conceptualization. But what is presented is the world as glimpsed in experience, and it is *this* that requires conceptualization.[11] Insofar as I grasp what I experience, I grasp it only in virtue of the conceptualization I then bring to bear upon it. How I conceptualize it is a part of how I experience it. My judgements about my experiences are thus criterial of them. There is no room for a gap – even for a gap that I can, mysteriously, always bridge successfully – between experience and its avowal.[12]

Wittgenstein explains this feature of avowals of experience by asking how we learn to make, for example, pain reports. We do so, he suggests,[13] because we are taught to say we have pains in circumstances where we are exhibiting more primitive pain behaviour, crying, nursing the affected part and so on. Our verbal reports come to *replace* this behaviour. It follows that if the primitive expressions of pain are criterial for its occurrence then the verbal reports which supersede them will be as well. There is no way in which they may be mistaken. They may, of course, be insincere. But so might the crying they replace be a pretence rather than a genuine expression of pain. In neither case is there a gap between sensation and response because the response is made on the basis of noticing that the experience obtains. The primitive response simply occurs; the verbal one may too, and is, in any case, not made on the basis of any criteria, be they inward or outward ones.[14]

Conclusion

What we have tried to do in this chapter is to sketch the outlines of a view of experience neither functionalist nor Cartesian. It depends upon locating the qualitative character of experience not in some special non-representational content, but in the way that intentional content is made available to a specific sort of subject. What it is like to be such a subject, and thus to have the experiences distinctive of her, is not private, but shareable by subjects of her sort. But this is not to be thought of as achieved through a functional resemblance that enables such subjects to simulate each other's experiential states. Rather, what it is like to have these experiences is understood through a grasp of how they furnish reasons for belief and action. These reasons are not only those that make belief and action reasonable in the light of the experience, but those that make them understandable because we register them as normal reactions to it. It is through them that our experiences are made public and can, indeed, become the subject of our own thought and talk.

Yet the reason-giving account of experience offered here may still seem unsatisfying. It may be conceded that experiences do provide reasons in the ways that we have sketched, but questioned whether this does bring out what is distinctive of experience itself, by contrast with the having of thoughts, say. And at this point the seemingly intrinsic phenomenal properties that we have rejected may be resorted to as the supposedly required differentiating factor. We, by contrast, will have to supply such a factor without postulating elements over and above those involved in the acquisition of reasons.

We can do so, perhaps, by noticing the *unity* of experience, the fact that the features of an experience – the colours and shapes perceived, for example, the pains or pleasures thereby felt, and so forth – are unified into a state with a single subjective character rather than composing, as would thoughts, a number of distinct states. In the reason-giving account of experience what this amounts to is that acquiring a reason for one belief, that there is something red against the green, say, *is* a reason for acquiring another, that it is a moving figure, and so on. It is, importantly, also a reason for desire and action, for wanting to attract the figure's attention, for example, for following it with one's eye, and much, much more. All this, we may suppose, is part and parcel of one and the same visual experience, one in which I attend to and identify one thing rather than others, have these feelings – of pleasure tinged with anxiety, rather than alarm, say – and these behavioural reactions. It is not a jumble of separate experiences, but a unity in virtue of the way that different responses it provides reasons for relate to and interact with one another. And this unity is inextricably linked to an experience's complexity and richness – the indefinite number of beliefs and so on for which it furnishes reasons and its scope for exploration, in the course of which it provides reasons for fresh beliefs, desires and actions. It is all this, we might conclude by observing, that poets and novelists seek to convey in expressing experiences. They do not attempt the impossible task of communicating ineffable phenomenal properties.

The reason-giving account can, we suggest, cope with the problems posed by the knowledge argument and the inverted spectrum and absent qualia examples met with in the previous chapter. Very briefly, what monochromatically confined Mary lacks in this account is a certain kind of *reason* for her beliefs and so on. She does not know what it is like to see red, say, just because she cannot ground her judgements about her environment on the sorts of reasons a visual experience of redness would provide. She is not, therefore, able to grasp how people are able to make such judgements in the circumstances they do. This is not to fail to have knowledge of some mysterious property of experience. It is to fail to have knowledge of a perfectly ordinary one, but one not accessible on the basis of physical facts alone precisely because it requires a certain perspective to appreciate it.

The man whose experience of green is hypothesized as being like our experience of red must, in the reason-giving account, be supposed to have a reason for thinking that what he sees is red although he judges "It is green". Can we imagine that? This is very doubtful. The mere imagining of a rearrangement of colours in his visual field will not suffice, for this, of course, would give us reasons for *different* judgements and reactions from the ones we make, whereas the inverted spectrum subject makes the same ones. There is no way, then, in which we can see him as having reasons for what he does. But, by the same token, we cannot think of him as seeing red, since this would give him reasons for doing *other* than as he does. In fact, we would treat him as seeing green on the presumption of rationality, and treat any evidence to the contrary he may subsequently produce as indicative of some pathology.

Absent qualia would comprise the condition of one for whom there was *nothing* it was like to be in a state which for us would constitute an experience. We are to imagine him doing and believing just what we do, but having no reason for this, rather, we may suppose, as we are sometimes capable of doing ourselves when we absentmindedly but skilfully negotiate our environment while fixing our attention on something else. Here our behaviour and belief formation are to be explained by causal mechanisms operating independently of the subject's capacity to provide herself with reasons.

This example of what we do automatically, without the mediation of thought, contrasts illuminatingly with the case in which our behaviour *expresses* our thoughts and feelings. In both cases we, as observers, see a person's body negotiate her environment; and in the Cartesian picture that is *all* that we see. But this fails to bring out the difference between the cases, a difference that places the former, automatic movement example in the same category as, say, the behaviour of a beetle, and the latter, expressive case in a strikingly contrasting one. For here, as we argued earlier, our shared perspective on the world enables us to see the body as being expressive of the agent's outlook on it. It is in the explanation of behaviour viewed in this light that our talk of reasons is rooted. And so, it may be suggested, it is only because we possess this mode of embodiment that we can be viewed as *subjects* of thoughts and feelings that furnish reasons. It is to this topic that we turn in the final chapter.

157

Further reading

A very good, short introduction to Wittgenstein's philosophy of mind can be found in Peter Hacker's *Wittgenstein on human nature* (London: Phoenix, 1997). Nagel's approach is best understood by reading his *The view from nowhere* (Oxford: Oxford University Press, 1986). Aspects of it, and of Wittgensteinian themes, appear in John McDowell's challenging *Mind and world* (Cambridge, Mass.: Harvard University Press, 1994). Wittgenstein and Heidegger are illuminatingly brought together in Stephen Mulhall's *On being in the world* (London: Routledge, 1990), which provides a route into material from the phenomenological tradition that our own study has entered, and which Gregory McCulloch's *The mind and its world* (London: Routledge, 1995) also brings to bear on the analytic tradition.

Chapter 8

The embodied subject

Mentality

In this final chapter it is time to review the state of play in the philosophy of mind and to draw some tentative conclusions of our own. The key questions, as we have seen, are what it is that makes something a mental state and how such states explain behaviour. The Cartesian answer is that a mental state is a conscious state, and, because wholly accessible to consciousness, a state of a substance that is in principle independent of bodies in the external world, namely the mind. Such mental states explain bodily behaviour through a mysterious interface with the body, which thereby moves to bring about results recommendable to reason. What supposedly differentiates creatures with minds from lower animals is, indeed, that the former's acts are done for reasons, and thus via the intervention of the mind, while the latter's occur only through a chain of physical causes. For some consideration to play the role of a reason thus requires it to be scrutinized by the subject and appreciated as a reason. For, though Descartes himself has an abstract and impersonal view of the connections that the light of reason reveals to us, this image of light gives an essential role to the subject of consciousness as seeing these connections by means of this light. Things count as reasons for her only in virtue of the subject's first personal perspective upon them. That she must play this role in order to judge and act for reasons explains, we may note, why the states that can count as reasons must be conscious states.

The functionalist paradigm we have been examining in previous chapters contrasts sharply with this, of course. Mental states are functional states playing their specified parts in the explanation of behaviour, most centrally in providing the agent's reasons for action. But here their status as reasons is explicated in terms of their abstract relations to other states and to behaviour – without the need for their subject to play a role in scrutinizing the content of her states. Their status as reasons, that is to say, does not depend upon this, or indeed any, way in which they reflect her first personal perspective. It is a corollary that consciousness, or accessibility to consciousness, can claim no special place in marking her states out as mental states. Those states that are essentially conscious, for example experiences of pain or vivid visual sensation, are, we have seen, difficult for functionalists to cope with. In particular, even if an account of the conscious character of experiences can be offered (in terms of internal monitoring, say), this character seems inessential to the part that experiences can play as reasons for belief or action.

Here, then, is a contrast between Cartesianism and functionalism in which the latter has arguably lost one of the advantages of the former, namely its capacity to take some account of the fact that reasons explain actions in terms of the agent's perspective (where this means something other than merely the sum total of her beliefs or other reason-providing states), in particular where that perspective confronts the world through experience. It loses it in order to avoid the mysterious metaphysic of a mental substance whose existence is constituted by its continuous self-scrutiny.

It is the comprehensiveness of this self-scrutiny that makes the Cartesian an internalist about the content of her mental states. Paradoxically, without the need for such self-scrutiny the functionalist usually remains an internalist, and now it is because we function in no way different in kind from lower animals – through a chain of physical causes within the body, each, in its essence, independent of anything beyond.

The view of mental states that we have offered as an alternative to both Cartesianism and current functionalism rejects internalism. But it is closer to the former than the latter in trying to reclaim the notion that it is essential to mentality that it presents a subject's perspective upon her world.[1] The world in question is not, as in Cartesianism, a world of ideas, but of objects in her physical environment. Her perspective upon them constitutes a class of relationships with them in virtue of which her actions in this environment can be explained. She believes of the cup before her that it contains coffee, and drinks from it eagerly, for example. That the world appears to her thus is what gives her reasons for her acts, and it is essentially as providing such reasons that make her acts appropriate that mental states are to be understood. The point of characterizing them as constituted by perspectivity is to capture the way they do so – a way that cannot, we have argued, be captured in terms of their abstract logical relations, or their material causal ones. We have, therefore, provided interconnected answers to the questions of what is involved in having a mental state and the question of how mental states make our behaviour intelligible. To have a mental state is to be a subject with a perspective or point of view on to the world, a perspective constituted by the responses to that world which it makes appropriate. Here it is crucial that the world that we have a point of view on is the world of objects not of ideas, and that our responses to it bring about transformations upon those objects. The subjectivity at issue here is an embodied subjectivity – of which we shall say more below.

Desire

We can illustrate the conception of the mental with the case of desire, construed in a broad sense as a mental state that motivates an agent to bring about some state of affairs. In philosophical thinking about desire two models are dominant.[2] In one model of desires our basic desires are simply brute facts about us, facts explained biologically or in some other way in terms of the causal encounters we have with an environment. Other desires are derived from these by means of instrumental calculations based on our beliefs. We shall refer to this as the brute desire model.

Some version of this model of desire seems to inform most naturalizing theories of the explanation of behaviour which treat the belief/desire pattern as central.[3] For, under it, desires specify the ends of action and beliefs the means for attaining them. A reason for action is thus normally a suitable belief/desire pair. But the only way a desire itself can be explained as being reasonable is in terms of its aptness for achieving the agent's most general goals, and these are basic. In such naturalizing theories desires are internal states of an organism interacting in specified ways with other states and issuing in behaviour. Indeed, functionalism identifies them in just this way. But they are in no sense cognitive. It is supposedly through beliefs alone that the subject gains access to the world, though beliefs alone are motivationally inert. Beliefs influence behaviour only through their interaction with desires, which, in the limiting case, produce actions without beliefs, as when, moved by a desire to move my leg, I move it, without having any belief to the effect that by moving this bit of me I move my leg. If mentality consists in the possession of states that function in ways that provide a certain sort of explanation of behaviour, then desires construed in the manner just described are central to the picture this involves.

We can contrast with this a model of desire that sees the subject's cognitive relation to her world as being fundamental to her having reasons for her acts. Here the Cartesian conception of reason which we sketched in the preceding section comes into play.[4] By its light we arrive at judgements of what is good, and what is good is a real property of the world, independent of an agent's psychological states and of its possible effects upon her. That something is good provides a reason for action since certain actions, namely those that aim at the good, are appropriate to it. A rational creature will need no other motivation for performing them. Desire, in this story, is a psychological state whose proper employment is to mediate between the recognition of the good and the achievement of it. We may, therefore, call this the rational desire model.

In this model of desire it is not internal motivational states that are paradigmatic of the mental, but states analogous to perception in that they disclose real properties, albeit, in the Cartesian formulation, not properties dependent upon the existence of an external world. What it is to be conscious – to think, as Descartes regarded it – is for a subject to apprehend these properties and to appreciate their connections, however imperfectly. Furthermore, insofar as we are rational agents we bring our behaviour into line with these cognitions. Being rational is for Descartes, as for Davidson, a requirement of mentality, but whereas for Davidson, as we have seen,[5] rationality is something we read into the subject's course of action, for Descartes it is something she herself must see as a way of regulating it. She does so by taking up a perspective on the considerations that provide her with reasons and detecting in them the properties in virtue of which they do so.

Desirability

The two models of desire that we have sketched are both profoundly unsatisfactory. The brute desire model suggests a quite unrealistic reduction of all intentional behaviour to that which we explain in terms of basic drives or other fundamental mechanisms. It is implausible to assume that the multiplicity of reasons we have for acting terminate in an appeal to such states. Moreover, this fails to reveal at all why the actions for which we have reasons should recommend themselves to us as achieving anything *worth* desiring, since it is a feature of the way that brute desires simply assail us that they lack this character. Yet the rational desire model is no more appealing. It fails adequately to explain why recognizing that some end is good should *motivate* us to achieve it. These defects are mirrored in the more general accounts of mentality which, tacitly or otherwise, exploit these models. Functionalism, on the one hand, fails to bring out how our ordinary psychological explanations are normative, Cartesianism how the subject's perspective can connect with physical behaviour – a problem recognized by Descartes as we have seen,[6] in his insistence that the soul does not stand to the body simply as a pilot to his boat.

Yet the dilemma set out here is, readers may recognize, also one familiar in moral philosophy. On the one hand stands naturalism, which locates moral value in the fact that something answers to human (or animal) desires. But then moral value would be dependent upon facts about desire which we could imagine being otherwise and which we could not, in their turn, subject to moral scrutiny. On the other hand stands the non-naturalist view which locates moral value in facts independent of desires; but now it is hard to see how such facts could motivate us to moral acts. Both views are realist in that the facts they allude to in locating value are taken to be discoverable features of the world and thus subject to true or erroneous judgements. They are also objectivist in the special sense we noted in the previous chapter, namely that these facts are taken to be detectable in principle from any subject's point of view.

Now John McDowell has argued[7] that we can escape the dilemma without abandoning realism by adopting what is, in effect, a subjectivist conception of moral values. Moral values are real features of the world, but are detectable only to creatures like ourselves equipped to respond to them in a characteristic way. But this way is precisely to find them as calling for action that brings about the good and eliminates the bad. The response required to recognize value *is* that of pursuing it, so that recognition of value and motivation go hand in hand. Yet the moral response may be made to the wrong object. Although in a world without desires there would be no moral values to be recognized, for it is only in virtue of the responses that desires make possible that the world has any moral shape, the values there are do not depend upon the *particular* desires we have, and these could be imagined differently.

This account of moral value can be taken over, with modifications, into a general characterization of desire which similarly escapes the dilemma of the brute and rational desire models by resort to a subjectivist conception of desirability. To desire something, on this alternative model, is essentially to find something desirable. To find something desirable, however, is not to judge that it has some objective property in virtue of which it should be desired. For one could make that judgement without being moved by the desirability it imputes. Rather, to find something desirable is already to be moved to an appropriate response. Indeed it is the capacity for such a response that underpins the concept of desirability. Yet it would be a mistake to think that the notion of desirability could be reduced to a disposition to bring about such a response as the first model would suggest. For that would be to miss out the key feature here. The desirability of the object is what makes the response reasonable or appropriate. It brings it within the scope of reasons which on reflection can be modified, for in the light of such reflection I can judge my response to be misguided. It is this feature that allows such desirability to be counted as a real feature of the world, albeit a perspectival one.

This model, therefore, combines the motivational features of the brute desire model with the normative ones of its rational desire competitor. Moreover, the model illustrates some very general features of mental states which we have already noticed; on the one hand their normativity and perspectivity, on the other hand the essential connection of these features with behavioural responses – a characteristic we shall now give a little more attention to.

The experience of desire

Descartes' reason for denying that he stood to his body as a pilot to his ship was that the pilot felt nothing at damage done to the vessel, while the mind was affected by bodily affliction, and, one might add, is affected by physical gratification too. What this demonstrates is that, while the pilot needs to draw upon general principles as to what his responsibilities are and what is good for his charge, we have no such need of normative principles in determining at least some of our reactions to the effects of the environment upon our bodies. Pains and physical pleasures elicit immediate responses, not just as producing physical reactions, but as presenting those reactions as being appropriate, other things being equal, in the circumstances that give rise to them. They are appropriate because the situation is experienced as desirable or undesirable in some way – the rose bush as painfully prickly; its flowers as intoxicatingly perfumed. In these experiences desire is felt because the desirability or otherwise of its objects is felt. It is in such experiences that one gets a grasp of what it is for something to be desirable.

What we are arguing here is that the subjective character of experience discussed in the last chapter is fundamental to having a perspective on the world. For the world to appear as it does from a particular point of view with its specific saliences is for a subject to have experiences of the world in which its saliences are disclosed. In these the appropriateness of certain responses to the world and the way it is experienced as salient go together. Their appropriateness is not assessed in terms of pre-existing desires or general goals. Instead, such desires and goals emerge to characterize the subject's perspective and norms of action from the subjective character of her experiences.

The point, as we noticed earlier,[8] is derived from Heidegger, whose own picture emerged from opposition to the Cartesian tendency in his mentor, Husserl. That we can experience the world as having value, as containing desirable and undesirable things, stands in need of an explanation that a purely rationalistic account cannot give. But the explanation is not to be had in terms of a naturalistic postulation of pre-existing desires. Rather, that what we experience evokes the primitive reactions which it does, and has the intentional content it has, reveals that it matters to us because of what we are essentially, namely creatures whose world *is* salient to them in ways prior to the formation of specific desires and plans. In other words, that a specific experience has its subjective character shows that we are creatures whose relation to the world is perspectival and normative.

Heidegger's own example to illustrate this is fear.[9] First, in fear, something, real or imaginary, is experienced as fearsome – a particular mode of undesirability. Secondly, something specific is feared, which is what gives fear its intentional content. Thirdly, and underpinning the fact that this object is experienced with the particular subjective character it presents, the subject fears *for* something. What specifically matters does so, and matters in the particular troubling manner it does, because the subject is concerned for herself[10] in a certain way. But the way she is concerned for herself cannot be elucidated except in terms of the perspective she takes on the world and the norms she brings to bear on her actions in it. A fear of heights, for example, shows itself in a person's attending to features of his situation which others might not attend to, and in taking precautions that seem to them inappropriate. What he fears for – perhaps, we might say, his control over his body – is intelligible only to the extent that we can share his perspective and norms. To do that is to see how heights can have the sort of salience for him that they do.

What we fear for exemplifies why things matter to us, or their salience, as we have termed it. To return to the dis-analogy from Descartes at the start of this section, the fact of experience shows that our bodies matter to us as the ship does not matter to its pilot, namely as the unmediated ground of anything mattering.[11] At which point it is time to turn our attention to what conception of the body is required by an account of the mind anchored, in the way we have suggested, in embodied subjectivity.

Beyond the Cartesian body

The body we encounter, if we encounter a body at all, when we read modern texts in the philosophy of mind is invariably the body as described by the medico-physical sciences. This is the body-as-object; the body, you will recall, that Keith Campbell describes as a "mass of matter" and an "assemblage of flesh, bones, and organs which the anatomist anatomizes".[12] It is something entirely objectified and understood exclusively and exhaustively in terms of the causal-mechanical laws governing all material things. This conception of the human body is so deeply suffused within our culture, both inside and outside philosophy classrooms, that it has become almost unthinkable that there may be alternative models available. Yet it is an idea with a history: an idea, as we have said, that owes much of its parentage to Descartes and his contemporaries in the seventeenth century. Despite this, when one reads Descartes' own work closely, one is made aware that he is not entirely happy with this himself and that a different conception of the body struggles for recognition within his writings. This is the body, he says in the *Sixth meditation*, "which by some special right I call 'mine'".[13] He recognizes that there is something significantly different about this body which means that it is not simply one object amongst others but has its own unique status. Thus, he continues,

my belief that this body, more than any other, belonged to me had some justification. For I could never be separated from it, as

> I could from other bodies; and I felt all my appetites and emotions in, and on account of, this body; and finally, I was aware of pain and pleasurable ticklings in parts of this body, but not in other bodies external to it. . . . I was not able to give any explanation of all this, except that nature taught me so.[14]

In other words he has a distinctive acquaintance with his own body. His experience of this body is both quantitatively and qualitatively different from his experience of other bodies: not only does its presence have a permanence that perceived objects do not, but it also presents itself as a field of unmediated sensations. Elsewhere he concedes that the identity conditions for human bodies are different from those for other bodies in that, in the latter case, what determines whether an object is the same object is whether it is the same parcel of matter, whereas in the former case this is determined by whether or not it is the body of the same person.[15] As he was unable to theoretically accommodate either set of observations, he then goes on to draw a distinction between the living body, as known in experience, and the body grasped abstractly in the understanding.[16] So, in the end, Descartes makes little of these insights and the orthodox Cartesian view, the view we have largely inherited, continued to posit the human body as a wholly objectified, organic machine.

Phenomenology of the body

It is interesting to note, however, that these non-orthodox Cartesian speculations themselves have a resonance in twentieth-century philosophy – though commonly not within the tradition in which most modern philosophy of mind takes place. In the foregoing passage, and at other points in the *Sixth meditation*, Descartes comes close to articulating a conception of the body as the "lived-body"; this conception is at odds with the orthodox Cartesian conception of the body as something understood in abstraction by the medico-physical sciences. This distinction was something explored in depth by philosophers in the phenomenological tradition: thinkers as diverse as Husserl, Marcel, Heidegger and Merleau-Ponty.[17] What impressed these philosophers were precisely the sorts of considerations that impressed and worried Descartes: for each of us, our bodies are the only objects we each, so to speak, know from within. When Marcel famously declared "my body is mine in so far as for me the body is not an object but, rather, I *am* my body",[18] he was not referring to the body as understood by science. His body, he wanted to say, is not simply one object among others but is the object at the very centre of his world. According to the phenomenologist where the orthodox Cartesian conception goes wrong, and thus, by extension, the scientism of the dominant programme, is in positing the abstracted understanding of the body-as-object as ontologically basic. The body, it insists, is really nothing more than a mass of matter: that is how the body really is. But this is not the body we first encounter in our everyday lives or know through living our embodiment.

On the contrary, as Merleau-Ponty argues, the naturalistic picture of the body "as a chemical structure or an agglomeration of tissues, is formed, by a process of impoverishment, from a primordial phenomenon of the body-for-us, the body of human experience or the perceived body".[19] The body as it is lived is therefore a phenomenon that is prior to, and acts as a ground for, any conceptualization we make of the body as a physiological thing. By losing sight of this fact, the immaterialism of Descartes' dualism and the physicalism of the dominant paradigm, both born of Descartes' original and mutually exclusive two-part division of the world into *res cogitans* and *res extensa*, cannot account for our actual experience of embodiment. Our experience of our own bodies teaches us a new mode of existence which is neither simply a pure subjective being-for-itself, such as Descartes' self-contained mind, nor a pure objective being-in-itself, such as the body-object that this conception of mind stands over against, but is a mixture of the two. It is an "ambiguous mode of existing" which calls into question the traditional subject/object dichotomy on which all Cartesian philosophies are based, regardless of whether they privilege one side or the other of that divide. In something of a reflection of Descartes' conclusion that the unity of body and soul can only be known through experience and is not fully capturable in the understanding, Merleau-Ponty argues that our awareness of this mode of existence is "not a thought", but something we have to live. Thus he says,

> If I try to think of it as a cluster of third person processes – "sight", "motility", "sexuality" – I observe that these "functions" cannot be interrelated, and related to the external world, by causal connections, they are all obscurely drawn together and implied in a unique drama. Therefore the body is not an object. For the same reason, my awareness of it is not a thought, that is to say, I cannot take it to pieces and reform it to make a clear idea. Its unity is always implicit and vague. . . . I have no means of knowing the human body other than that of living it, which means taking up on my own account the drama which is being played out in it, and losing myself in it. . . . Thus the experience of one's body runs counter to the reflective procedure which detaches subject and object from each other, and which gives us only the thought about the body, or the body as an idea, and not the experience of the body or the body in reality.[20]

The difference between Merleau-Ponty and Descartes is that the former embraces this awareness of the body as primary, whereas for Descartes, he says, it finally always "remains subordinated to our knowledge of it through the medium of ideas". Embracing the primacy of this experience compels us to give up a dogmatic adherence to the above dichotomy and acknowledge a third mode of existence that unites its two terms. From this alternative perspective, therefore, the body, before anything else, is a fundamental dimension of the human subject's existence. The human subject was seen by Merleau-Ponty to be something that stands above the simplistic dualistic opposition between an objectified mechanistic body and an immaterial soul, however this opposition arises, so that in its case we can no longer speak of an "either/or". The human subject is first and foremost a bodily subject, or an incarnate subjectivity, so that the human body, while obviously something material, does not belong simply to the material order of things. In fact it has its own, albeit ambiguous, mode of existence, which Cartesian categories cannot capture.

This is what Marcel and Merleau-Ponty mean when they say that the body is not an object. In fact Merleau-Ponty goes further than this denial and insists that the human body is itself a subject.[21] Descartes' non-orthodox reflections only capture part of the body's significance. As Merleau-Ponty asserts, the permanence of a perceived object is compatible with its total absence from the perceptual field, but this is not true of the body. One's body is not simply that object which one perceives more than any other, or that object which just happens to accompany all one's perceptions, both of which seem implied by Descartes. It cannot be either of these things, for its total absence, or even a radical variability in its perspective, is actually inconceivable. Perceptual objects present themselves as *before us* and open to exhaustive exploration, but the body presents itself as *with us* and our ability to explore it is severely curtailed. The most important of these limitations stem from the fact that the body itself is the focal point of action and perception: it is itself a perspective, a point of view, and, moreover, a point of view upon which one cannot take a point of view. Its total absence and variability in its perspective are inconceivable, Merleau-Ponty argues, because its permanence and invariability in perspective are the conditions for perceptual objects presenting themselves perspectivally or, indeed, at all. Thus, it seems that in rediscovering the lived-body we must also revise our understanding of the relation between the body itself and the world; the conclusion being that our orthodox understanding, based simply on an empirical analysis of causal connections, must be supplanted by an understanding based on a phenomenological analysis of a primordial dialogue of mutual implication between body and world.

Spatiality and embodiment

Merleau-Ponty explores different ways in which this manifests itself, though it is sufficient for our purposes to look at only one: the spatial orientation of our perceptual experience. Whether these reflections in the end show that the body is a subject in its own right is problematic.[22] Indeed, it is not clear that he need go so far as this. What they do show is that the status of the body is, as he said, ambiguous – it needs to be thought of as both a material object and part of our subjective being. What Marcel and Merleau-Ponty should have perhaps stated more clearly, and less hyperbolically, is that it is not so much that the body is not an object, but that it is not *simply* an object as characterized in the orthodox Cartesian understanding.

The content of perceptual experience is not orientated absolutely or in itself, but is arranged according to a network of egocentric spatial relations. The directions such as "up", "down", "in front of", "to the right" and so on, which constitute this network are relative; but to what are they relative? Merleau-Ponty answers that we must discover the "absolute within the sphere of the relative". What is important here is undoubtedly the human body; but not simply as a thematized, perceived, or objectified body, occupying objective space as a sign of orientation; rather it is the lived-body as the potentiality of actions and the vehicle of one's being-in-the-world. One does not position oneself in the world by continually perceiving a particular thematized object, one's body, relative to the other thematized objects it encounters. This is why Merleau-Ponty speaks of the spatiality of the body being unlike the spatiality of perceived objects; it is a third kind of spatiality distinct from that of content or form, a spatiality of *situation* rather than simply a spatiality of *position*. Thus, "here" expresses the body's presence in the world and determines this presence as being-to-the-world. The world responds by presenting itself egocentrically as a possible habitat for an embodied subject and, as such, is structured as a field of potential action for this subject. Merleau-Ponty therefore stresses the importance of the subject's embodiment and the fact that this is of a kind which is essentially characterized by the subject's sensory and volitional involvement with the world. It is only as a bodily agent functioning in the world that this egocentric structuring of perceptual experience has any meaning for the subject and that directions such as "up" and "down" have any significance.

Why is this? Why do these spatial orientations require the subject to be embodied and an agent? Our grasp on the spatial orientations "up" and "down", for example, is determined by two interrelated facts: that we are asymmetrical bodies operating within a gravitational field. Merleau-Ponty is right to insist that the spatiality of the perceived world cannot result, as he says, from the "simple summation" of the material arrangement of the human body; the asymmetrical nature of our bodies alone does not determine the perceptual structure. This spatiality is not a response to a Cartesian body-object, a mass of matter with a particular arrangement of its parts. On the other hand neither is our corporeal architecture entirely irrelevant, so that this also cannot be determined by agency alone. Taken in isolation, neither the fact that our bodies have a particular physical structure nor the fact that we are agents accounts for the significance that these spatial directions have for us. It is only when the two come together that they have the significance that they do; the spatiality of the perceived world is a reply to both the body's dimensions *and* its capacity for purposeful action.

Unlike symmetrical or uniform objects such as beach-balls, we have a top and a bottom, a front and a back and so on, so in order to achieve what Merleau-Ponty calls a "behavioural optimum", and thereby gain the enjoyment of space, we must align our asymmetrical structures to gravity and to the world and its objects with which we interact. Similarly, what determines the top of an object for us is that when it is appropriately aligned with gravity its function is unimpeded: a beach-ball has no top or bottom for it can function in any alignment; but a typewriter is only of use if it is the right way up. Up and down are thus not simply perceiver dependent; but then neither are they determined by reference to a paradigm object in perception, either the objectivized human body or, say, the surface of the earth – they are primarily determined by our capacity to move and act as asymmetrical objects in a gravitational field. Nevertheless, gravity is not an indispensable factor in these determinations, for we carry our structural asymmetries with us into space. Such considerations are therefore equally important in a weightless environment, for in order to act we still have to achieve a behavioural optimum and so align our asymmetrical bodies appropriately with whatever it is with which we wish to interact. Thus the spatial structure of what I perceive is directly connected with my need to achieve coherence in action. This is something more recently remarked upon by Gareth Evans:

Egocentric spatial terms are the terms in which the content of our spatial experiences would be formulated, and those in which our immediate behavioural plans would be expressed. This duality is no coincidence: an egocentric space can exist only for an animal in which a complex network of connections exist between perceptual input and behavioural output.[23]

In other words, spatial information embedded within a particular perceptual experience can have significance for a subject only insofar as it has a place in the network of these connections. Both Merleau-Ponty and Evans point to the essential interconnectedness of perception and agency and how the subject's perceptions are spatially structured so as to govern the subject's purposeful and goal-directed actions.[24] But our discussion above reveals that this is only necessary if the subject is a physical organism operating within the boundaries set by its particular corporeal architecture and the nature of its physical environment. Thus, the significance of these spatial orientations emerges in response to two factors; that the perceived world is also a world of potential action (the objects of perception are identical to the objects of purposeful action), and that the subject is embodied in this world as an agent and not simply a causal system. But it seems clear that being embodied also means being a part of the objective order. In other words, it follows from this that while it is true that the spatiality of the subject is not simply one of position, it is also the case that it is not simply one of situation either; it is one of both position and situation. Having a perspective on the world means being both a subjectivity and part of that world itself.

The egocentric field reveals that the subject has a point of view on the world (situation) *qua* embodied subject, but the significance of this requires the subject to be conceived of as a physicality, that is as itself an item in the objective order (position). If this were not the case, as Evans notes, it is difficult to imagine how the subject's egocentric space is a *space* at all. To think of oneself as being located must also mean that one can think of one's situation "from the objective point of view". Therefore, there must be some coincidence between positions represented in the subject's egocentric or phenomenal spatial thinking and those conceived under a larger spatial representation of the world: the subject's egocentric space must be mappable onto public space so that a particular position on one is also a particular position in the other.[25] Surely this is correct; especially if the subject's sensory experiences are supposed to be experiences of an independently existing world through which it moves. It follows that the same must be true of the body: the lived-body itself is also an object in the world.[26] Hence, the egocentric field only has significance for a subject that is embodied as both a physicality and as a set of capacities. Merleau-Ponty overstates the case when he says, "What counts for the orientation of the spectacle is not my body as it in fact is, as a thing in objective space, but as a system of possible actions, a virtual body with its phenomenal 'place' defined by its task and situation."[27] In fact it is determined by both.

What is then clear is that we have multiple but equally important discourses with different ways of thinking about the body. However, it is natural, if not inescapable, to think that these different discourses refer to one and the same body – that the body, as Merleau-Ponty himself put it, is a single reality. This may be the case, especially since, in each case, the body appears as a materiality, but it does not necessarily mean that we can group these multiple discourses under one over-arching explanatory scheme. If this is so, this may be a lesson with a more general application.

Metaphysical questions: multiple narratives

The characterization of the body articulated in the last section is distinct from that offered by the discourses of medical science. It is, nonetheless, part of a materialist discourse, in the sense that it in no way requires the existence of any kind of immaterial substance and, moreover, it does requires that the body be itself a material object occupying a spatial position and standing in certain spatio-temporal relations to other such bodies. The accounts of the material, however, found within the discourses of embodied subjectivity are distinct from those informing reductive physicalism. One consequence of this is that the material world is not fully articulatable from within the domain of physicalist science; nor is it clear that such physicalist discourses play a foundational role in its articulation. Intentional discourses, we have been claiming, are *sui generis* ways of describing that reality which do not require vindication from physicalist sources.

To refuse scientific discourse a privileged position in the articulation of our world and insist on a multiplicity of discourses, all needed to make sense of it, is to explicitly adopt a pluralist metaphysics. In this picture not all conceptual frameworks can be integrated together to form a single unified picture. We need multiple narratives to make sense of the world, which do not all weave into a single systematic account. It is not the case, in this view, that all the descriptive and explanatory projects in which we are engaged can be ultimately integrated into and determined by a single scientific explanatory project.

The kind of picture we are resisting is spelt out in a recent article by Kim Sterelny.[28] Sterelny works with the metaphor of a tree: "The idea is that the tree is rooted in fundamental physical kinds and processes. Through various different branches, all scientific kinds depend on that taproot . . . kinds (and the laws expressed in terms of them) further out on the branches need to be explained by kinds and laws closer to the root."[29] Of course not all kinds are natural kinds (although they have some connection with the tree if we assume that all kinds supervene, in the ontological sense, on these fundamental kinds). However, kinds that are not natural kinds, in Sterelny's picture, do not do genuine explanatory work; "a notion . . . is explanatory only to the extent that it can be incorporated into the tree".[30] It is plausible to assume that our intentional kinds are natural kinds, he says, because they appear to do genuine explanatory work. The task is then to fit them onto the tree. This picture, or one very much like it, is the metaphysical framework informing much modern philosophy of mind. It works as a presupposition and most of its proponents offer no defence of it other than its supposed plausibility. We are resisting this picture because intentional discourses, as we have argued, cannot be fitted within it. They do genuine explanatory work but they do not have a place on the tree.

We have put forward two key and interconnected reasons why everyday psychological descriptions cannot be integrated into a tree of scientific natural kinds. First, such discourses are necessarily perspectival; and secondly, they play a role in explanatory projects distinct from that of bringing particular instances under general regularities.

Genuine explanations

Much of the motivation for the metaphysical picture illustrated by Sterelny's tree is a conception of the explanatory work to which our intentional kinds are put. The assumption is made that all genuine explanatory work is causal explanatory work, and that our psychological kinds do such causal explanatory work in much the same way that theoretical kinds do in science. One move that can be made against such an assumption has been highlighted in the rest of the book. There we have been emphasizing the very distinctive kind of intelligibility that is tied up with our psychological descriptions. Central to this has been the rendering of the agent's responses to the world as being rational or appropriate, in various distinct kinds of ways. This is the standard move made by theorists who have opposed reductionist conceptions of the mind. Rationalizing explanations occupy a different explanatory space from causal explanations, the argument goes, and so do not need to be integrated into a common framework.

Neat as this is, it is also too simple. For we clearly do use causal notions within our psychological framework. We make causal interventions in the world by manipulating psychological states; we try to surprise him into admitting his guilt, we persuade her into taking the holiday by describing it in glowing terms, and so on. Moreover, most everyday psychological explanations have conditional implications that echo those of causal claims. If Maureen did not find playing with Barbie dolls pleasurable, then she would not have set off to her friend's house. If the swan had not looked black, I would not have believed it was black. So dismissing causality from the sphere of psychological discourse just does not seem possible.

Allowing it in, however, does not necessarily force the picture of the unified tree. The discourses surrounding causality are themselves multiple and they cannot all be forced under a single schema. Here we need to revisit some of the motivations driving reductive functionalism. One assumption, which derived from explanatory physicalism, was that all causal interactions be constituted out of causal interactions at the physical level. A connected one was the assumption of the completeness of physics. If psychological states play a causal explanatory role in relation to behaviour, and we also expect complete neuro-physiological explanations, then it looked as if the behaviour would be over-determined. Functionalism answers both these anxieties by construing our mentalist causal explanations as place-holders for the scientific account.[31] But it seems inappropriate for a whole range of cases, not just the psychological one, to assume that whenever we have a causal explanation not in physicalist terms then the properties it invokes must be functional ones. When we explain why the sea bird's eggs do not fall off the narrow sea cliffs, we do so in terms of their distinctive shape. Yet having such a shape is not a functional property.

If we reject the pull of explanatory physicalism, by rejecting the view that all causal interactions must be justified by their relations to those at the micro-particulate level, then we can look for the justification of causal claims at the psychological level from within their own framework. Such justification is anchored in the conditional and counterfactual claims and regularities (if not laws) which the non-physicalist mode of description makes visible. By attributing a desire for a sandwich to John, I can explain his going to the buffet and anticipate what Peter will do if he gets hungry. I can also predict their responses should the buffet be closed.

Supervenience revisited

Is it possible to adopt such metaphysical pluralism and still accept that psychological discourses supervene on physicalist ones? If not, in what sense can we claim that our position is a materialist one? In our discussion of the concept of supervenience, in Chapter 2, we unpacked two strands. The first strand was an asymmetric indiscernibility relation. Two items (events, states, people, locations or worlds – depending on the scope of the claim) cannot alter in terms of their psychological descriptions without altering in terms of their physical descriptions. Another way of expressing this is that two items cannot share all their physical properties and differ psychologically. We have seen how such claims are difficult to defend if the items concerned are individual events or human bodies. But if the claims are extended to cover whole worlds, or more plausibly extended locales, such a claim seems constitutive of a minimalist materialism.

There was a second and more robustly ontological supplement to the indiscernibility claim. This gave ontological priority to the physical properties. The physical properties were seen as being fundamental. The true physical descriptions of items were those in virtue of which all further descriptions, if true, were true. It was this further demand that fitted into the picture of Sterlney's tree.

It was, of course, one of the strongest arguments for functionalism that it could satisfy this demand.

Within the metaphysical pluralism which, we are suggesting, we can reject the second strand of the supervenience claim. That is, we reject the ontological priority of the physicalist characterizations of the material; the claim that the physical descriptions are those in virtue of which all other descriptions, if true, are true. It is however possible to do this without rejecting the first strand of the claim, that of asymmetric indiscernibility. Accepting it sets up a constraint on the relationship between two discourses: they must each be applied in a way that respects it. However, within the framework that we have been suggesting, this claim is not a consequence of the metaphysical privilege assigned to physicalist ways of describing the world. It is rather a consequence of the "logical grammer" of our psychological discourses. As became clear in Chapter 7, our grasp of the subjectivity of others is anchored in the expressive power of the body. Two bodies with exactly the same micro-particulate arrangements within a stable context would then be perceived as expressive of the same kind of subjectivity. This makes the psychological case much closer to the aesthetic one. It also makes clear why the mental and physical modes of description cannot float completely free of one another. The expressive power of a body requires that the body be *apt* for such expression. The analogy with the aesthetic case is instructive, for the sculptor, for example, can only work with certain kinds of material.

It is, however, important to see just how minimal such a supervenience claim is. It does not commit us to being able to specify in physicalist terms the application conditions of the alternative conceptual apparatus. We can perhaps bring this home in the following way. The claim of indiscernibility implies that if we have two items that share all their physical properties, then they will be of the same psychological kinds. But, of course, if two items shared all their physical properties, including spatial temporal position and relational properties, we would not have two items at all. They would be identical. So the claim has to be that if two items share all the same *relevent* physical properties, then they will have the same psychological properties. This is a familiar move from the discussions of the relation of moral and aesthetic properties and natural ones.[32] What counts as a relevant similarity, however, is not something that can be settled from within the physical/natural level of description. That is, we cannot state in purely physical/ natural terms in what way states must be similar if they are to share their psychological/evaluative properties. This is a moral or aesthetic question in one case and a psychological one in the other. It involves what psychological descriptions apply to particular physical configurations. This relates to the point made in Chapter 3, where we argued that projectible conditions for psychological concepts cannot be specified in non-psychological terms.

To resist a strong supervenience claim is to resist a foundational role for physicalist descriptions while recognizing that alternative ways of conceptualizing the material, and making it intelligible, do not operate quite independently of each other. Here it is worth revisiting an example of Kim's which we used in Chapter 2.[33] Kim was discussing the activity of a sculptor working a piece of marble. His emphasis was on the fact that this was physical work, and, in illustration of the claims of supervenience, he points out that once the physical work is done nothing further remains to be done for it also to be the case that she has produced something with a certain aesthetic character. Nonetheless, from the perspective of the sculptor, this misrepresents the nature of the process. She is set on producing a pleasing shape. That is the conceptualization that informs her action and yields the transformation in the stone. It is also the case that in producing the pleasing shape nothing more needs to be done to produce certain physical changes in the stone.

Adopting a minimal supervenience thesis does, however, cast some light on the vexed question of over-determination. Accepting autonomous explanatory accounts at the psychological level with causal implications risks, as we noted in Chapters 2 and 5, putting forward two independent sets of causally sufficient conditions for behaviour. Actually, the issue is not quite that. We have already noted the ambiguity attaching to the term "behaviour". What our psychological states explain, our intentional acts and the expressive responses of our bodies, are not identical with any of the *explananda* of physical explanations. When we explain Maureen setting off to her friend's house in terms of its desirability, no explanation of her bodily movements as physically construed is given. But it nonetheless remains the case that if the option had not struck her as desirable, then such movements as she does make would not have occurred, and it is at least plausible to assume that such movements will have some physicalist explanation. Here the supervenience claim can help. The presence of physically sufficient conditions for movements does not rule out the possibility that in concrete contexts other conditions may be necessary for it: namely, those which supervene on the physical ones. This much follows from the recognition that ascribing mentality makes demands of the physicality of the bodies of those to whom it can be ascribed. What does not follow is that the intentional explanations of actions and the physical explanations of movements are competitors in the same explanatory space.

Naturalism revisited

To reject a position for subjectivist notions on Sterelny's tree is to reject a certain kind of naturalist picture that is dominant in modern philosophy of mind, a picture captured by the model of the tree. It would, however, be quite misleading to read this position as one in which mentality and thereby subjectivity are not natural phenomena. In an earlier chapter we remarked that it is an entirely natural fact about us that we are the kind of creatures to whom the world can appear as salient, the kind of creatures who can learn to apply concepts to that world, and so on. In our discussion of the content of experience it also became clear that such content could not be articulated independently of the expressive possibilities of our bodies, mediated by culture and context. Moreover the intentional content of our thoughts is anchored in indexical relations to objects which require an embodied subjectivity. What is being rejected is a scientific naturalism that seeks to understand mental phenomena by allocating them a place on the tree.

We have argued that we should not expect investigation at the extensional functional level to provide insight into what *constitutes* mentality; but this does not preclude such investigation having relevence of another kind. Much neurological empirical investigation is concerned to establish the physical causal base for distinct kinds of psychological capacities. As we made clear in earlier chapters, it is an important and entirely legitimate area of empirical scientific research to investigate what kinds of functional and physical organization *enable* a creature to have a point of view onto the world and thereby have psychological states.[34] What such investigations do not do, however, is to cast light on what it is to have psychological states; that question cannot be addressed from within that project (although it is one that that project needs an answer to in order to inform its investigations). One way of looking at the matter would be this: certain physical conditions are required if we are to have mentality at all. Different kinds of subjectivity rest on the expressive possibilities of bodies, and these have physiological requirements. Intentional acts require certain kinds of physical mechanisms to be in place and uncovering these physical enabling conditions also contributes to making intelligible how material bodies of certain physically characterizable kinds can be such as to instantiate mentality. The mistake, however, is to construe the investigation of such enabling conditions as investigations into what is constitutive of subjectivity.[35]

This helps to make clear that the distinct discourses of the body which occupy different explanatory spaces and carry with them distinct modes of intelligibility are nonetheless not completely autonomous or distinct from one another. José Luis Bermudez has asked "how can we explain the personal level fact that an amputee tries to walk with both legs . . . without bringing in sub-personal level facts?"[36] Of course, no one is suggesting that such, in his terminology, sub-personal-level facts, have no bearing. They form enabling (or disabling) conditions of personal-level discourse. What we have been at pains to point out, however, is the different kind of explanatory task that each level performs. Explaining the amputee's response as a response expressive of certain sensations, or as part of an ongoing project with the world as it appears to her, makes intelligible her attempts to act in a certain way. This kind of intelligibility is not conveyed by talk of what is going on in her central nervous system. To take a slightly different example, consider seasonal affective disorder. We have been hearing, in recent years, of this condition, a depression apparently caused by lack of sufficient exposure to sunlight. Knowing its cause, however, does not cast light on the phenomenon itself. To do this we might make reference to sunlight in a very different way; capturing how the world appears to the depressive is commonly done in terms of the metaphors of it appearing grey and overcast. One of the central concerns of this book has been to prevent us mistaking explanations of the first sort for those of the second.

Throughout the book we have been concerned to address the key issues that motivate the dominant paradigm in philosophy of mind and give due recognition to the force of its arguments. However, we have not simply engaged with this paradigm, but have also attempted to unsettle the picture it gives us of what philosophy of mind is about. Within this current paradigm there are a large number of detailed accounts of psychological phenomena. We have suggested alternative ways in which these psychological phenomena can be understood; but, it would also be fair to say, we have not produced a similarly detailed account ourselves. This would be an ambitious undertaking and one that would take us well beyond the scope of the present book. We recognize, however, that such a task is a necessary one if one is to give a satisfying answer to the fundamental metaphysical questions confronting anyone investigating current concerns in the philosophy of mind.

Further reading

The relevant part of Merleau-Ponty's thought is most fully expressed in Part 1 of his *Phenomenology of perception*, Colin Smith (trans.) (London: Routledge & Kegan Paul, 1962). Monica Langer's *Merleau-Ponty's "Phenomenology of perception"* (London: Macmillan, 1989) is an excellent guide and commentary. For a more critical appraisal, which also sets his work in context, see Richard Zaner, *The problem of embodiment: some contributions to a phenomenology of the body* (The Hague: Martinus Nijhoff, 1964). Recent works that adopt approaches sympathetic to ours include John McDowell, *Mind and world* (Cambridge, Mass.: Harvard University Press, 1994); Gregory McCulloch, *The mind and its world* (London: Routledge, 1995); and Jennifer Hornsby, *Simple mindedness* (Cambridge, Mass.: Harvard University Press, 1997). Although different to our own, Huw Price has been championing a form of metaphysical pluralism for a number of years: see especially the recent symposium with Frank Jackson, "Naturalism and the fate of the M-worlds", *Proceedings of the Aristotelian Society*, Supp. Vol. **71**, 1997, pp. 247–82.

Notes

Chapter 1. The Cartesian legacy

1. T. Kuhn, *The structure of scientific revolutions* (Chicago: University of Chicago Press, 1962), pp. 10–22.
2. Although "materialism" and "physicalism" are terms that are normally used interchangeably, throughout this book we shall use them in the restricted senses adumbrated here.
3. J. Cottingham, R. Stoothoff & D. Murdoch (eds), *The philosophical writings of Descartes* [2 vols] (Cambridge: Cambridge University Press, 1984), vol. 1, p. 127. The phrase itself, originally in French not Latin, occurs in the *Discourse on the method* (as above), but essentially the same argument is rehearsed again and again throughout Descartes' corpus. See the *Meditations* (*ibid.*, vol. 2, p. 17), the *Principles of philosophy* (*ibid.*, vol. 1, p. 195), and *The search for truth* (*ibid.*, vol. 2, pp. 409–10).
4. See C. Taylor, "Overcoming epistemology", in *Philosophical arguments* (Cambridge, Mass.: Harvard University Press, 1995), pp. 1–19.
5. Cottingham, Stoothoff & Murdoch (eds), *The philosophical writings of Descartes*, vol. 1, p. 224.

6. K. Campbell, *Body and mind* (London: Macmillan, 1970), p. 2.
7. What Merleau-Ponty called an existence *"partes extra partes"*. The complaint is not that this, the anatomist's or mortician's conception of the body, is illegitimate; but that it is not the *only* conception available, least still that it is how the body really is. The body of a living person can also be viewed as a synergic system or what Richard Zaner calls a "contexture" – a system whose constituent parts are organized by a unifying principle beyond the parts themselves. M. Merleau-Ponty, *Phenomenology of perception* (London: Routledge & Kegan Paul, 1962), p. 73; and R. M. Zaner, *Context of self* (Chicago: Ohio University Press, 1981), pp. 22 ff.
8. Merleau-Ponty, *Phenomenology of perception*, p. 351.
9. This analogy appears in *The passions of the soul*, § 6, Cottingham, Stoothoff & Murdoch (eds), *The philosophical writings of Descartes*, vol. 1, pp. 329–30, and at the end of the *Treatise on man*, *ibid.*, vol. 1, pp. 104 and 108. His soulless physiology is defended at the beginning of the *Description of the human body*, *ibid.*, vol. 1, pp. 314–16.
10. According to Descartes, both require physiological changes to take place. After all, sensations, especially sense perception, involve the function of specialized bodily organs and the imagination, he thought, involved the perception by the mind of images in the brain (on the surface of the pineal gland, see below).
11. Cottingham, Stoothoff & Murdoch (eds), *The philosophical writings of Descartes*, vol. 1, p. 224.
12. *Ibid.*, vol. 2, p. 19. See also Part 1, § 9 of the *Principles of philosophy*, *ibid.*, vol. 1, p. 195.
13. *Ibid.*, vol. 2, p. 113.
14. The exception, for Descartes, were thoughts about God. In the *Third meditation*, on the basis of the principle that the efficient cause of something must have as much reality as the thing caused, Descartes argues that God must exist in order for us to have thoughts about God. Cottingham, Stoothoff & Murdoch (eds), *The philosophical writings of Descartes*, vol. 2, pp. 28–35. For discussion of this argument see J. Cottingham, *Descartes* (Oxford: Blackwell, 1986), pp. 48–55.
15. This is a particular form of a more general problem, the difficulty of understanding across differences in perspective. In this case the difference is between the perspectives of particular individuals; but we could formulate similar questions in terms of societies, cultural groups, peoples in different historical periods, people of different race or gender, different sentient species (not just

human beings), and so on. See K. Lennon & M. Whitford (eds), *Knowing the difference* (London: Routledge, 1994).

16. For two contrasting approaches to this problem see A. J. Ayer, "One's knowledge of other minds", in *Essays in philosophical psychology*, D. F. Gustafson (ed.) (London: Macmillan, 1964), pp. 346–64; and N. Malcolm, "Knowledge of other minds", *ibid.*, pp. 365–76.

17. Cottingham, Stoothoff & Murdoch (eds), *The philosophical writings of Descartes*, vol. 2, p. 161.

18. J. Cottingham, R. Stoothoff, D. Murdoch & A. Kenny (eds), *The philosophical writings of Descartes: the correspondence* (Cambridge: Cambridge University Press, 1991), p. 365. For discussion of Descartes' views on animals, see J. Cottingham, "'A brute to the brutes?': Descartes' treatment of animals", *Philosophy* **53**, 1978, pp. 551–9.

19. Cottingham, Stoothoff & Murdoch (eds), *The philosophical writings of Descartes*, vol. 1, p. 140.

20. Not evaluative in the sense of being morally evaluative; but in the sense that, if I am a rational agent, I *ought to* or *should* believe α or do β, given my (other) beliefs and desires. Causal explanations simply describe patterns or regularities in the way things are. For further discussion, see Chapter 3.

21. J. Cottingham (ed.), *Descartes' conversation with Burman* (Oxford: Clarendon Press, 1976), p. 28.

22. Cottingham, Stoothoff & Murdoch (eds), *The philosophical writings of Descartes*, vol. 1, p. 340.

23. This account occurs in Part 1 of *The passions of the soul*; perhaps the fullest treatment he gives to the mind/body relationship. See Cottingham, Stoothoff & Murdoch (eds), *The philosophical writings of Descartes*, vol. 1, pp. 328–48. Cf. *Treatise on man, ibid.*, vol. 1, pp. 99–108. It has been suggested how a youthful Descartes was greatly influenced in his thinking by seeing the Francinis' hydraulically operated statues in the grotto of the royal gardens at Saint Germain on the outskirts of Paris (a sort of seventeenth-century Euro-Disney). See J. Jaynes, "The problem of animate motion in the seventeenth century", *Journal of the History of Ideas* **31**, 1970, pp. 219–34.

24. Cottingham, Stoothoff, Murdoch & Kenny (eds), *The philosophical writings of Descartes: the correspondence*, p. 227.

25. Imagine the unlucky golfer who is simultaneously struck by a meteor and a bolt of lightning while having a heart attack, each of which would be sufficiently fatal on their own. Her death is over-

determined. The worry is not that such things happen at all, we know they do, but that cases of over-determination in nature are rare and that dualism would require them to be the norm with respect to a large category of physical events, namely those that go to make up the bodily movements of human beings and other relevant organisms.

26. M. Merleau-Ponty, *Signs*, R. C. McCleary (trans.) (Evanston, Illinois: Northwestern University Press, 1964), p. 11.

27. G. Ryle, *The concept of mind* (London: Hutchinson, 1949), p. 21.

28. The most obvious example of which was La Mettrie who, in *Machine man*, saw himself as carrying through to fruition a project entirely consistent with Descartes' teachings. La Mettrie, *Machine man and other writings*, A. Thomson (ed.) (Cambridge: Cambridge University Press, 1996).

Chapter 2. Reductionalism and the road to functionalism

1. For classical accounts see J. Mackie, *The cement of the universe* (Oxford: Clarendon Press, 1974); and C. Hempel, *Aspects of scientific explanation* (New York: The Free Press, 1965).

2. D. Hume, *Enquiries concerning human understanding and concerning the principles of morals*, P. H. Nidditch (ed.), 3rd edn (Oxford: Clarendon Press, 1975). Mackie, *The cement of the universe*.

3. There is some debate concerning whether probabilistic links form an objective feature of the world or simply reflect our ignorance of further relevent factors.

4. This issue is discussed in J. Mackie, *Truth, probability and paradox* (Oxford: Clarendon Press, 1973) and in D. Lewis, *Counterfactuals* (Oxford: Blackwell, 1973).

5. See the discussion in Chapter 2 of K. Lennon, *Explaining human action* (London: Duckworth, 1990).

6. Donald Davidson, however, has a different account. See D. Davidson, "Mental events", in *Essays on actions and events* (Oxford: Oxford University Press, 1980), pp. 207–27.

7. Empirical generalizations are normally distinguished from generalities that simply follow from our agreement to use terms in a particular way. However, the difference between *a priori* and empirical generalizations becomes somewhat muddied if we accept that some terms are implicitly defined by their role in such

explanations. For a discussion see Lennon, *Explaining human action*, Chapter 3.

8. Discussed in R. Boyd, "Natural kinds, homeostatis and the limits of essentialism". Unpublished manuscript (Department of Philosophy, Cornell University, 1984).

9. See R. Keat and J. Urry, *Social theory as science* (London: Routledge & Kegan Paul, 1975), Part 1.

10. H. Putnam, "Explanation and reference" and "The meaning of meaning", in *Mind language and reality, philosophical papers*, vol. 2 (Cambridge: Cambridge University Press, 1975), pp. 196–214 and 215–71 respectively; S. Kripke, *Naming and necessity* (Cambridge, Mass.: Harvard University Press, 1980); R. Boyd, "On the current status of the issue of scientific realism", *Erkenntnis* **19**, 1983, pp. 45–90.

11. Plato, *Phaedrus* 265e.

12. C. Hempel, "The logical analysis of psychology", in N. Block, *Readings in philosophy of psychology,* vol. 1 (Cambridge, Mass.: Harvard University Press, 1980); B. F. Skinner, *Science and human behavior* (New York: Macmillan, 1953); for further discussion also see Chapter 2 in J. Kim, *Philosophy of mind* (Colorado: Westview Press, 1996).

13. Classical statements of the type/type identity theory are U. T. Place, "Is consciousness a brain process", *British Journal of Psychology* **47**, 1956, pp. 44–50; H. Feigl, "The 'mental' and the 'physical'", in *Minnesota studies in philosophy of science*, vol. 2, H. Feigl, M. Scriven & G. Maxwell (eds) (Minneapolis: University of Minnesota Press, 1958); J. J. C. Smart, "Sensations and brain processes", *Philosophical Review* **68**, 1959, pp. 141–56.

14. For a discussion of distinctions between type and token identity theories see C. McDonald, *Mind-body identity theories* (London: Routledge, 1989).

15. See the discussion in Chapter 2 of Lennon, *Explaining human action.*

16. P. Oppenheim & H. Putnam, "Unity of science as a working hypothesis", in H. Feigl *et al.*, *Minnesota studies in the philosophy of science*, vol. 2.

17. E. Nagel, *The structure of science* (London: Routledge & Kegan Paul, 1961).

18. Kim, *Philosophy of mind*, pp. 69–70.

19. *Ibid.*, pp. 233–6.

20. This argument began to emerge in the late 1960s. For an early version see H. Putnam, *Mind and language and reality* (Cam-

bridge: Cambridge University Press, 1975), Chapters 18, 20 and 21.

21. Davidson, "Mental events".
22. Lennon, *Explaining human action*, Chapter 2.
23. For some influential eliminativist views see P. Churchland, "Eliminativist materialism and the propositional attitudes", *Journal of Philosophy* **78**, 1981, pp. 67–90, and *Matter and consciousness* (Cambridge, Mass.: Bradford Books/MIT Press, 1988); S. Stich, *From folk psychology to cognitive science: the case against belief* (Cambridge, Mass.: MIT/Bradford Books, 1983).
24. See for example L. Rudder Baker, *Saving belief: a critique of physicalism* (Princeton: Princeton University Press, 1987), Chapter 3; L. Rudder Baker, *Explaining attitudes* (Cambridge: Cambridge University Press, 1987); S. Stich, *Deconstructing the mind* (Oxford: Oxford University Press, 1996).
25. G. E. Moore, *Principia ethica* (Cambridge: Cambridge University Press, 1903); R. M. Hare, *The language of morals* (Oxford: Oxford University Press, 1952).
26. Davidson, "Mental events".
27. The strength of these claims depends on how we interpret the strength of the "must". See D. Charles, "Supervenience, composition and physicalism", in *Reduction, explanation and realism*, D. Charles & K. Lennon (eds) (Oxford: Clarendon Press, 1992), pp. 265–96.
28. For a discussion of global versus local supervenience claims see G. Currie, "Individualism and global supervenience", *British Journal for the Philosophy of Science* **35**, 1984, pp. 345–58; J. Kim, "'Strong' and 'global' supervenience revisited", *Philosophy and Phenomenological Research* **48**, 1987, pp. 315–26, reprinted in J. Kim, *Supervenience and mind* (Cambridge: Cambridge University Press, 1993), pp. 79–91.
29. See Chapter 1 of D. Braddon-Mitchell & F. Jackson, *Philosophy of mind and cognition* (Oxford: Blackwell, 1996); and Chapter 1, § 2 in D. Chalmers, *The conscious mind: in search of a fundamental theory* (Oxford: Oxford University Press, 1996).
30. Kim, *Philosophy of mind*, p. 222.
31. For further and detailed discussion of the supervenience relation see Kim, *Supervenience and mind*.
32. See J. Haugeland, "Weak supervenience", *American Philosophical Quarterly* **19**, 1982, pp. 93–103.
33. J. A. Fodor, "Special sciences, or: the disunity of science as a working hypothesis", *Synthese* **28**, 1974, pp. 97–115, reprinted in

Representations (Cambridge, Mass.: MIT Press, 1981), pp. 127–45.

34. Kim, *Philosophy of mind,* p. 151.
35. *Ibid.*
36. *Ibid.*, p. 152.
37. *Ibid.*, p. 151.
38. J. Heil and A. Mele (eds), *Mental causation* (Oxford: Oxford University Press, 1993); and C. McDonald & G. McDonald (eds), *Philosophy of psychology* (Oxford: Blackwell, 1995).
39. Lennon, *Explaining human action*, Chapter 6.
40. See Introduction and papers by A. Cussins and D. Papineau in Charles & Lennon (eds), *Reduction, explanation and realism.*
41. D. Lewis, "How to define theoretical terms", *Journal of Philosophy* **67**, 1970, pp. 427–46.
42. For a defence of common-sense functionalism see Braddon-Mitchell & Jackson, *Philosophy of mind and cognition.*
43. For a defence of scientific functionalism see G. Rey, *Contemporary philosophy of mind: a contentiously classical approach* (Oxford: Blackwell, 1997).

Chapter 3. Computational models of mind

1. The classical use of the term "intentionality" to capture the directedness of thought onto a content is found in F. Brentano, "The distinction between mental and physical phenomena", in *Realism and the background of phenomenology*, R. M. Chisholm (ed.) (Atascadero, CA.: Ridgeway Publishing, 1960), pp. 39–61.
2. For a good overview of issues surrounding intentionality, see J. Perry, "Intentionality 2", in *A companion to the philosophy of mind*, S. Guttenplan (ed.) (Oxford: Blackwell, 1994).
3. For a discussion of the structure of practical reason see K. Lennon, *Explaining human action* (London: Duckworth, 1990), Chapter 1.
4. D. Davidson, "Actions, reasons and causes", in *Essays on actions and events* (Oxford: Clarendon Press, 1980), pp. 3–19.
5. C. Cherniak, *Minimal rationality* (Cambridge, Mass.: MIT Press, 1986).
6. Davidson, "Actions, reasons and causes".
7. See Lennon, *Explaining Human Action*, Chapter 2.
8. J. A. Fodor, "The big idea: can there be a science of mind?", *The Times Literary Supplement*, 3 July 1992, pp. 5–7.

9. See T. Crane, *The mechanical mind* (London: Penguin, 1995), pp. 141–9.

10. "You connect the causal properties of a symbol with its semantic properties via its syntax . . . we can think of its syntactic structure as an abstract feature of its . . . shape. Because, to all intents and purposes, syntax reduces to shape, and, because the shape of a symbol is a potential determinant of its causal role, it is fairly easy to imagine symbol tokens interacting causally in virtue of their syntactic structure . . . in much the same way that the geometry of a key determines which locks it will open." J. A. Fodor, "Fodor's guide to mental representation", in *A theory of content and other essays* (Cambridge, Mass.: MIT Press, 1990).

11. Crane, *The mechanical mind*, p. 146.

12. J. A. Fodor, *The language of thought* (New York: Thomas Crowell, 1975).

13. D. Braddon-Mitchell & F. Jackson, *Philosophy of mind and cognition* (Oxford: Blackwell, 1996), Chapters 10 and 11.

14. J. A. Fodor, *Psychosemantics* (Cambridge, Mass.: Bradford Books/ MIT Press, 1987).

15. J. A. Fodor, "Propositional attitudes", *Monist* **61**, 1978, pp. 501– 23, reprinted in *Representations* (Cambridge, Mass.: MIT Press, 1981), pp. 177–203.

16. D. C. Dennett, "Intentional systems", *Journal of Philosophy* **8**, 1971, pp. 87–106.

17. Crane, *The mechanical mind*, pp. 156–60.

18. At this level, too, computationism has disputes with connectionism.

19. J. A. Fodor, "Methodological solipsism considered as a research strategy in cognitive psychology", *Behavioural and Brain Sciences* **3**, 1980, pp. 63–73.

20. D. Davidson, "Replies", in *Essays on Davidson: actions and events*, B. Vermazen & M. Hintikka (eds) (Oxford: Oxford University Press, 1985).

21. J. McDowell, "Functionalism and anomolous monism", in *Actions and events: perspectives on the philosophy of Donald Davidson*, E. LePore & B. McLaughlin (eds) (Oxford: Blackwell, 1985), pp. 387– 98.

22. J. Searle, "Consciousness, intentionality and the background", in *The rediscovery of the mind* (Cambridge, Mass.: MIT Press, 1992), p. 182.

23. *Ibid.*, p. 180.

24. J. Hornsby, "Physicalist thinking and conceptions of behaviour", in *Subject, thought, and context*, P. Pettit & J. McDowell (eds) (Oxford: Clarendon Press, 1986), pp. 95–115.

25. McDowell, "Functionalism and anomalous monism", p. 389.

26. *Ibid.*, p. 396.

27. M. Heidegger, *Being and time*, J. Macquarrie & E. Robinson (trans.) (Oxford: Blackwell, 1967). We shall discuss this further in Chapters 5 and 7.

28. T. Nagel, *The view from nowhere* (Oxford: Oxford University Press, 1986).

29. M. Davies, "Meaning and semantic knowledge", *Proceedings of the Aristotelian Society*, Supp. vol. **71**, 1997. See http:/www.blackwellpublishers.co.uk/aristsoc.htm.

30. K. Lennon, "Reduction, causality and normativity", in *Reduction, explanation and realism*, D. Charles & K. Lennon (eds) (Oxford: Clarendon Press, 1992), pp. 225–38.

Chapter 4. The content of thought

1. Also known as *individualism*. Internalist functionalism is sometimes known as "short arm" functionalism, by contrast with the "long arm" variety which reaches right out, as it were, to objects in the external world.

2. The classic functionalist picture is that which aims at a reduction of psychological states to physical states characterized in terms of their functional roles, where these roles do not make any essential reference to what lies beyond the physical organism. Much, though as we shall see not all, scientific functionalism is of this kind, but so-called common-sense functionalism can be similarly construed (see Chapter 2).

3. For this sort of example see H. Putnam, *Reason, truth and history* (Cambridge: Cambridge University Press, 1981), Chapter 1.

4. S. Kripke, "A puzzle about belief", in *Meaning and use*, A. Margalit (ed.) (Dordrecht: Reidel, 1979), pp. 239–83. One must suppress one's incredulity at the example in order to focus on the theoretical issues it raises.

5. H. Putnam, "The meaning of 'meaning'", in *Language, mind and knowledge*, K. Gunderson (ed.) (Minneapolis: University of Minnesota Press, 1975), pp. 131–93.

6. Putnam, *Reason, truth and history*, p. 227.

7. Putnam, "Meaning of 'meaning'", p. 227.
8. T. Burge, "Individualism and the mental", *Midwest Studies in Philosophy* **4**, 1979, pp. 73–121.
9. H. Putnam, *Representation and reality* (Cambridge, Mass.: MIT Press, 1991), p. 33.
10. J. Searle, *Intentionality* (Cambridge: Cambridge University Press, 1983), p. 212.
11. See A. Bilgrami, *Belief and meaning* (Oxford: Blackwell, 1992), p. 198.
12. B. Russell, *Problems of philosophy* (London: Williams & Norgate, 1912), Chapter 5.
13. Notice that the existence of a *body* is here presupposed, together with its spatial properties. An internalist who wished to forego this also would need a different argument against Russellian thought.
14. See J. Hornsby, "Physicalist thinking and conceptions of behaviour", in *Subject, thought and context*, P. Pettit & J. McDowell (eds) (Oxford: Clarendon Press, 1986), pp. 95–115.
15. See, for example, N. Block, "An advertisement for a semantics for psychology", in *Mental representation*, S. P. Stitch & T. A. Warfield (eds) (Oxford: Blackwell, 1994), pp. 81–141.
16. See J. A. Fodor, "Banish discontent", in W. G. Lycan, *Mind and cognition* (Oxford: Blackwell, 1990), p. 424.
17. We are here allowing for the sake of argument that generalized content does not pose a problem for internalism. This is very doubtful, not only because it is unclear that there are the required general terms which lack an indexical element but because the *application* of general terms seems to require it.
18. See J. A. Fodor, *A theory of content* (Cambridge, Mass.: Bradford Books/MIT Press, 1990), Chapter 3.
19. For discussion see R. Cummins, *Meaning and mental representation* (Cambridge, Mass.: MIT Press, 1989), Chapter 4.
20. J. A. Fodor, *Psychosemantics* (Cambridge, Mass.: Bradford Books/ MIT Press, 1987), Chapter 4.
21. See, for example, R. Millikan, "Biosemantics", *Journal of Philosophy* **86**, 1989, pp. 281–97, reprinted in *Mental representation*, S. P. Stich & T. A. Warfield (eds), pp. 243–58.
22. Due to D. Davidson "Knowing one's own mind", *Proceedings and Addresses of American Philosophical Association* **60**, 1987, pp. 441–58.
23. See F. Dretske, *Explaining behaviour* (Cambridge, Mass.: Bradford Books/MIT Press, 1988).

24. Indeed, it may even fall into it. For teleological theories impose no limits in principle on the way the believer's world can be, given the beliefs she has. They only impose limits on the way the world was when the structures that realize those beliefs were formed, however they have been transmitted to her now.

25. Cf. J. Hornsby, *Simple mindedness* (Cambridge, Mass.: Harvard University Press, 1997), Chapter 12, especially pp. 217–20 – "Postscript: externalism". Hornsby too aims to offer an account of content that "accommodates [externalism] effortlessly, as it were" (p. 218).

Chapter 5. Anti-reductionist alternatives

1. D. Davidson, *Essays on actions and events* (Oxford: Oxford University Press, 1980), p. 231.

2. *Ibid.*, and D. C. Dennett, *Brainstorms: philosophical essays on mind and psychology* (Montgomery, Vt: Bradford Books/MIT Press, 1978).

3. D. Davidson in *A companion to the philosophy of mind*, S. Guttenplan (ed.) (Oxford: Blackwell, 1994).

4. Davidson, *Essays on actions and events*, p. 222.

5. Guttenplan, *A companion to the philosophy of mind*, p. 232.

6. D. C. Dennett, "Intentional systems", *Journal of Philosophy* 8, 1971, pp. 87–106.

7. D. Davidson, "Mental events", in *Essays on actions and events*. For discussion see Chapter 2.

8. Dennett in *A companion to the philosophy of mind*, S. Guttenplan (ed.), p. 240.

9. *Ibid.*, p. 230.

10. See the discussion in J. Hornsby, "Physics, biology and commonsense psychology", in *Reduction, explanation and realism*, D. Charles & K. Lennon (eds) (Oxford: Oxford University Press, 1992), pp. 155–77.

11. For some writers this view is not satisfactory because it does not accommodate Descartes' causal intuitions.

12. Compare the discussion of positivism and realism in Chapter 2, § 1.

13. D. C. Dennett, "Real patterns", *Journal of Philosophy* **89**, 1991, pp. 27–51.

14. Davidson is not so vulnerable to this suggestion as, for reasons outside the scope of this chapter, he attributes intentionality only

to creatures with a language who have a grasp of the distinction between truth and falsity. See D. Davidson, "Thought and talk", in *Inquiries into truth and interpretation* (Oxford: Oxford University Press, 1984), pp. 155–70.

15. Guttenplan (ed.), *A companion to the philosophy of mind*, p. 232.
16. Davidson, *Inquiries into truth and interpretation*, pp. 158–9.
17. There is some disagreement concerning whether Davidson should be read as advocating a two-stage epistemological process or as a direct interpretationalist.
18. This does not resolve the issue of indeterminacy. What remains, however, results solely from the general under-determination issue, not from an additional indeterminacy attaching to the mental even when we have fixed on a physicalist theory.
19. Here we are characterizing a possible position rather than attributing it to someone.
20. K. Lennon, *Explaining human action* (London: Duckworth, 1990), Chapter 3.
21. See Davidson in Guttenplan (ed.), *A companion to the philosophy of mind*.
22. See W. Child, *Causality, interpretation and the mind* (Oxford: Clarendon Press, 1994); J. Hornsby, *Simple mindedness* (Cambridge, Mass.: Harvard University Press, 1997); and L. Rudder Baker, *Explaining attitudes* (Cambridge: Cambridge University Press, 1987).
23. C. Taylor, *Human agency and language: philosophical papers*, vol. 1, and *Philosophy and the human sciences: philosophical papers*, vol. 2 (Cambridge: Cambridge University Press, 1985).
24. C. Taylor, "Self interpreting animals", in *Human agency and language*, vol. 1, pp. 45–76, and "Interpretation and the sciences of man", in *Philosophy and the human sciences*, vol. 2, pp. 15–57.
25. Taylor, *Human agency and language*, vol. 1, p. 18.
26. G. McCulloch, *The mind and its world* (London: Routledge, 1995).
27. M. Heidegger, *Being and time*, J. Macquarrie & E. Robinson (trans.) (Oxford: Blackwell, 1967).
28. *Ibid.*, § 32, pp. 190–91.
29. McCulloch, *The mind and its world*, pp. 150–51.
30. J. McDowell, *Mind and world* (Cambridge, Mass.: Harvard University Press, 1994), p. 78.
31. *Ibid.*, p. 84.
32. Taylor, *Human agency and language*, vol. 1, p. 53.
33. N. Scheman, "Anger and the politics of naming", in *Engenderings* (London: Routledge, 1993).

34. S. Mulhall, *On Being in the world: Wittgenstein and Heidegger on seeing aspects* (London: Routledge, 1990).

35. L. Wittgenstein, *Philosophical investigations* (Oxford: Blackwell, 1958).

36. K. Lennon, "Feminist epistemology as local epistemology", *Proceedings of the Aristotelian Society*, Supp. vol. **71**, 1997, pp. 37–54.

Chapter 6. The content of experience

1. Though see J. Searle, *The rediscovery of the mind* (Cambridge, Mass.: MIT Press, 1992) and G. Strawson, *Mental reality* (Cambridge, Mass.: MIT Press, 1994).

2. See T. Nagel, "What is it like to be a bat?", in *Mortal questions* (Cambridge: Cambridge University Press, 1979) for the introduction of this notion, and for this application see for example N. Block, "Consciousness", in *Companion to the philosophy of mind*, S. Guttenplan (ed.) (Oxford: Blackwell, 1994).

3. We may have reflexive consciousness of a strange thought, of course, but that contrasts with the first-order consciousness of something peculiar involved in a peculiar feeling. This does not imply that conscious thoughts are necessarily conscious only in the sense that we have reflexive consciousness of them. We may need a further notion of consciousness here to cover these cases, perhaps that of what occurs in a stream of consciousness, as when our consciousness of the world through perception is seamlessly interwoven with thoughts about it.

4. F. Jackson, "Epiphenomenal qualia", *Philosophical Quarterly* **32**, 1982, pp. 127–36, reprinted in *Mind and cognition*, W. G. Lycan (ed.) (Oxford: Blackwell, 1990), pp. 469–77.

5. See D. Lewis, "What experience teaches", in *Mind and cognition*, Lycan (ed.), pp. 499–519.

6. For example, T. Horgan, "Jackson on physical information and qualia", *Philosophical Quarterly* **34**, 1984, pp. 147–53.

7. N. Block & J. A. Fodor, "What psychological states are not", *Philosophical Review* **81**, 1972, pp. 159–81.

8. G. W. Leibniz, "Monadology" (1714), *Basic writings*, G. Montgomery (trans.) (La Salle: Open Court, 1957), p. 254.

9. Compare Bob Kirk's "Giant" in *Raw feeling* (Oxford: Oxford University Press, 1994), pp. 117–23.

10. See S. Shoemaker, *The first person perspective and other essays* (Cambridge: Cambridge University Press, 1996), p. 121.
11. Block & Fodor, "What psychological states are not".
12. Kirk, *Raw feeling*, p. 33.
13. See H. Putnam, *Reason, truth and history* (Cambridge: Cambridge University Press, 1981), p. 81.
14. D. C. Dennett, "Quining qualia", in *Mind and cognition*, Lycan (ed.), pp. 526–36.
15. See W. G. Lycan, *Consciousness* (Cambridge, Mass.: MIT Press, 1987), Chapter 6 and *Consciousness and experience* (Cambridge, Mass.: MIT Press, 1996), Chapter 2.
16. P. Carruthers, "Brute experience", *Journal of Philosophy* **86**, 1989, p. 263.
17. It may seem puzzling that we can know what it is like to be very angry *without* attending to one's state. But, contrary to the reflexive consciousness view of experience, we can. For more on what is involved see the following chapter.
18. Now it is evident that this picture could be shared either by theorists who think of qualia as independent of reflexive consciousness or by those who think of them as constituted by it. Physicalists will hold that qualia are really physical or functional properties of mental states. Thus they are not *really* intrinsic, only seemingly so. Where the two theories differ is that first-order theories, as we may dub them, hold that qualia are physical properties involved in mediating between input and output, and not necessarily the object of self-scanning processes; second-order theories hold that they are properties of a system engaged in just such scanning processes as well as the mediating processes involved in an experiential state.
19. C. Peacocke, *Sense and content* (Oxford: Oxford University Press, 1983), pp. 12–13 and 16–17.
20. J. Westphal, "White", *Mind* **95**, 1986, pp. 311–28.
21. M. Schlick, "Form and content: an introduction to philosophical thinking", *Gesammelte Aufsatze* (Vienna, 1938), pp. 151–249. Reprinted in *Philosophical papers*, H. L. Mulder & B. F. B. van de Velde-Schlick (eds) (Dordrecht: Reidel, 1979), vol. 2, pp. 285–369. The distinction here originates with Kant.
22. L. Wittgenstein, *Philosophical investigations* (Oxford: Blackwell, 1958), § 243.
23. *Ibid.*, § 258.
24. Logical grammar is what confers sense on an expression by establishing a distinction between correct and incorrect uses of it.

25. *Ibid.*, § 293.
26. It may seem that this conception also animates the inner perception model of conscious experience. For the features of experience which are, on this account, brought to consciousness through inner perception, surface in properties that are supposedly directly discriminatable by their subject. But notice that if these features are really functional features, then the phenomenal properties through which they surface in consciousness do not need to be regarded as private. The notion of a phenomenal property, as introduced in the section on intentionalism, is not necessarily that of a private property.

Chapter 7. Subjects of experience

1. T. Nagel, "What is it like to be a bat?", in *Mortal questions* (Cambridge: Cambridge University Press, 1979).
2. *Ibid.*, p. 167.
3. *Ibid.*, p. 173.
4. *Ibid.*, p. 175.
5. For example, D. Armstrong, *A materialist theory of mind* (London: Routledge, 1968).
6. Nagel, *Mortal questions*, p. 207.
7. See J. Heal, "Replication and functionalism", in *Language, mind and logic*, J. Butterfield (ed.) (Cambridge: Cambridge University Press, 1986), pp. 135–50.
8. L. Wittgenstein, *Philosophical investigations* (Oxford: Blackwell, 1958), § 285.
9. The account of experience developed in this section is not simply a form of functionalism, individuating experiences in terms of the beliefs and behaviour to which they give rise usually. For, unlike functionalism, our account treats experience as essentially subjective, and accomplishes this by emphasizing the normativity and perspectivity of the connections between an experience and the beliefs, desires and acts that it explains.
10. Wittgenstein, *Philosophical investigations*, p. 178.
11. For discussion see J. McDowell, *Mind and world* (Cambridge, Mass.: Harvard University Press, 1994).
12. This is not to admit that everything we *say* about our experiences is correct. The avowals in question are serious and sincere statements, unclouded by considerations of what we ought to say in the

circumstances on the basis of our general beliefs and so forth. As such they may be an idealization, for other criteria can conflict with what one says and reveal defects in it.

13. Wittgenstein, *Philosophical investigations*, § 244.

14. Judgements about what experience we are having, then, are not founded on reasons. This explains why there is nothing that it is like to *experience* a higher-order consciousness, that is, an awareness of our experience. For if to have experience is to have reasons for belief as to what is presented in it, then to be conscious of experience by way of a further experience would be to have reasons for belief as to the occurrence of ground-level experience. But if our belief as to its occurrence is not mediated by reasons, then there is no experiential content for higher-order consciousness to have. This is enough to dispose of the inner perception model of higher-order consciousness we raised doubts about in the preceding chapter. Indeed, Nagel's approach to experience, wedded, as he would wish it to be, to a Wittgensteinian attack on the Cartesian picture, opens up a new range of possibilities for thinking about psychological phenomena generally from the traditional ones still pressed into service, as we have seen, in present-day functionalism.

Chapter 8. The embodied subject

1. This is unsurprising since it draws on ideas in phenomenology that have their roots in Husserl's rethinking of the Cartesian project of pure enquiry.

2. The subsequent discussion is heavily dependent on Thomas Nagel's distinction between what he calls *unmotivated* desires, like appetites and some emotions, and *motivated* desires which, by contrast with these, are arrived at by deliberation; though our distinction between brute and rational desires does not precisely correspond to his. See T. Nagel, *The possibility of altruism* (Oxford: Oxford University Press, 1970), pp. 29–30.

3. For example, F. Dretske, *Explaining behaviour* (Cambridge, Mass.: Bradford Books/MIT Press, 1988). For an argument for the influence of the model there, see G. F. Schueler, *Desire* (Cambridge, Mass.: MIT Press, 1995), pp. 124–46.

4. Charles Taylor disputes this, in effect, Platonic reading of Descartes in *Sources of the self* (Cambridge: Cambridge University Press, 1989), Chapter 8.

5. See Chapter 5 above.
6. See Chapter 1 above. The example comes from the *Sixth meditation*.
7. See especially J. McDowell, "Are moral requirements hypothetical imperatives?", *Proceedings of the Aristotelian Society*, Supp. Vol. **52**, 1978, pp. 13–29; J. McDowell, "Non-cognitivism and rule-following", in *Wittgenstein: to follow a rule*, S. Holkman & C. Leich (eds) (London: Routledge, 1981), pp. 141–62; and J. McDowell, "Values and secondary qualities", in *Morality and objectivity*, T. Honderich (ed.) (London: Routledge, 1985), pp. 110–29.
8. See Chapter 5 above.
9. M. Heidegger, *Being and time* (Oxford: Blackwell, 1967), pp. 179–82. Stephen Mulhall usefully draws the parallel with McDowell's account of value in *Heidegger and "Being and time"* (London: Routledge, 1996), pp. 77–9.
10. This is not to deny that one may fear for others, as Heidegger acknowledges, but "what one 'is apprehensive about' is one's Being-with the Other, who might be torn away from one"; *Being and time*, p. 181.
11. Descartes himself, of course, was quite unable to draw this conclusion. His explanation of pain and so on is as confused modes of thought that God has providentially implanted in us to preserve our bodies.
12. K. Campbell, *Body and mind* (London: Macmillan, 1970), p. 2. See Chapter 1.
13. J. Cottingham, R. Stoothoff & D. Murdoch (eds), *The philosophical writings of Descartes* [2 vols] (Cambridge: Cambridge University Press, 1984), vol. 2, p. 52.
14. *Ibid.*, vol. 2, pp. 52–3.
15. J. Cottingham, R. Stoothoff, D. Murdoch & A. Kenny (eds), *The philosophical writings of Descartes: the correspondence* (Cambridge: Cambridge University Press, 1991), pp. 242–3. What he says is that, "provided that a body is united with the same rational soul, we always take it as the body of the same man, whatever matter it may be or whatever quantity or shape it may have; and we count it as the whole or entire body, provided that it needs no additional matter in order to remain joined to this soul".
16. *Ibid.*, p. 225.
17. Probably the best single-volume introduction to phenomenology is M. Hammond, J. Howarth & R. Keat, *Understanding phenomenology* (Oxford: Blackwell, 1991). A more thorough examination of the relevant views of some of these philosophers can be found in

R. M. Zaner, *The problem of embodiment; some contributions to a phenomenology of the body* (The Hague: Martinus Nijhoff, 1964).

18. G. Marcel, *Reflections and mystery*, R. Hague (trans.) (London: Harvill Press, 1950), p. 100.

19. M. Merleau-Ponty, *Phenomenology of perception*, C. Smith (trans.) (London, Routledge & Kegan Paul, 1962), p. 351.

20. *Ibid.*, pp. 198–9.

21. In most of the secondary literature the term "body-subject" is used to capture his thinking here, though Merleau-Ponty himself refers to the body variously as a "natural subject", a "natural 'I'", or the "subject of perception" rather than as a "body-subject".

22. We need not rehearse these difficulties here. Merleau-Ponty sometimes argues that *before anything else* the body is a body-subject, a privileging that leaves him open to the accusation that his thought continued to operate with the same presuppositions as a more traditional philosophy of consciousness.

23. G. Evans, *The varieties of reference* (Oxford: Oxford University Press, 1982), p. 154.

24. Cf. B. Brewer, "Self-location and agency", *Mind* **101**, 1992, pp. 17–34. Brewer says, "Egocentric spatial perception enables a subject to keep track of the changing spatial relations between himself and salient environmental objects in precisely the way required appropriately to modulate his spatial behaviour with respect to such objects."

25. Evans, *The varieties of reference*, pp. 162–4. Evans conceives of this "larger spatial representation" in terms of a cognitive map: a non-indexical conception of the subject's environment. The subject's capacity to think objectively about the world is manifested in its ability to grasp and utilize such a map by relating its experiences to it. It seems that Evans was exercised by a worry that, as the subject's right to be thinking about positions in space objectively conceived depends upon the roles these have played in its past life, this mode of thinking is "contaminated" by, if not reducible to, an egocentric mode of thinking (see Chapter 7, Appendix 3, pp. 264–5). However, perhaps this merely shows the interrelatedness of the two modes of spatial thinking, not that one is more fundamental than the other. As Thomas Baldwin points out, Evans's worry shows that the content of an objective thought is fixed by the egocentric mode but not that it is exhaustively determined by it. T. Baldwin, "Phenomenology, solipsism and egocen-

tric thought", *Proceedings of the Aristotelian Society*, Supp. Vol. **62**, 1988, pp. 27–43.

26. Cf. *Ibid.*, p. 41. Baldwin argues, correctly in our view, that these two conceptions of the body are interdependent: "there is no way to hold a phenomenal conception of one's body without also recognising that the objective conception applies to it. . . . One's understanding of action would be completely mysterious unless intrinsic to one's conception of oneself as an agent was an understanding of oneself as located within objective space and interacting causally with objects in the environment. . . . To a considerable extent the converse also holds: I cannot think of an object as my body unless I can think of it as constituting my point of view and means of basic action."

27. Merleau-Ponty, *Phemonology of perception*, pp. 249–50.

28. K. Sterelny, "Why naturalise representation?", in *Prospects for intentionality*, K. Neander & I. Ravenscroft (eds) Working papers in Philosophy 3, Research School of Social Sciences, Australian National University, 1993, pp. 133–40.

29. *Ibid.*, pp. 136–7.

30. *Ibid.*, p. 137.

31. See J. Campbell, "A simple view of colour", in *Reality, representation and projection*, J. Haldane & C. Wright (eds) (Oxford: Oxford University Press, 1993), pp. 261–4.

32. J. Griffin, "Values, reduction, supervenience, and explanation by ascent", in *Reduction, explanation and realism*, D. Charles and K. Lennon (eds) (Oxford: Clarendon Press, 1992), pp. 297–322.

33. J. Kim, *Philosophy of mind* (Colorado: Westview Press, 1996), p. 222.

34. For a discussion of the relation between enabling and constitutive conditions see J. McDowell, "The content of perceptual experience", *Philosophical Quarterly* **44**, 1994, pp. 190–205.

35. In our discussion of Daniel Dennett in Chapter 3 we noted his concern with showing how physical systems could be such as to instantiate intentional systems. He saw work in artificial intelligence as contributing towards this project. However, in his later account of consciousness – *Consciousness explained* (Boston: Little, Brown, 1991) – this project is construed in a much stronger way. The "quasi content" attributed to sub-personal states is there viewed as giving an account of all there is to consciousness at the personal level. But this is to read the work at the sub-personal level in a different way from that suggested in his original interpretationalism, for now the enabling condi-

tions are read as constitutive. This is precisely the move we are resisting.

36. J. L. Bermudez, "Syntax, semantics and levels of explanation", *Philosophical Quarterly* **45**, 1995, pp. 361–7.

Bibliography

Armstrong, D. *A materialist theory of mind* (London: Routledge, 1968).

Ayer, A. J. One's knowledge of other minds. See Gustafson (ed.), 1964, pp. 346–64.

Baker, G. & K. J. Morris. *Descartes' dualism* (London: Routledge, 1996).

Baldwin, T. Phenomenology, solipsism and egocentric thought. *Proceedings of the Aristotelian Society*, supp. vol. **62**, pp. 27–43, 1988.

Bermudez, J. L. Syntax, semantics, and levels of explanation. *Philosophical Quarterly* **45**, pp. 361–7, 1995.

Bermudez, J. L., A. Marcel & N. Eilan (eds). *The body and the self* (Cambridge, Mass.: MIT Press, 1995).

Bilgrami, A. *Belief and meaning* (Oxford: Blackwell, 1992).

Block, N. An advertisement for a semantics for psychology. See Stich & Warfield (eds), 1984, pp. 81–141.

Block, N. (ed.). *Readings in philosophy of psychology* [2 vols] (Cambridge, Mass.: Harvard University Press, 1980).

Block, N. & J. A. Fodor. What psychological states are not. *Philosophical Review* **81**, pp. 159–81, 1972.

Block, N., O. Flanagan & G. Güzeldere (eds). *The nature of consciousness* (Cambridge, Mass.: MIT Press, 1997).

Borst, C. V. (ed.). *The mind-brain identity theory* (Toronto: Macmillan, 1970).

Boyd, R. Natural kinds, homeostasis, and the limits of essentialism. Unpublished manuscript (Department of Philosophy, Cornell University, 1984).

Boyd, R. On the current status of the issue of scientific realism. *Erkenntnis* **19**, pp. 45–90, 1983.

Braddon-Mitchell, D. & F. Jackson. *Philosophy of mind and cognition* (Oxford: Blackwell, 1996).

Brentano, F. The distinction between mental and physical phenomena. See Chisholm (ed.), 1960, pp. 39–61.

Brewer, B. Self-location and agency. *Mind* **101**, pp. 17–34, 1992.

Broad, C. D. *The mind and its place in nature* (London: Kegan Paul, Trench, Trubner, 1925).

Brown, S. C. (ed.). *Philosophy of psychology* (New York: Macmillan, 1974).

Burge, T. Cartesian error and the objectivity of perception. See Pettit & McDowell (eds), 1986, pp. 117–36.

Burge, T. Individualism and causation in psychology. *Pacific Philosophical Quarterly* **70**, pp. 303–22, 1989.

Burge, T. Individualism and self-knowledge. *Journal of Philosophy* **85**, pp. 649–63, 1988.

Burge, T. Individualism and the mental. *Midwest Studies in Philosophy* **10**, pp. 73–121, 1979.

Burge, T. Other bodies. See Woodfield (ed.), 1982, pp. 97–120.

Butterfield, J. (ed.). *Language, mind and logic* (Cambridge: Cambridge University Press, 1986).

Campbell, J. A simple view of colour. See Haldane & Wright (eds), 1993, pp. 261–4.

Campbell, K. *Body and mind* (London: Macmillan, 1970).

Carruthers, P. Brute experience. *Journal of Philosophy* **86**, pp. 258–69, 1989.

Chalmers, D. *The conscious mind: in search of a fundamental theory* (Oxford: Oxford University Press, 1996).

Charles, D. Supervenience, composition and physicalism. See Charles & Lennon (eds), 1992, pp. 265–96.

Charles, D. & K. Lennon (eds). *Reduction, explanation and realism* (Oxford: Clarendon Press, 1992).

Cherniak, C. *Minimal rationality* (Cambridge, Mass.: MIT Press, 1986).

Child, W. *Causality, interpretation and the mind* (Oxford: Clarendon Press, 1994).

Chisholm, R. M. (ed.). *Realism and the background of phenomenology* (Atascadero, CA: Ridgeway Publishing, 1960).

Churchland, P. M. Eliminative materialism and the propositional attitudes. *Journal of Philosophy* **78**, pp. 67–90, 1981. Reprinted in Lycan (ed.), 1990, pp. 206–23.

Churchland, P. M. Folk psychology and the explanation of human behaviour. *Proceedings of the Aristotelian Society*, supp. vol. **62**, pp. 209–21, 1988.

Churchland, P. M. *Matter and consciousness: a contemporary introduction to the philosophy of mind* (Cambridge, Mass.: Bradford Books/MIT Press, 1988).

Churchland, P. M. & P. S. Churchland. Could a machine think? *Scientific American* **262**, pp. 32–7, 1990.

Churchland, P. S. *Neurophilosophy: toward a unified understanding of the mind-brain* (Cambridge, Mass.: Bradford Books/MIT Press, 1986).

Cockburn, D. (ed.). *Human beings* (Cambridge: Cambridge University Press, 1991).

Cottingham, J. "A brute to the brutes?": Descartes' treatment of animals. *Philosophy* **53**, pp. 551–9, 1978.

Cottingham, J. *Descartes* (Oxford: Blackwell, 1986).

Cottingham, J. (ed.). *Descartes' conversation with Burman* (Oxford: Clarendon Press, 1976).

Cottingham, J., R. Stoothoff & D. Murdoch (eds). *The philosophical writings of Descartes* [2 vols] (Cambridge: Cambridge University Press, 1984).

Cottingham, J., R. Stoothoff, D. Murdoch & A. Kenny (eds). *The philosophical writings of Descartes: the correspondence* (Cambridge: Cambridge University Press, 1991).

Crane, T. (ed.). *The contents of experience* (Cambridge: Cambridge University Press, 1992).

Crane, T. *The mechanical mind* (London: Penguin, 1995).

Crary, J., M. Feher, H. Foster & S. Kwinter (eds). *Fragments for a history of the human body* [3 vols] (New York: Zone Books, 1989).

Cummins, R. *Meaning and mental representation* (Cambridge, Mass.: MIT Press, 1989).

Currie, G. Individualism and global supervenience. *British Journal for the Philosophy of Science* **35**, pp. 345–58, 1984.

Davidson, D. Actions, reasons, and causes. See Davidson, 1980, pp. 3–19.

Davidson, D. *Essays on actions and events* (Oxford: Oxford University Press, 1980).

Davidson, D. *Inquiries into truth and interpretation* (Oxford: Oxford University Press, 1984).

Davidson, D. Knowing one's own mind. *Proceedings and Addresses of the American Philosophical Association* **60**, pp. 441–58, 1987.

Davidson, D. Mental events. See Davidson, 1980, pp. 207–27.

Davidson, D. Radical interpretation. See Davidson, 1984, pp. 125–39.

Davidson, D. Thought and talk. See Davidson, 1984, pp. 155–70.

Davies, M. Meaning and semantic knowledge. *Proceedings of the Aristotelian Society*, supp. vol. **71**, 1997. See http://www.blackwellpublishers.co.uk/aristsoc.htm.

Davies, M. & G. W. Humphreys (eds). *Consciousness* (Oxford: Blackwell, 1993).

Dennett, D. C. *Brainstorms: philosophical essays on mind and psychology* (Montgomery, Vt.: Bradford Books/MIT Press, 1978).

Dennett, D. C. *Consciousness explained* (Boston: Little, Brown, 1991).

Dennett, D. C. *The intentional stance* (Cambridge, Mass.: Bradford Books/MIT Press, 1987).

Dennett, D. C. Intentional systems. *Journal of Philosophy* **8**, pp. 87–106, 1971.

Dennett, D. C. Quining qualia. See Lycan (ed.), 1990, pp. 526–36.

Dennett, D. C. Real patterns. *Journal of Philosophy* **89**, pp. 27–51, 1991.

Dretske, F. *Explaining behavior: reasons in a world of causes* (Cambridge, Mass.: Bradford Books/MIT Press, 1988).

Dretske, F. *Naturalizing the mind* (Cambridge, Mass.: MIT Press, 1995).

Dretske, F. Reasons and causes. *Philosophical Perspectives* **3**, pp. 1–15, 1989.

Dreyfus, H. *What computers can't do* (New York: Harper, 1972).

Dreyfus, H. Why computers must have bodies in order to be intelligent. *Review of Metaphysics* **21**, pp. 13–32, 1967.

Dreyfus, H. & H. Hall (eds). *Husserl, intentionality, and cognitive science* (Cambridge, Mass.: Bradford Books/MIT Press, 1982).

Dreyfus, H. & J. Haugeland. The computer as a mistaken model of the mind. See Brown (ed.), 1974, pp. 247–58.

Evans, G. *The varieties of reference* (Oxford: Oxford University Press, 1982).

Feigl, H., M. Scriven & G. Maxwell (eds). *Minnesota studies in philosophy of science* (Minneapolis: University of Minnesota Press, 1958).

Fodor, J. A. Banish discontent. See Lycan (ed.), 1990, pp. 420–38.

Fodor, J. A. The big idea: can there be a science of mind? *The Times Literary Supplement*, 3 July 1992, pp. 5–7.

Fodor, J. A. Fodor's guide to mental representation. See Fodor, 1990, pp. 3–29.

Fodor, J. A. *The language of thought* (New York: Thomas Crowell, 1975).

Fodor, J. A. Methodological solipsism considered as a research strategy in cognitive psychology. *Behavioral and Brain Sciences* **3**, pp. 63–73, 1980. Reprinted in Fodor, 1981, pp. 225–53.

Fodor, J. A. Propositional attitudes. *Monist* **61**, 1978, pp. 501–23. Reprinted in Fodor, 1981, pp. 177–203.

Fodor, J. A. *Psychosemantics: the problem of meaning in the philosophy of mind* (Cambridge, Mass.: Bradford Books/MIT Press, 1987).

Fodor, J. A. *Representations: philosophical essays on the foundations of cognitive science* (Cambridge, Mass.: MIT Press, 1981).

Fodor, J. A. Special sciences, or: the disunity of science as a working hypothesis. *Synthese* **28**, pp. 97–115, 1974. Reprinted in Fodor, 1981, pp. 127–45.

Fodor, J. A. *A theory of content and other essays* (Cambridge, Mass.: Bradford Books/MIT Press, 1990).

Gaukroger, S. *Descartes: an intellectual biography* (Oxford: Oxford University Press, 1995).

Gilbert, P. H. *Human relationships* (Oxford: Blackwell, 1991).

Gilbert, P. H. Immediate experience. *Proceedings of the Aristotelian Society* **92**, pp. 233–50, 1992.

Griffin, J. Values, reduction, supervenience, and explanation by ascent. See Charles & Lennon (eds), 1992, pp. 297–322.

Gunderson, K. (ed.). *Language, mind and knowledge* (Minneapolis: University of Minnesota Press, 1975).

Gustafson, D. F. (ed.). *Essays in philosophical psychology* (London: Macmillan, 1964).

Guttenplan, S. (ed.). *A companion to the philosophy of mind* (Oxford: Blackwell, 1994).

Hacker, P. *Wittgenstein: on human nature* (London: Phoenix, 1997).

Haldane, J. & C. Wright (eds). *Reality, representation and projection* (Oxford: Oxford University Press, 1993).

Hammond, M., J. Howarth & R. Keat. *Understanding phenomenology* (Oxford: Blackwell, 1991).

Hare, R. M. *The language of morals* (Oxford: Oxford University Press, 1952).

Harré, R. *Physical being* (Oxford: Blackwell, 1991).

Haugeland, J. Weak supervenience. *American Philosophical Quarterly* **19**, pp. 93–103, 1982.

Heal, J. Replication and functionalism. See Butterfield (ed.), 1986, pp. 135–50.

Heidegger, M. *Being and time*, J. Maquarrie & E. Robinson (trans.) (Oxford: Blackwell, 1967).

Heil, J. *Philosophy of mind* (London: Routlege, 1998).

Heil, J. & A. Mele (eds). *Mental causation* (Oxford: Oxford University Press, 1993).

Hempel, C. *Aspects of scientific explanation* (New York: The Free Press, 1965).

Hempel, C. The logical analysis of psychology. See Block, 1980, vol. 1.

Holtzman, S. H. & C. M. Leich (eds). *Wittgenstein: to follow a rule* (London: Routledge, 1981).

Honderich, T. (ed.). *Morality and objectivity* (London: Routledge, 1985).

Honderich, T. (ed.). *The Oxford companion to philosophy* (Oxford: Oxford University Press, 1994).

Horgan, T. From supervenience to superdupervenience: meeting the demands of a material world. *Mind* **102**, pp. 555–86, 1993.

Horgan, T. Jackson on physical information and qualia. *Philosophical Quarterly* **34**, pp. 147–53, 1984.

Horgan, T. Mental quausation. *Philosophical Perspectives* **3**, pp. 47–76, 1989.

Horgan, T. Supervenience and microphysics. *Pacific Philosophical Quarterly* **63**, pp. 29–43, 1982.

Horgan, T. Supervenient qualia. *Philosophical Review* **96**, pp. 491–520, 1987.

Hornsby, J. Physicalist thinking and conceptions of behaviour. See Pettit & McDowell (eds), 1986, pp. 95–115.

Hornsby, J. Physics, biology, and common-sense psychology. See Charles & Lennon (eds), 1992, pp. 155–77.

Hornsby, J. *Simple mindedness* (Cambridge, Mass.: Harvard University Press, 1997).

Hume, D. *Enquiries concerning human understanding and concerning the principles of morals*, P. H. Nidditch (ed.) (Oxford: Clarendon Press, 1975).

Inwood, M. *Heidegger* (Oxford: Oxford University Press, 1997).

Jackson, F. Epiphenomenal qualia. *Philosophical Quarterly* **32**, pp. 127–36, 1982. Reprinted in Lycan (ed.), 1990, pp. 469–77.

Jackson, F. Naturalism and the fate of the M-worlds. *Proceedings of the Aristotelian Society*, supp. vol. **71**, pp. 269–82, 1997.

Jackson, F. What Mary didn't know. *Journal of Philosophy* **83**, pp. 291–5, 1986.

Jackson, F. & P. Pettit. Functionalism and broad content. *Mind* **97**, pp. 381–400, 1988.

Jackson, F. & P. Pettit. In defence of folk psychology. *Philosophical Studies* **59**, pp. 31–54, 1990.

Jaynes, J. The problem of animate motion in the seventeenth century. *Journal of the History of Ideas* **31**, pp. 219–34, 1970.

Keat, R. & J. Urry. *Social theory as science* (London: Routledge & Kegan Paul, 1975).

Kenny, A. *Descartes* (Bristol: Thoemmes Press, 1995).

Kim, J. *Philosophy of mind* (Colorado: Westview Press, 1996).

Kim, J. "Strong" and "global" supervenience revisited. *Philosophy and Phenomenological Research* **48**, pp. 315–26, 1987. Reprinted in Kim, 1993, pp. 79–91.

Kim, J. *Supervenience and mind* (Cambridge: Cambridge University Press, 1993).

Kirk, R. *Raw feeling* (Oxford: Oxford University Press, 1994).

Kripke, S. *Naming and necessity* (Cambridge, Mass.: Harvard University Press, 1980).

Kripke, S. A puzzle about belief. See Margalit (ed.), 1979, pp. 239–83.

Kuhn, T. *The structure of scientific revolutions* (Chicago: University of Chicago Press, 1962).

Langer, M. *Merleau-Ponty's "Phenomenology of perception"* (London: Macmillan, 1989).

Leder, D. *The absent body* (Chicago: University of Chicago Press, 1990).

Leder, D. Medicine and paradigms of embodiment. *Journal of Medicine and Philosophy* **9**, pp. 29–44, 1984.

Leder, D. (ed.). *The body in medical thought and practice* (Dordrecht: Kluwer Academic Publishing, 1992).

Leibniz, G. W. *Basic writings*, G. Montgomery (trans.) (La Salle: Open Court, 1957).

Lennon, K. *Explaining human action* (London: Duckworth, 1990).

Lennon, K. Feminist epistemology as local epistemology. *Proceedings of the Aristotelian Society*, supp. vol. **71**, pp. 37–54, 1997.

Lennon, K. Reduction, causality, and normativity. See Charles & Lennon (eds), 1992, pp. 225–38.

Lennon, K. & M. Whitford (eds). *Knowing the difference* (London: Routledge, 1994).

LePore, E. & B. McLaughlin (eds). *Actions and events: perspectives on the philosophy of Donald Davidson* (Oxford: Blackwell, 1985).

Lewis, D. *Counterfactuals* (Oxford: Blackwell, 1973).

Lewis, D. How to define theoretical terms. *Journal of Philosophy* **67**, pp. 427–46, 1970.

Lewis, D. What experience teaches. See Lycan (ed.), 1990, pp. 499–519.

Loar, B. *Mind and meaning* (Cambridge: Cambridge University Press, 1981).

Loewer, B. & G. Rey (eds). *Meaning in mind* (London: Routledge, 1991).

Lycan, W. G. *Consciousness* (Cambridge, Mass.: MIT Press, 1987).

Lycan, W. G. *Consciousness and experience* (Cambridge, Mass.: MIT Press, 1996).

Lycan, W. G. (ed.). *Mind and cognition: a reader* (Oxford: Blackwell, 1990).

McCulloch, G. *The mind and its world* (London: Routledge, 1995).

McDonald, C. (ed.). *Mind-body identity theories* (London: Routledge, 1989).

McDonald, C. & G. McDonald (eds). *Philosophy of psychology: debates on psychological explanation* (Oxford: Blackwell, 1995).

McDowell, J. Are moral requirements hypothetical imperatives? *Proceedings of the Aristotelian Society*, supp. vol. **52**, pp. 13–29, 1978.

McDowell, J. The content of perceptual experience. *Philosophical Quarterly* **44**, pp. 190–205, 1994.

McDowell, J. Functionalism and anomolous monism. See LePore & McLaughlin (eds), 1985, pp. 387–98.

McDowell, J. *Heidegger and "Being and time"* (London: Routledge, 1996).

McDowell, J. *Mind and world* (Cambridge, Mass.: Harvard University Press, 1994).

McDowell, J. Non-cognitivism and rule-following. See Holtzman & Leich (eds), 1981, pp. 141–62.

McDowell, J. Values and secondary qualities. See Honderich (ed.), 1985, pp. 110–29.

McGinn, C. *The character of mind* (Oxford: Oxford University Press, 1982).

McGinn, C. *Mental content* (Oxford: Blackwell, 1989).

McGinn, C. *The problem of consciousness: essays towards resolution* (Oxford: Blackwell, 1991).

McGinn, M. *Wittgenstein and the "Philosophical investigations"* (London: Routledge, 1997).

Mackie, J. *The cement of the universe* (Oxford: Clarendon Press, 1974).

Mackie, J. *Truth, probability and paradox* (Oxford: Clarendon Press, 1973).

213

McLaughlin, B. P. (ed.). *Dretske and his critics* (Oxford: Blackwell, 1991).

Malcolm, N. Knowledge of other minds. See Gustafson (ed.), 1964, pp. 365–76.

Marcel, G. *Reflections and mystery*, R. Hague (trans.) (London: Harvill Press, 1950).

Margalit, A. (ed.). *Meaning and use* (Dordrecht: Reidel, 1979).

Merleau-Ponty, M. *Phenomenology of perception*, C. Smith (trans.) (London: Routledge & Kegan Paul, 1962).

Merleau-Ponty, M. *Signs*, R. C. McCleary (trans.) (Evanston, Ill.: Northwestern University Press, 1964).

La Mettrie, J. O. de. *Machine man and other writings*, A. Thomson (ed.) (Cambridge: Cambridge University Press, 1996).

Millikan, R. Biosemantics. *Journal of Philosophy* **86**, pp. 281–97, 1989. Reprinted in Stich & Warfield (eds), 1994, pp. 243–58.

Millikan, R. *Language, thought, and other biological categories: new foundations for realism* (Cambridge, Mass.: MIT Press, 1984).

Moore, G. E. *Principia ethica* (Cambridge: Cambridge University Press, 1903).

Moravia, S. *The enigma of the mind: the mind-body problem in contemporary thought* (Cambridge: Cambridge University Press, 1995).

Mulhall, S. *On being in the world: Wittgenstein and Heidegger on seeing aspects* (London: Routledge, 1990).

Nagel, E. *The structure of science* (London: Routledge & Kegan Paul, 1961).

Nagel, T. *Mortal questions* (Cambridge: Cambridge University Press, 1979).

Nagel, T. *The possibility of altruism* (Oxford: Oxford University Press, 1970).

Nagel, T. *The view from nowhere* (Oxford: Oxford University Press, 1986).

Neander, K. & I. Ravenscroft (eds). *Prospects for intentionality: working papers in philosophy 3* (Research School of Social Sciences, Australian National University, 1993).

Peacocke, C. *Sense and content* (Oxford: Oxford University Press, 1983).

Pettit, P. & J. McDowell (eds). *Subject, thought, and context* (Oxford: Clarendon Press, 1986).

Van Peursen, C. A. *Body, soul, spirit: a survey of the body-mind problem* (Oxford: Oxford University Press, 1966).

Place, U. T. Is consciousness a brain process? *British Journal of Psychology* **47**, pp. 44–50, 1956.

Polt, R. *Heidegger* (London: UCL Press, forthcoming).

Putnam, H. Explanation and reference. See Putnam, 1975, pp. 196–214.

Putnam, H. The meaning of "meaning". See Putnam, 1975, pp. 215–71.

Putnam, H. *Mind, language and reality: philosophical papers* (Cambridge: Cambridge University Press, 1975).

Putnam, H. *Reason, truth and history* (Cambridge: Cambridge University Press, 1981).

Putnam, H. *Representation and reality* (Cambridge, Mass.: MIT Press, 1991).

Rey, G. *Contemporary philosophy of mind: a contentiously classical approach* (Oxford: Blackwell, 1997).

Rudder Baker, L. *Explaining attitudes* (Cambridge: Cambridge University Press, 1987).

Rudder Baker, L. *Saving belief: a critique of physicalism* (Princeton: Princeton University Press, 1987).

Russell, B. *Problems of philosophy* (London: Williams & Norgate, 1912).

Ryle, G. *The concept of mind* (London: Hutchinson, 1949).

Scheman, N. *Engenderings* (London: Routledge, 1993).

Schlick, M. Form and content: an introduction to philosophical thinking. *Gesammelte Aufsatze* (Vienna, 1938), pp. 151–249. Reprinted in Schlick, 1979, vol. 2, pp. 285–369.

Schlick M. *Philosophical Papers*, H. L. Mulder & B. F. B. van de Velde-Schlick (eds) [2 vols] (Dordrecht: Reidel, 1979).

Schueler, G. F. *Desire* (Cambridge, Mass.: MIT Press, 1995).

Searle, J. R. *Intentionality: an essay in the philosophy of mind* (Cambridge: Cambridge University Press, 1983).

Searle, J. R. *Minds, brains and science: the 1984 Reith lectures* (London: BBC, 1984).

Searle, J. R. *The mystery of consciousness* (London: Granta Books, 1997).

Searle, J. R. *The rediscovery of the mind* (Cambridge, Mass.: MIT Press, 1992).

Shoemaker, S. *The first person perspective and other essays* (Cambridge: Cambridge University Press, 1996).

Shoemaker, S. *Identity, cause and mind: philosophical essays* (Cambridge: Cambridge University Press, 1984).

Skinner, B. F. *Science and human behavior* (New York: Macmillan, 1953).

Smart, J. J. C. Sensations and brain processes. *Philosophical Review* **68**, pp. 141–56, 1959.

Snowdon, P. Neutral monism. See Honderich (ed.), 1994, p. 618.

Spicker, S. F. *The philosophy of the body* (Chicago: Quadrangle Books, 1970).

Spiegelberg, H. *The phenomenological movement: a historical introduction* (London: Heinemann, 1962).

Sterelny, K. *The representational theory of mind: an introduction* (Oxford: Blackwell, 1990).

Sterelny, K. Why naturalise representation? See Neander & Ravenscroft (eds), 1993, pp. 133–40.

Stich, S. P. *Deconstructing the mind* (Oxford: Oxford University Press, 1996).

Stich, S. P. Do true believers exist? *Proceedings of the Aristotelian Society*, supp. vol. **65**, pp. 229–44, 1991.

Stich, S. P. *From folk psychology to cognitive science: the case against belief* (Cambridge, Mass.: Bradford Books/MIT Press, 1983).

Stich, S. P. & T. A. Warfield (eds). *Mental representation* (Oxford: Blackwell, 1994).

Strawson, G. *Mental reality* (Cambridge, Mass.: MIT Press, 1994).

Taylor, C. *Human agency and language*, vol. 1 of *Philosophical papers* (Cambridge: Cambridge University Press, 1985).

Taylor, C. Interpretation and the sciences of man. See Taylor, 1985, vol. 2, pp. 15–57.

Taylor, C. Overcoming epistemology. See Taylor, 1995, pp. 1–19.

Taylor, C. *Philosophical arguments* (Cambridge: Cambridge University Press, 1995).

Taylor, C. *Philosophy and the human sciences*, vol. 2 of *Philosophical papers* (Cambridge: Cambridge University Press, 1985).

Taylor, C. Self-interpreting animals. See Taylor, 1985, vol. 1, pp. 45–76.

Taylor, C. *Sources of the self* (Cambridge: Cambridge University Press, 1989).

Vermazen, B. & M. Hintikka (eds). *Essays on Davidson: actions and events* (Oxford: Oxford University Press, 1985).

Vesey, G. N. A. *The embodied mind* (London: George Allen & Unwin, 1965).

Vesey, G. N. A. (ed.). *Body and mind* (London: George Allen & Unwin, 1964).

Warner, R. & T. Szubka (eds). *The mind-body problem: a guide to the current debate* (Oxford: Blackwell, 1994).

Welton, D. (ed.). *Body and flesh: a philosophical reader* (Oxford: Blackwell, 1998).

Westphal, J. White. *Mind* **95**, pp. 311–28, 1986.

Wittgenstein, L. *Philosophical investigations* (Oxford: Blackwell, 1958).

Woodfield, A. (ed.). *Thought and object: essays on intentionality* (Oxford: Clarendon Press, 1982).

Zaner, R. M. *The problem of embodiment: some contributions to a phenomenology of the body* (The Hague: Martinus Nijhoff, 1964).

Zaner, R. M. The radical reality of the human body. *Humanitas* **2**, pp. 73–87, 1966.

Zaner, R. M. The subjectivity of the human body. *Main Currents in American Thought* **29**, pp. 117–20, 1973.

Zaner, R. M. The other Descartes and medicine. In *Phenomenology and the understanding of human destiny*, S. Skousgaard (ed.) (Lanham, Md.: University Press of America, 1981), pp. 93–119.

Zaner, R. M. *Context of self* (Chicago: Ohio University Press, 1981).

Index